AF889616

IMAGES
of America

SAN FRANCISCO'S EXCELSIOR DISTRICT

Excelsior

By Henry Wadsworth Longfellow

The shades of night were falling fast,
As through an Alpine village passed
A youth, who bore, 'mid snow and ice,
A banner with the strange device,
Excelsior!

His brow was sad; his eye beneath,
Flashed like a falchion from its sheath,
And like a silver clarion rung
The accents of that unknown tongue,
Excelsior!

In happy homes he saw the light
Of household fire gleam warm and bright;
Above, the spectral glaciers shone,
And from his lips escaped a groan,
Excelsior!

"Try no the Pass!" the old man said;
"Dark lowers the tempest overhead,
The roaring torrent is deep and wide!"
And loud that clarion voice replied,
Excelsior!

"Oh, stay," the maiden said, "and rest
Thy weary head upon this breast!"
A tear stood in his bright blue eye,
But still he answered, with a sigh,
Excelsior!

"Beware the pine-tree's withered branch!
Beware the awful avalanche!"
This was the peasant's last Good-night,
A voice replied, far up the height,
Excelsior!

At break of day, as heavenward
The pious monks of Saint Bernard
Uttered the oft-repeated prayer,
A voice cried through the startled air,
Excelsior!

A traveler, by the faithful hound,
Half-buried in the snow was found,
Still grasping in his hand of ice
That banner with the strange device,
Excelsior!

There, in the twilight cold and gray,
Lifeless, but beautiful, he lay,
And from the sky, serene and far,
A voice fell, like a falling star,
Excelsior!

IMAGES
of America

San Francisco's Excelsior District

Walter G. Jebe Sr.

ARCADIA

ISBN 0-7385-2889-7

Published by Arcadia Publishing
Charleston SC, Chicago IL, Portsmouth NH, San Francisco CA

Printed in Great Britain

Library of Congress Catalog Card Number: 2004109849

For all general information contact Arcadia Publishing at:
Telephone 843-853-2070
Fax 843-853-0044
E-mail sales@arcadiapublishing.com
For customer service and orders:
Toll-Free 1-888-313-2665

Visit us on the internet at http://www.arcadiapublishing.com

This book is dedicated to my wife, Vivian Ferrera Jebe (Noni), my daughter, Vivian Ann Jebe, and my son, Walter G. Jebe II, who have always been by my side and encouraged me in my life's work.

The author may be contacted via E-mail at wgjebesr@aol.com.

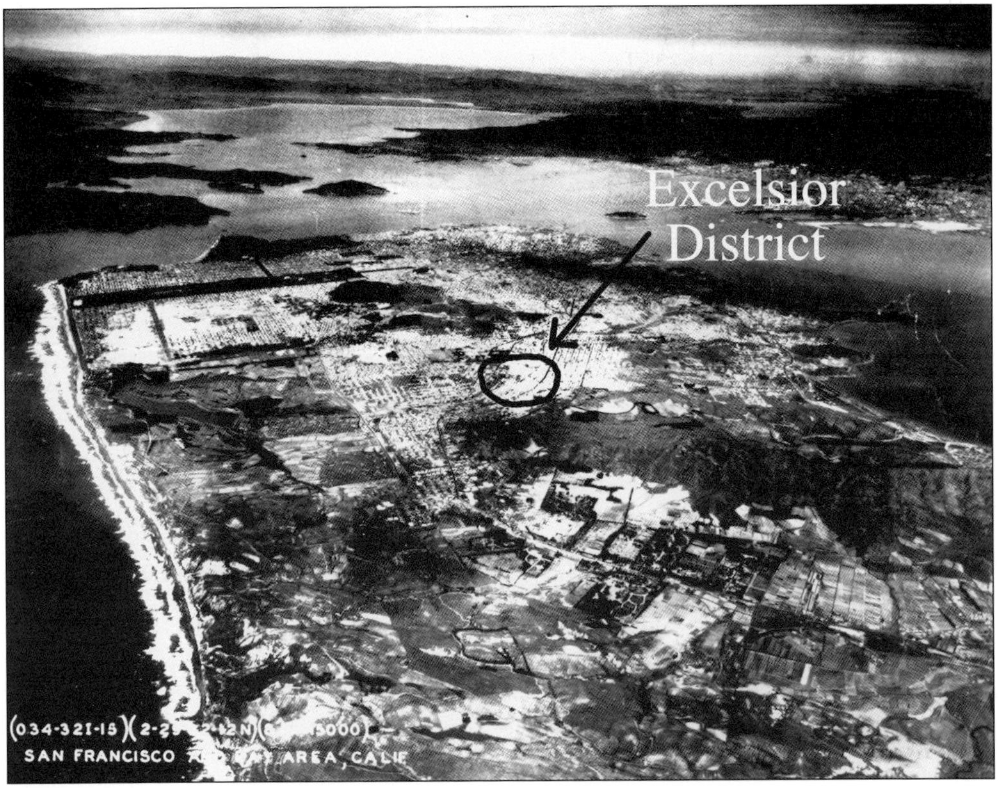

CONTENTS

ACKNOWLEDGMENTS

It would be nearly impossible to write and publish a book without acknowledging the kind and generous contributions made by my family, friends, associates, and fellow residents of the Excelsior District. The valued memories and sometimes mere fragments of local history held in the minds of the older residents such as John Consiglieri, and a host of others, enabled this work to materialize. Preserving the district's history has been a lifelong venture of mine. In the past, many City College and San Francisco State College professors referred their students to me for research information on the Excelsior District history for term papers and other school projects. Most of the photos, ephemera, and history in this book are from the author's private collections. Through general conversations with many old-timers who are no longer with us, the early days of the Excelsior District have been preserved and their memories of these historical facts will forever live in the pages of this book. However, it saddens me to realize that those who have come before us failed to leave an accounting of all the treasured memories of the Excelsior District. Those reading this book may consider investigating and recording the history of their own unique neighborhoods and families. A tremendous amount of the Excelsior's history has yet to be compiled, organized, and presented to the world. The Excelsior District played a prominent role in the history of San Francisco. My wish is that the publication of this book has kindled a spark that will light the path for future historians with a burning desire to preserve the history of not only the Excelsior District but their own locales.

I would like to express my gratitude to the following individuals who contributed to this effort, for without their input this project could not have been completed: my wife, Vivian Ferrera Jebe (Noni); my daughter, Vivian Jebe; my son, Walter Jebe II; Emil and Rose Ferrera; Alice Ferrara Lundin; Rebecca Silverberg; Martha Cohen of the Mayor's Office; John Poultney at Arcadia Publishing; Bonnie Sherk (Living Library); Dermot Philpott, former deputy chief of police, historian, and storyteller; and a very special thanks to Emily Powell, who brought to the surface the athletic history and the many fine accomplishments of the people who grew up in the Excelsior District and graduated from Balboa High School; and to Susan Goldstein of the San Francisco Public Library Archives; and Mr. Andy Harris, whose knowledge of computer operation and graphics is great. A special thanks to all of my faithful friends and customers throughout the years.

Organizing, planning, and enduring all of the difficulties to put this material together and get it to the publisher was like Eisenhower planning the 'D' Day invasion of Normandy. If I left anyone out, please forgive me.

"All you need to do to receive guidance is to ask for it and then listen" —Samoya Ramon

INTRODUCTION

Henry Wadsworth Longfellow's poem "Excelsior," written in 1841, was so popular that even cleaning maids could recite it by heart. Excelsior means "ever higher" and was intended to convey a sense of optimism about moving on. The Excelsior District and its exact location is little known to the average San Franciscan. One of several reasons for this book is to make the public aware of the importance of the Excelsior and its contributions to the city of San Francisco, not only in terms of its neighborhoods and buildings but its people.

The main street traversing the Excelsior District is Mission Street, but the true name is the El Camino Real, "The Kings Road." The El Camino Real, which starts at San Diego, travels to Sonoma, connecting all 21 California missions. The El Camino Real was the path followed by Fr. Junipero Serra and his fellow friars while establishing California's missions. On June 28, 1776, a few days before the signing of the Declaration of Independence in Philadelphia, a friar from Father Serra's group and Spanish soldiers passed through the area on their trek to the Laguna Dolores, located at today's Dolores and Sixteenth Street. There is no actual proof that Father Serra visited Mission Dolores, but the assumption is that he did since he was a head of the order and would have visited the mission at least once. If so, locals can feel honored that the saintly man passed through this area.

Lake Geneva was in the vicinity of Geneva and Cayuga Avenues and was a stop for travelers replenishing their water supplies. Islais Creek flows from Lake Geneva and empties into San Francisco Bay. Even though it is paved over with asphalt and homes, the creek still flows today under Cayuga Avenue and in the spring of 2004 flooded the basements of many homes located in the Cayuga Avenue area. The beautiful cafeteria at Balboa High School has been damaged by water and still is unusable at this writing because of the improper maintenance of sump pumps. The use of such pumps is not uncommon in San Francisco, and they can be found in buildings such as San Francisco City Hall and the San Francisco Main Library.

The Ohlone Indians were the original people of San Francisco, although they are still not recognized by the U.S. government. At one time there were about 170 Ohlones living in three villages throughout the San Francisco area, all governed by one chief.

The Excelsior area was part of "Rincon de las Salinas y Potrero Viejo," commonly referred to as Bernal Rancho, deeded to the Bernals on December 31, 1857.

In 1848 San Francisco was a sleepy little Spanish village with a population of about 800 people. After the discovery of gold this was no longer the case; by 1850 the greatest migration in American history had caused San Francisco to increase its population to 25,000 in only two years.

On April 15, 1869, the Excelsior Homestead was filed at city hall in books "C" and "D" and in the book of city maps on page 129. At this time some of the arrivals in San Francisco were European farmers and fishermen; the fishermen stayed near the northern shores to ply their trade while the farmers moved south toward the Excelsior. The first farmers in this area were Irish potato farmers, followed by the Italians, the Germans, and the Swiss who grew cabbages, cauliflower, Swiss chard, lettuce, artichoke, and other produce.

The majority of the Excelsior's population around 1880 to 1888 consisted of Italians, followed by the Germans and the Irish, with the balance being Middle European.

The earthquake of 1906 did very little damage to the Excelsior. As a result, many families migrated to the Excelsior from other parts of the city.

A historical note: Amazon Street was originally Greece, and Avalon was China. Japan became Excelsior, India is now Persia; however, some streets were eventually changed because of the anti-Asian fervor that gripped the country, which eventually lead to the Chinese Exclusion Act of 1882, in which immigration from China was prohibited altogether.

From World War I through World War II, the Excelsior District developed at a normal rate. According to Ron Faina of the Excelsior area, Crocker Amazon Park at Moscow and Geneva Avenues became a marshaling point for the U.S. Army during World War II and later a hospital for the U.S. Navy.

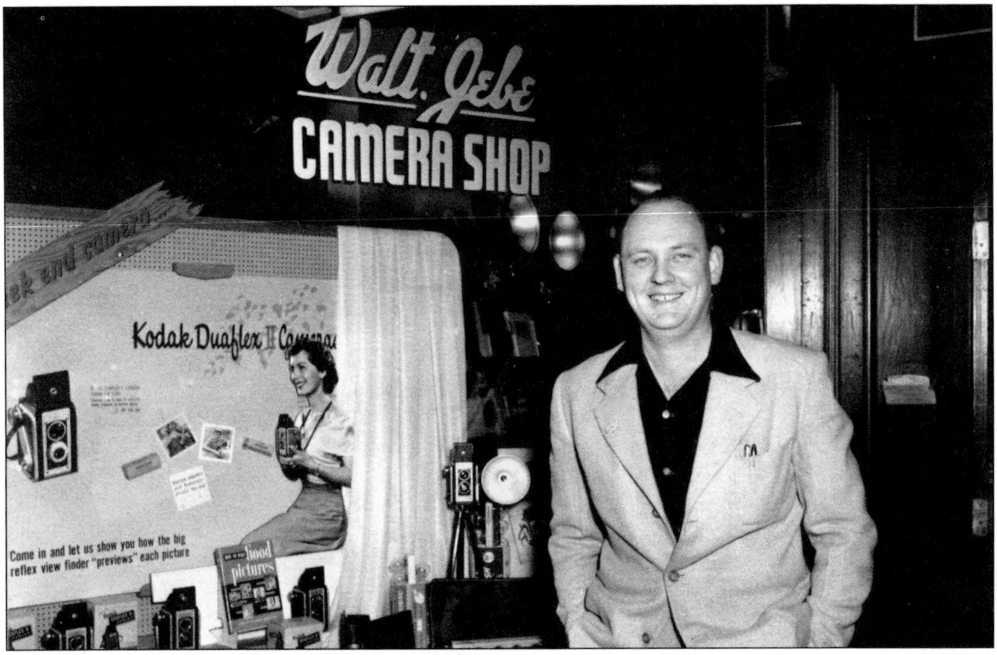

Welcome to the Excelsior. My name is Walter Jebe Sr. I was born in San Francisco at the German Hospital, August 15, 1924, later named the Franklin Hospital and currently Davies Hospital. When I was four years old we moved from Duncan Street in the Mission to the Excelsior District. I attended Excelsior, Monroe, and Balboa High Schools and Penn State for a while. After my release from the U.S. Army in World War II, I established Jebe's Camera Shop on Mission Street at Ocean Avenue in the Excelsior.

Most of the pictures in this book are from my large collection of San Francisco pictures. It must have been my customers and friends that got me interested in the history of the Excelsior. My neighbors were coming into my store, requesting copies and repairs of their old family pictures. Every so often, there was a picture that caught my attention. I would ask if they would permit me to make an extra copy for my private collection. Ninety-nine percent of the people were very happy to help me build my collection and preserve our history. I want to thank all of those grand customers of mine who were so helpful and made it possible for me to build my own collection. I might mention that those people who allowed their history to be shared with me and others were rewarded with a price break on their work. In this book, we will walk through the Excelsior District. Naturally, we will start at Mission Street, which was originally known as El Camino Real, or the Kings Road. This road was traveled by Fr. Junipero Serra and his band of friars, who established a chain of California missions from San Diego to Sonoma. Mission Dolores and the Presidio is where the city of San Francisco began, but eventually civilization moved south on the peninsula and clusters of people created settlements we now know as neighborhoods or districts. The Excelsior Homestead was part of the larger Bernal Rancho; a map of the Excelsior Homestead was filed in mid-1869 at the San Francisco City Hall.

One

EARLY DAYS AND AGRICULTURE

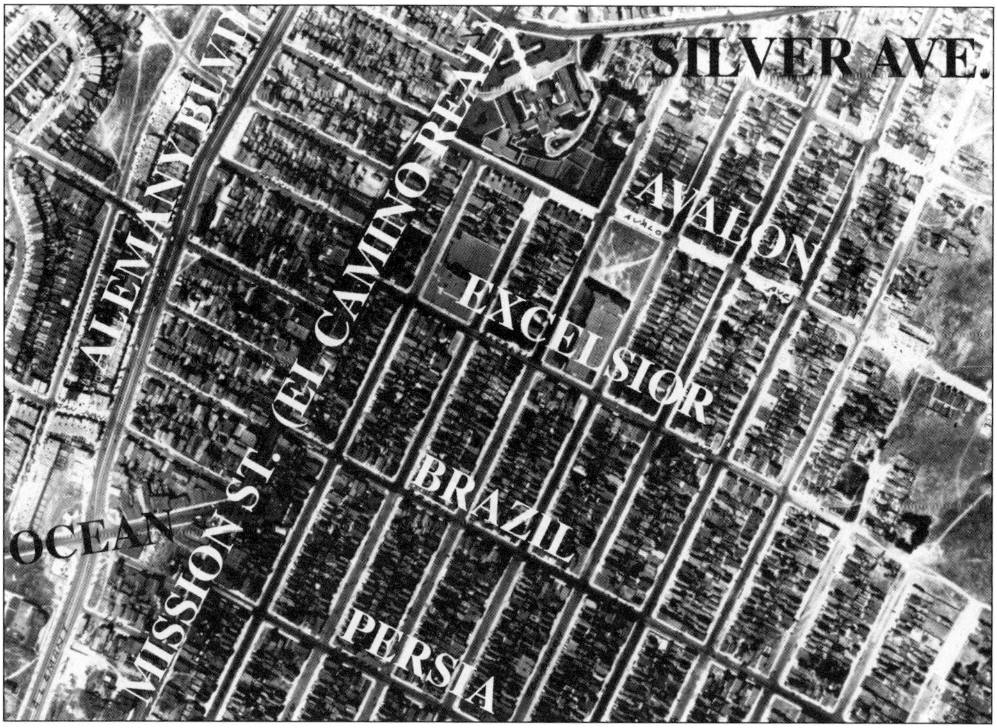

Prior to the 1970s, the Excelsior District was not indicated on any map. For 30 years, the author worked to get map makers to change the words "Outer Mission" to the proper designation, "Excelsior District." The major streets in the neighborhood have been marked in this early-1940s aerial photograph. The entrance to the Jewish Home for the Aged and Infirmed can be found at the intersection of Mission Street (El Camino Real) and Silver Avenue. To the left of the "B" in Alemany Boulevard is an elongated blank patch of ground that today is Cayuga Avenue. The significance of that bare patch is threefold: first, it is the bed of Islais Creek, which flows into the San Francisco Bay. Second, for many years the Barnum & Bailey traveling circus would pitch their huge tents in this area, along with their many animals, to the great excitement of the neighborhood's children. Third, it is today the location of very nice middle-class homes, although, due to Islais Creek, their basements are occasionally flooded. During a storm in the spring of 2004 the water reached a depth of eight feet. The Excelsior School is located at Excelsior and London while the Monroe School is located at Excelsior and Madrid.

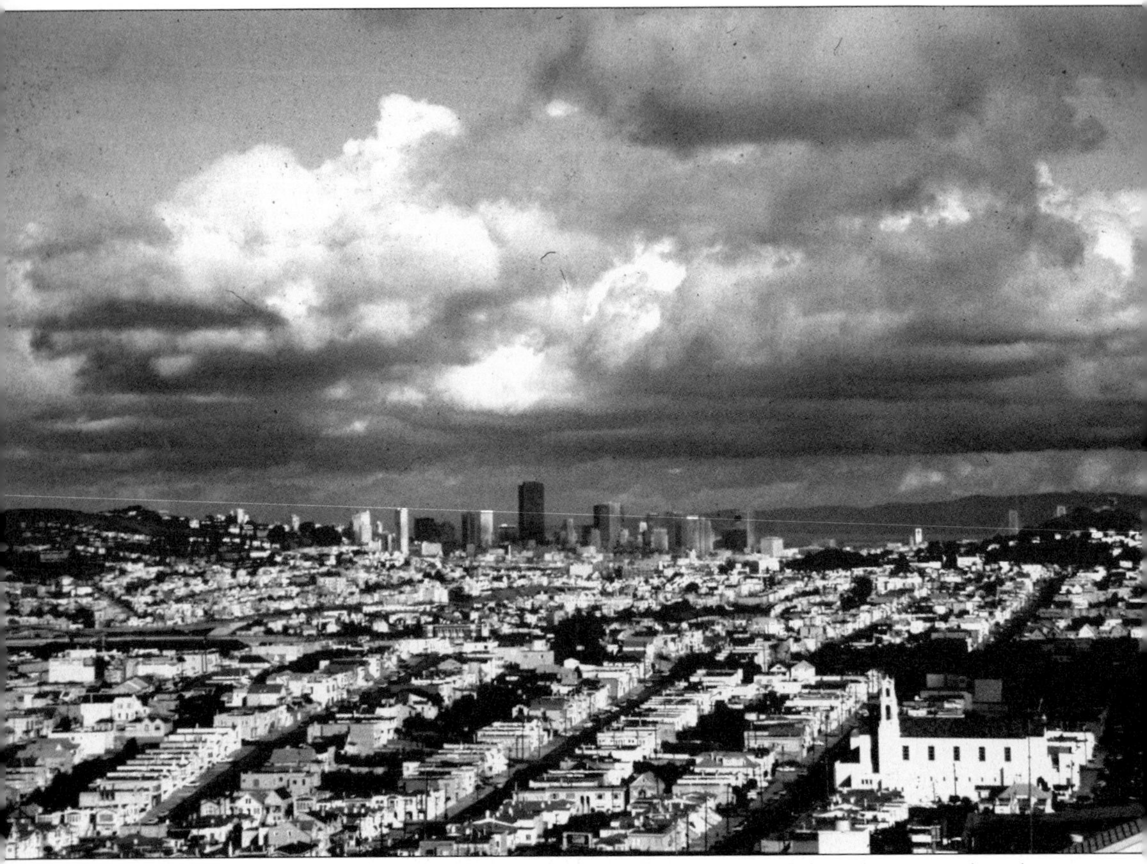

The homes in this picture cover a great period of time, as some of them have stood in the area since about 1870 while others were built yesterday. The downtown skyline and the Bank of America building are visible in the background. From the center of the Excelsior, the Transamerica Pyramid is hidden from view, directly behind the 779-foot-tall Bank of America building. Many other districts of San Francisco do not offer a view of downtown San Francisco and its skyline; thus the Excelsior has been a favorite location for movies.

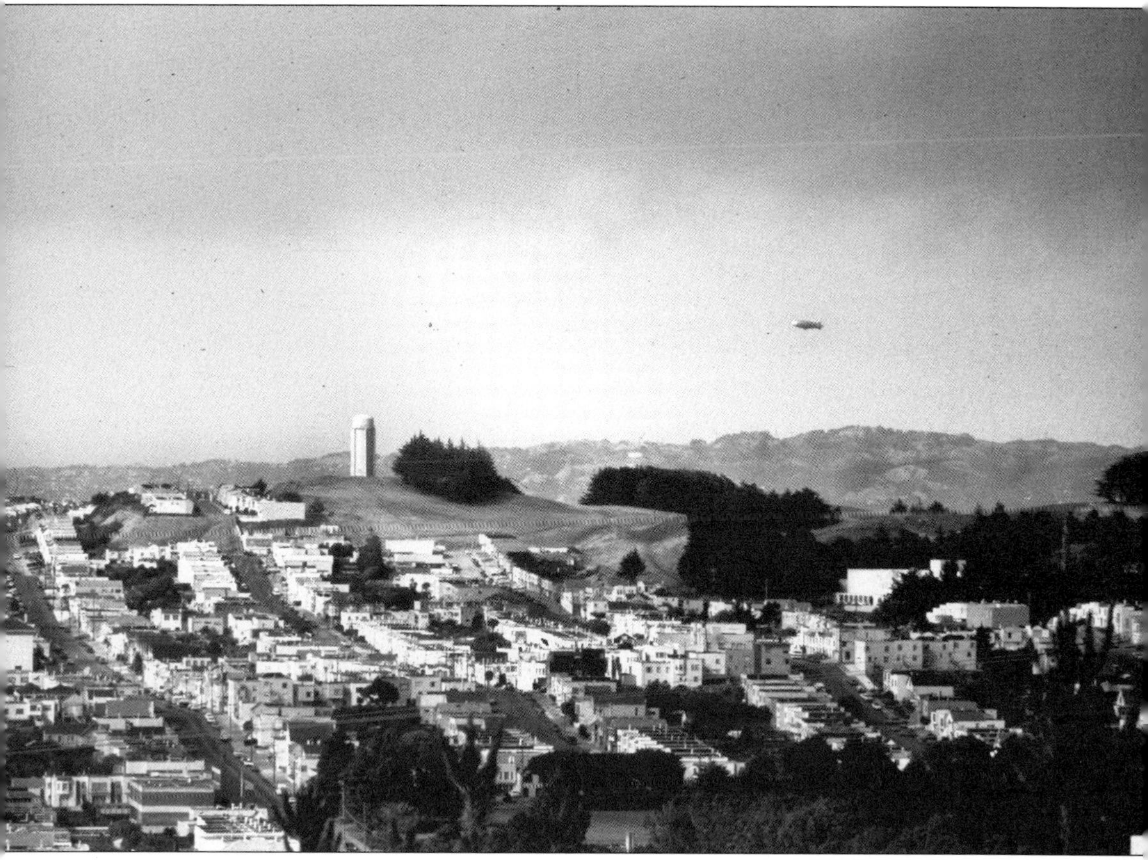

Looking north from Southern Hills, this *c.* 1970 photo shows one of the peaks of the Excelsior District: the landmark water tower off La Grande Avenue in McLaren Park, which provides water pressure for the area. The larger building in the lower left is the Cleveland Elementary School, located on Persia Avenue between Vienna Street and Athens. The large white building in the lower center right, nestled in the trees on the grounds of McLaren Park, is Luther Burbank Middle School on La Grande Avenue between Brazil and Persia Avenue. These two streets are among several entrances to McLaren Park. The Goodyear blimp flies high over Candlestick Park for either a Giants baseball or 49ers football game.

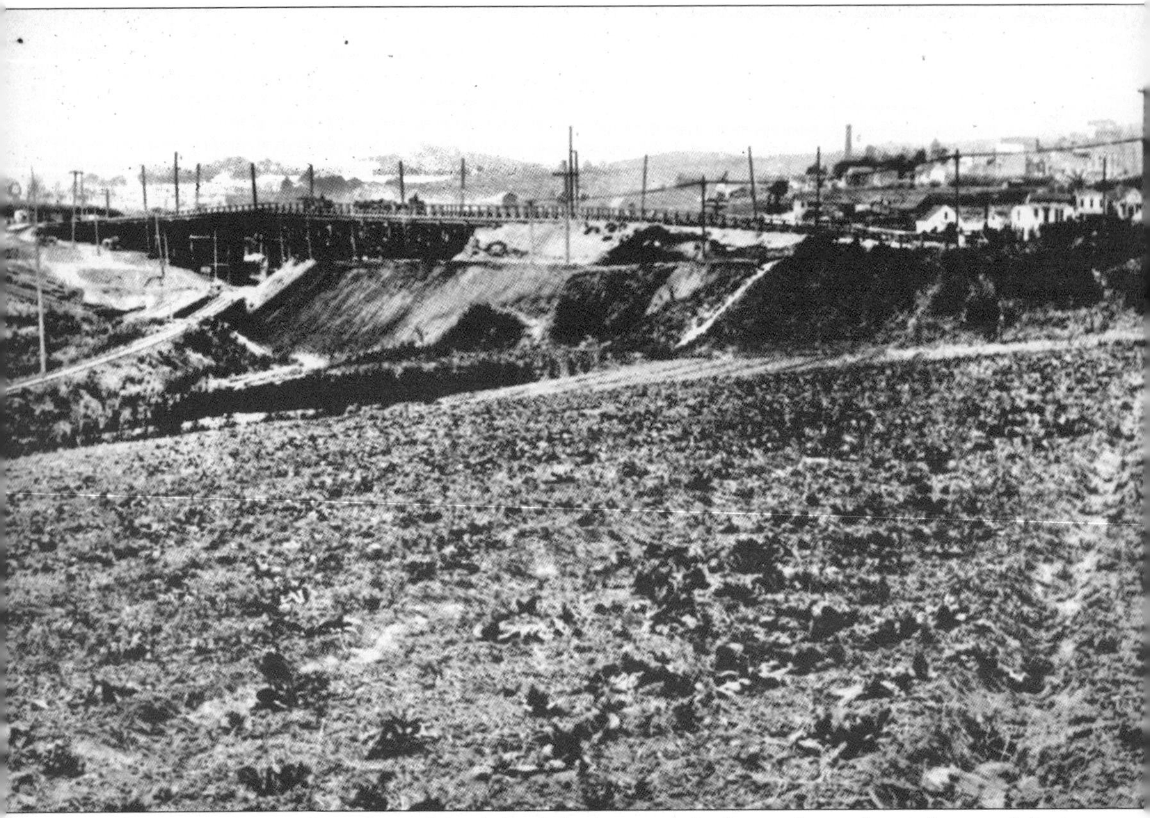

This *c.* 1905 view from Saint Mary's Park looking south shows the early viaduct on Mission Street crossing two interesting points: the trackwork of the Ocean Shore Railroad and the Islais Creek bed. Before the completion of this wooden viaduct, anyone going south on Mission Street (El Camino Real) had to go down a hill on the right side of this picture with their wagons and horses, cross Islais Creek, and continue up the left side toward the south. On the right end of Mission Street (El Camino Real) is Saint Mary's Park. Across Islais Creek going south (on the left), the following streets intersect Mission Street: Trumbull, Ney, Maynard, and Silver Avenue. Saint Mary's Park was the original location of Saint Mary's College, which stood on the site from 1863 to 1927 until it moved to Moraga, California. The college was founded by Joseph Sadoc Alemany, archbishop of San Francisco, after whom Alemany Boulevard is named.

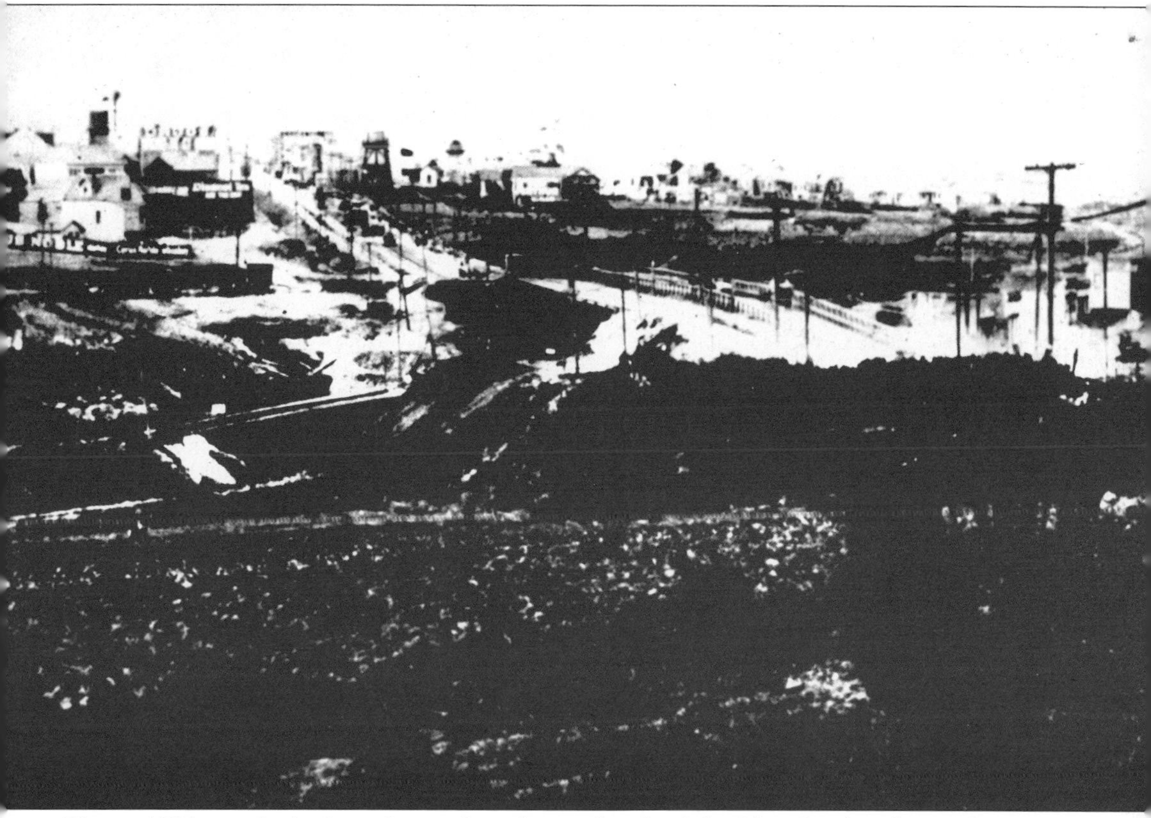

This *c.* 1906 view looks from the north to the south side of the Islais Creek gully. By this time the Ocean Shore Railroad had been completed and was carrying San Franciscans down the coast to Pacifica and Half Moon Bay. Note that railings have been added to the sides of the viaduct, perhaps in response to the influence of the Cyrus Noble Whiskey ad on the left—the first billboard of many to dot the hills surrounding the gulch that would eventually become Highway 280 and Alemany Boulevard. The Cyrus Noble sign is on Ney Street at Mission, the current location of Cala Foods. Directly down the hill at the bottom was once a large tannery building. As a youth the author and his friend Bill Laughrey would play with other children near the ponds in the creek near the tannery, catching Stickleback fish and sometimes falling into the water, much to the consternation of their mothers later in the day.

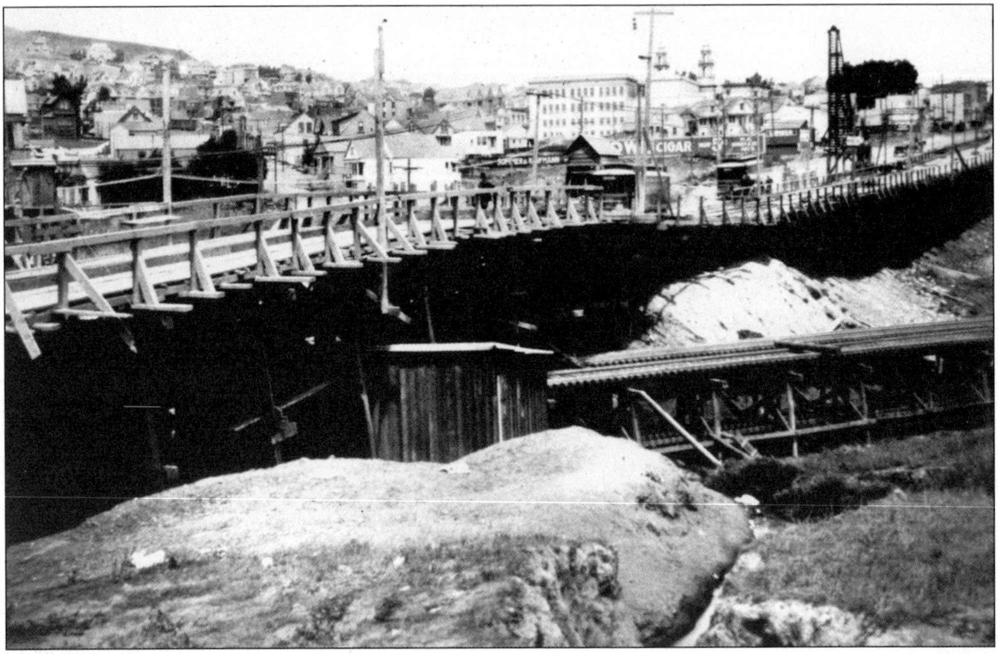

This mid-1920s view looks from the south side of the Islais Creek gully and the Ocean Shore Railroad (now Alemany Boulevard and Highway 280). Saint John the Evangelist Catholic Church and Saint John's School on Saint Mary's Avenue and Marsily can be seen in the upper center right, although Saint John's School no longer exists. A new Saint John's School was built on Mission Street but at the time of this writing is closed.

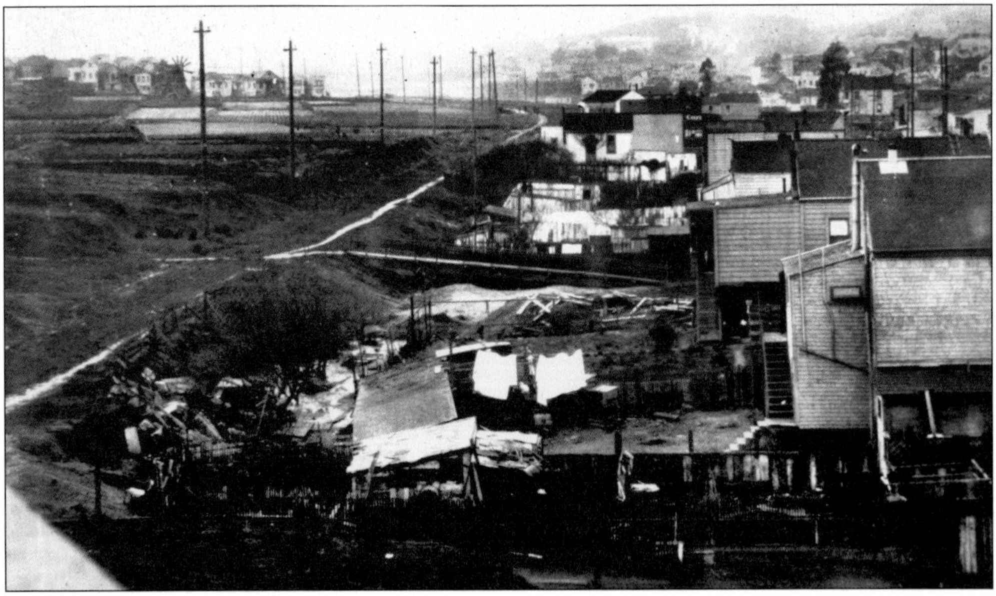

This *c.* 1920 view from the Mission Street viaduct looking southwest shows where Alemany Boulevard will later be situated (extreme left). To the center left beyond the two-line telephone poles are produce fields irrigated by a windmill located to the left of the first visible telephone pole. The pipe in the center carried water up from Islais Creek into an irrigation channel that also served as a footpath going south curving back toward Mission Street.

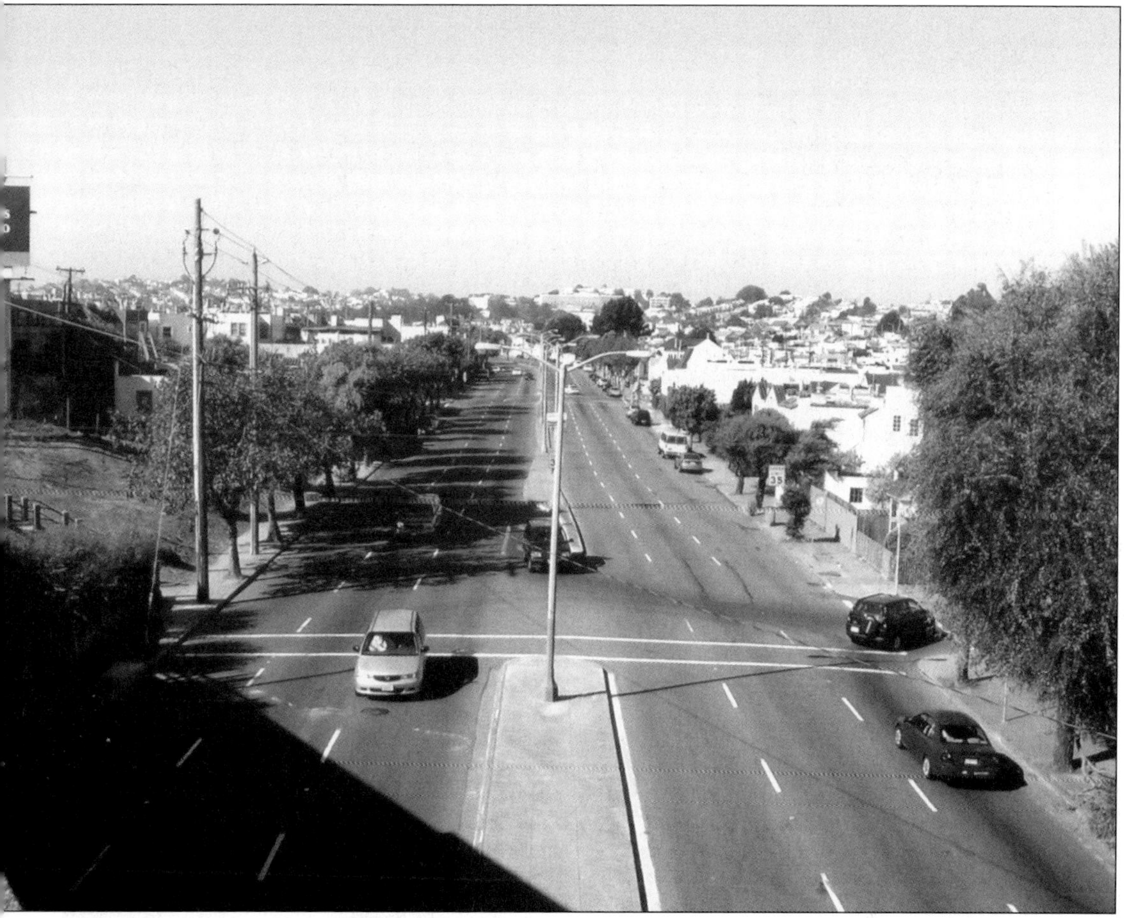

This photo shows Alemany Boulevard as it appears today, from the Mission Street viaduct looking southwest. Take note of the changes from the previous pictures. What is now Alemany Boulevard with its many nice homes was farmland, sand, and a great number of trees.

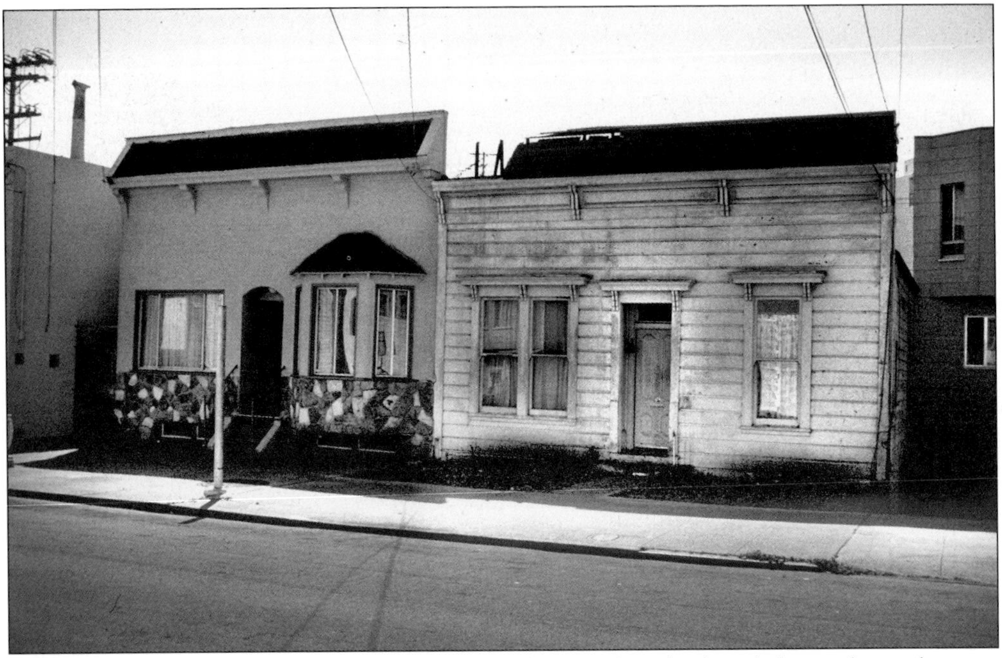

These homes on Cayuga Avenue and Still Street have their backyards located on what was once Islais Creek.

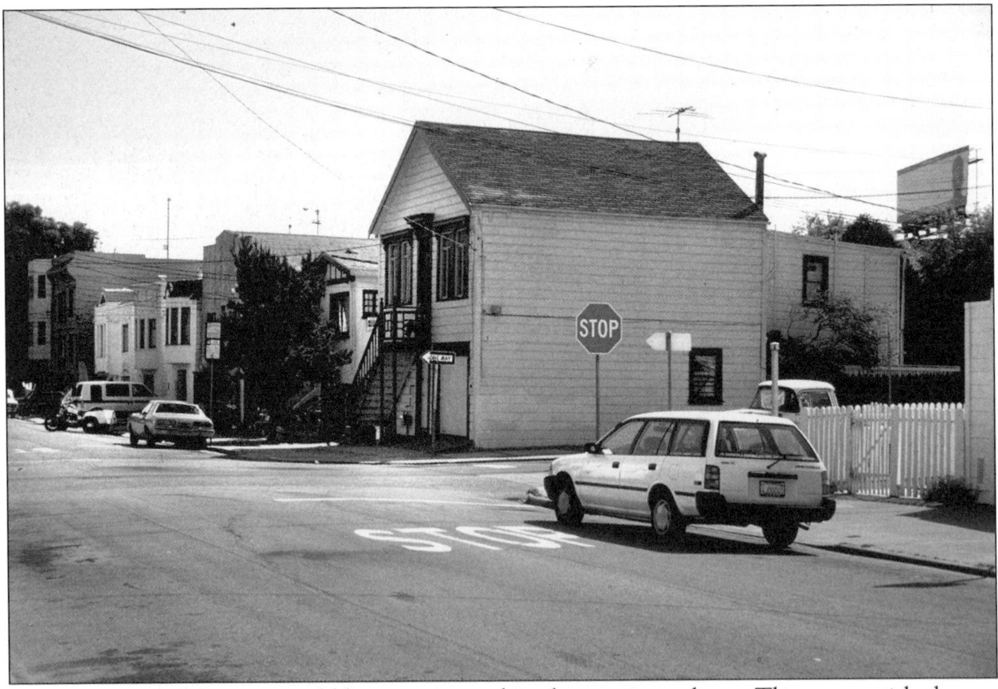

Here are more of those very old homes pictured in the previous photo. The street with the car is Cayuga Avenue while the one-way street sign is Lyell Street. Being the former bed of Islais Creek, Cayuga Avenue sometimes floods in this area.

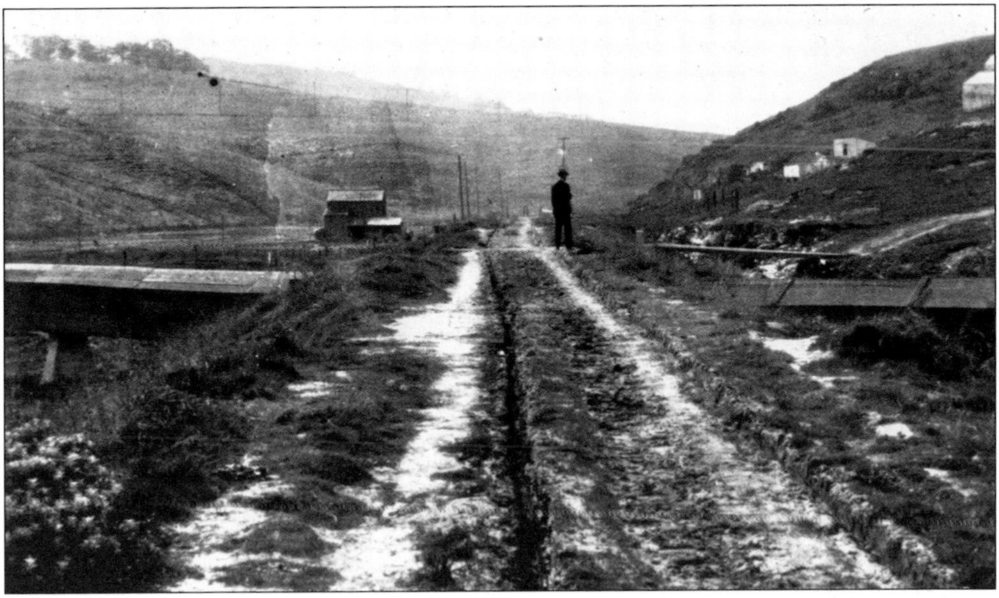

This view looking south shows the Islais Creek gully on the far left, which today is Highway 280 South. Note the wooden-covered aqueduct over the creek used for carrying water. In the center is the former track bed for the Ocean Shore Railroad. The pipe opposite the man in the photo was also used for water transportation.

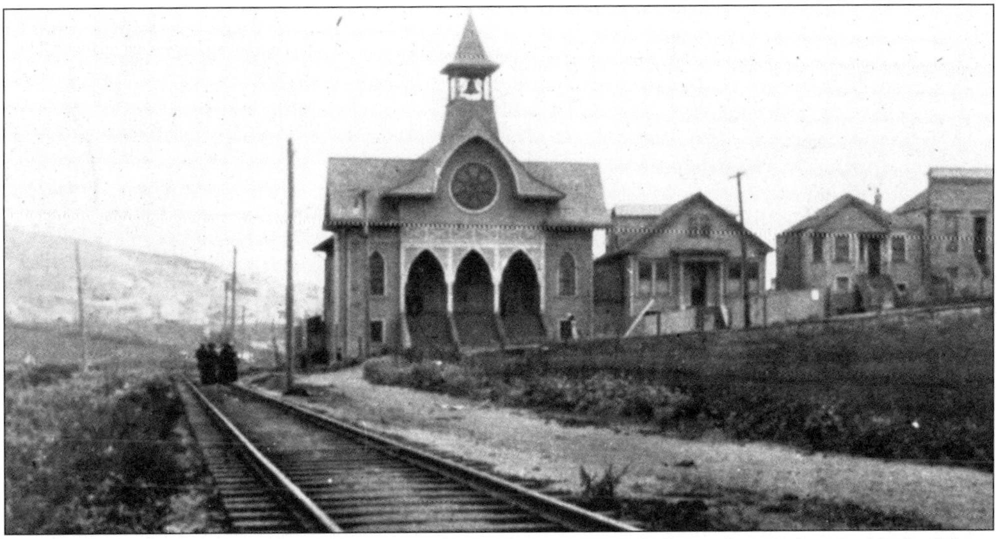

Corpus Christi Catholic Church was built for $7,000 and dedicated on May 9, 1888. When Corpus Christi was built, the Excelsior District was nothing but rolling hills with Italian, Swiss, and German farmers living in a few scattered houses. The Italian farmers in this southern end of San Francisco wanted a local priest who would give mass in the native language so that they would no longer have to travel to Saint Peter and Paul's Church in North Beach by horse and wagon to fetch one. The three-and-a-half-hour trip was an all day affair in one direction, and a few of the farmers would travel to North Beach on Saturday and bring the priest out to the Excelsior, who would then stay with a family overnight. Sunday mass was said in one of the local barns, and the priest was then returned to North Beach. Here, the Ocean Shore Railroad tracks run on what is now Alemany Boulevard and Santa Rosa Street.

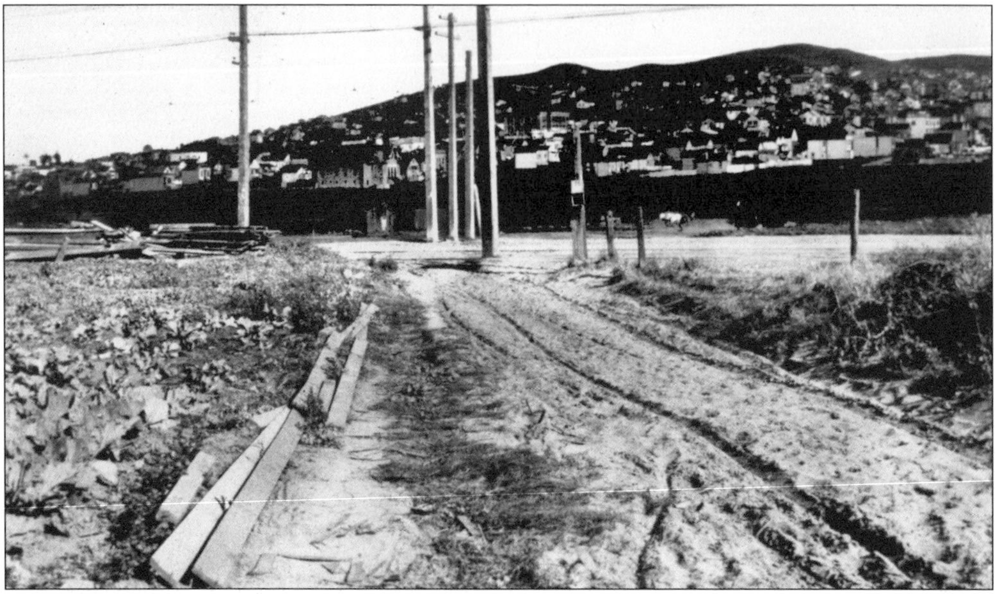

This view of the Excelsior District, believed to have been taken around 1895, looks across San Jose Avenue from what is now Balboa Park. Corpus Christi Church is just visible to the left of the telephone poles. At this time the hill was home to sheep, cattle, and dairy ranches. Today, most of that area is known as McLaren Park, the second largest park in San Francisco.

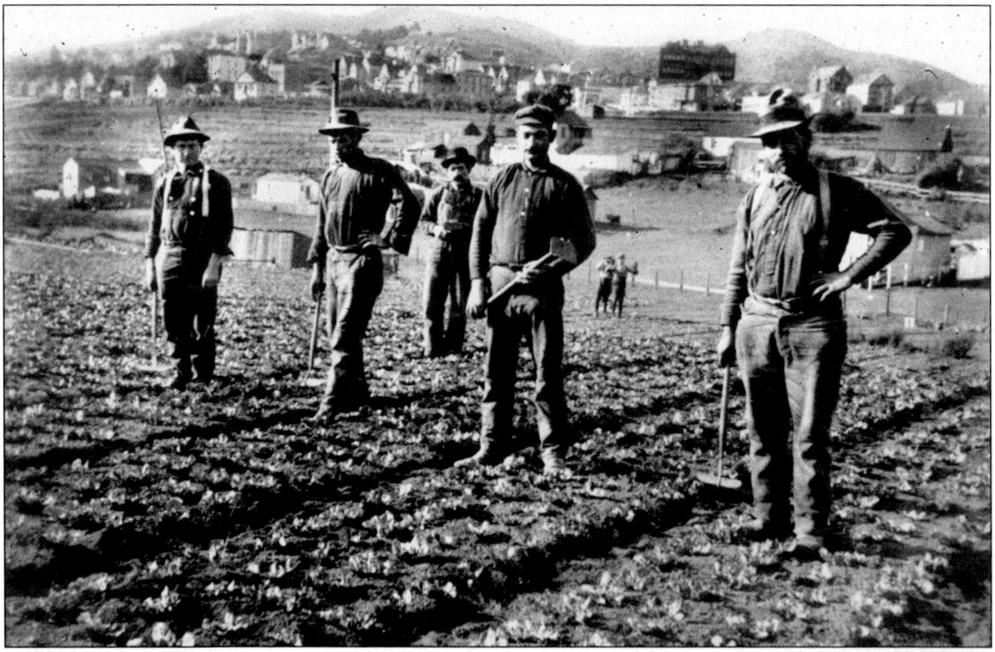

This photo shows early Italian, Swiss, and German farmers and was taken just off Mission and Maynard Streets. What grew well in this part of "The City" was Swiss chard, potatoes, zucchini, lettuce, basil, parsley, strawberries, certain tomatoes, string beans, Italian beans, cabbage, Brussels sprouts, artichokes, and other fresh vegetables, many grown for the San Francisco restaurants. The Westlake area, developed by Henry Dolelger, was primarily vegetable gardens until after World War II.

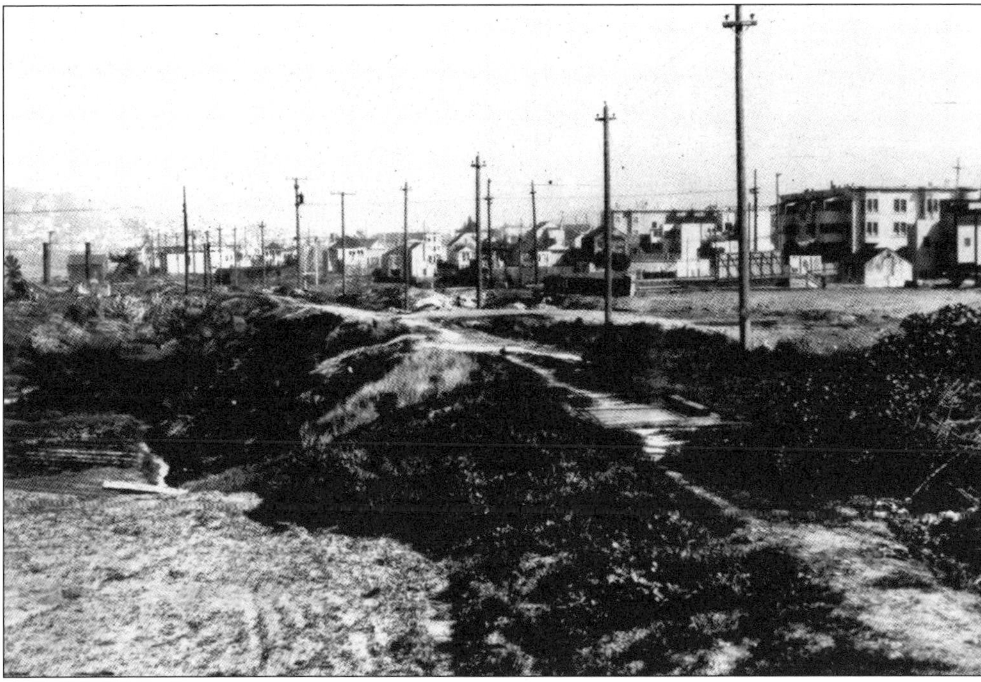

The area left of the telephone lines is now Alemany Boulevard. The large building on the right center is still standing on Mission Street at Onandaga. The area in the center of this picture is now the location of a very large telephone exchange.

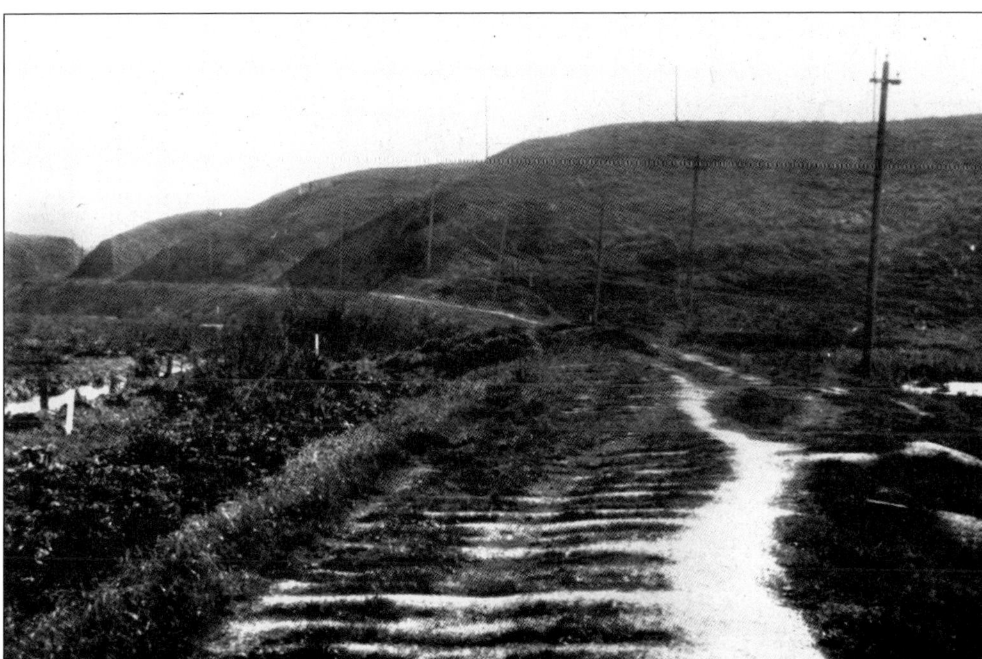

Another view of Islais Creek shows it gathering water from other tributaries and becoming larger as it nears the bay. Note the traces of the Ocean Shore Railroad; it ran along the creek in some areas before it was removed.

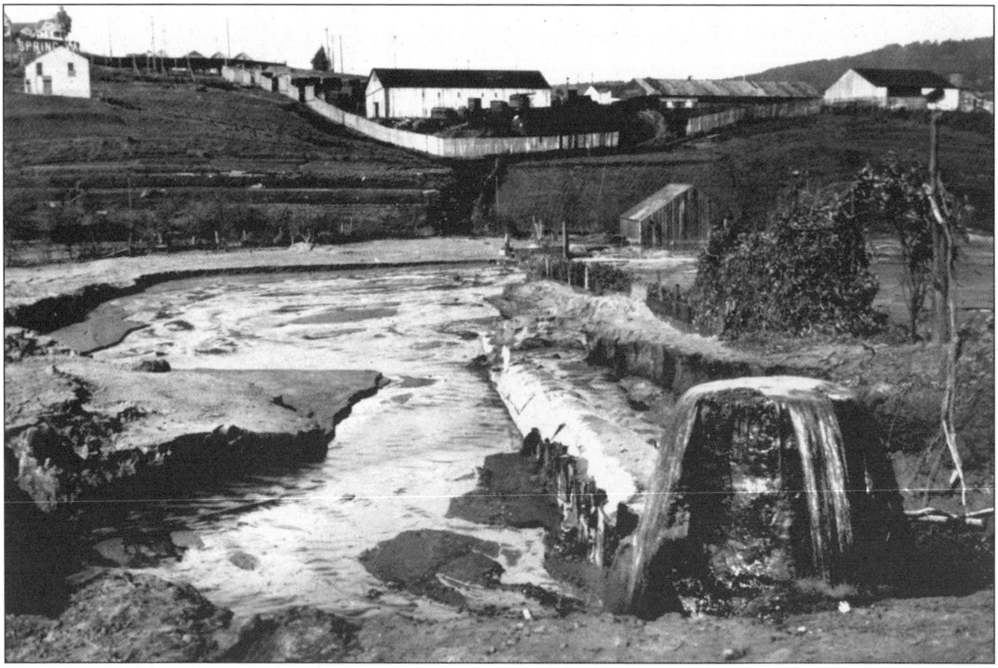

This was the location of Lake Geneva, the source of Islais Creek, which flowed the length of the Excelsior District, appearing just south of Geneva Avenue looking west. This photo is more documentation that this area was heavily farmed. The barns pictured here stored hay and feed and provided protection for cattle.

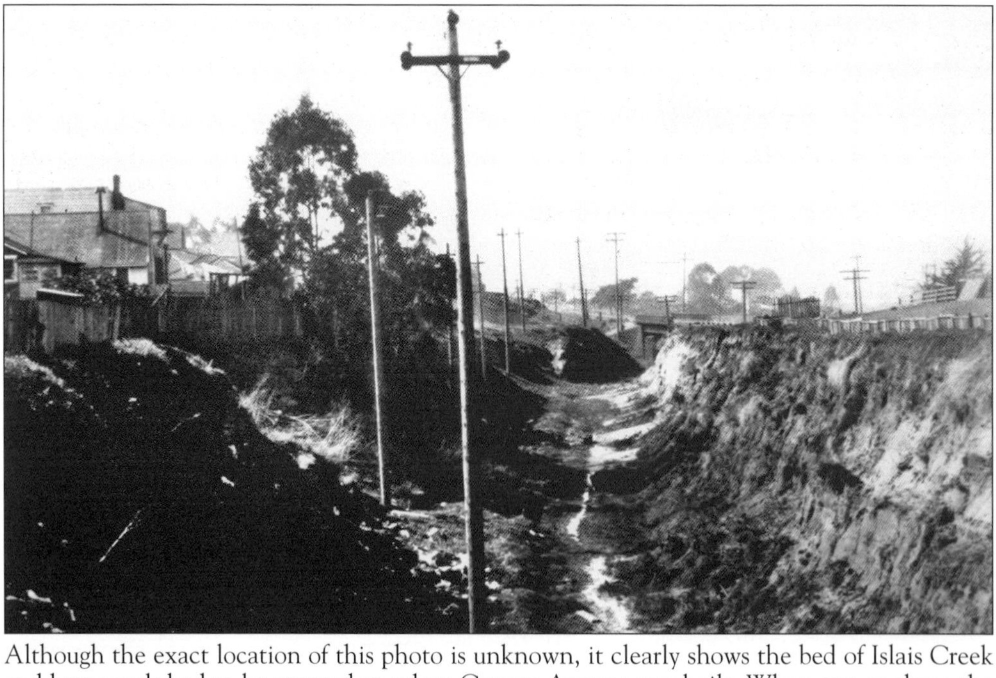

Although the exact location of this photo is unknown, it clearly shows the bed of Islais Creek and how much had to be covered up when Cayuga Avenue was built. When one analyzes the size of the creek's banks and its depth, it becomes obvious why Cayuga Avenue every so often reaches flood stage.

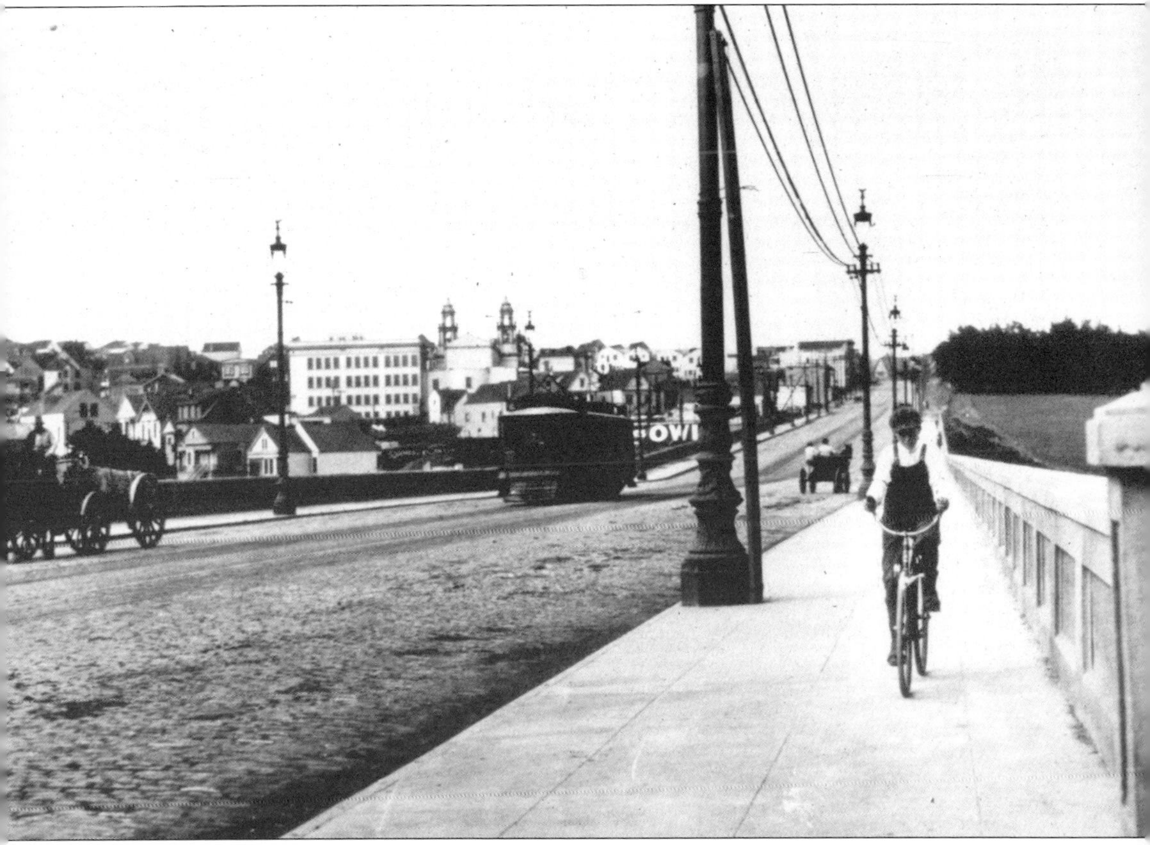

This image is of the Mission Street viaduct, built *c.* 1927, looking north. The streetcar appears to be the famous No. 40 that ran from Fifth and Market Streets to San Mateo. This car offered a special deluxe ride for 10¢ that featured closed doors at both ends to insulate passengers from the cold winter weather, overstuffed leather seats with polished brass fittings, and interior wood of polished mahogany. Note that the other form of transportation is the horse and wagon and that there is very little traffic on the street. Saint John's Catholic Church is shown just above the streetcar with Saint John's School next to it.

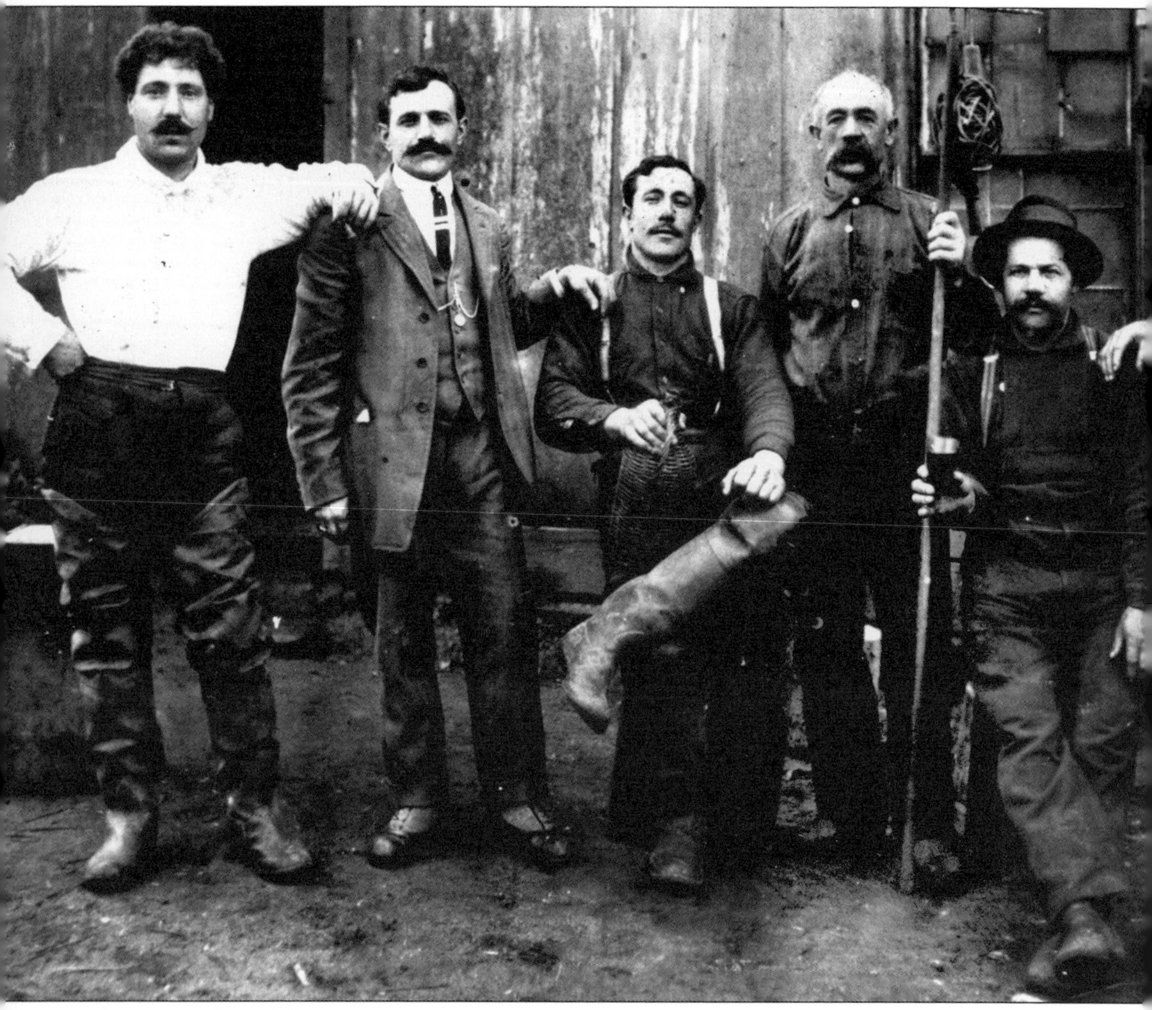

The nationality of this group of relaxed-looking group of local farmers is unknown. According to John Consiglieri, who was born in the Excelsior District in 1917 and still lives in the same house across from Corpus Christi Church, most of the farmers and dairy ranchers were Italian, Swiss, or German. This would also help to explain why the area just across the valley to Glen Park used be called Little Switzerland.

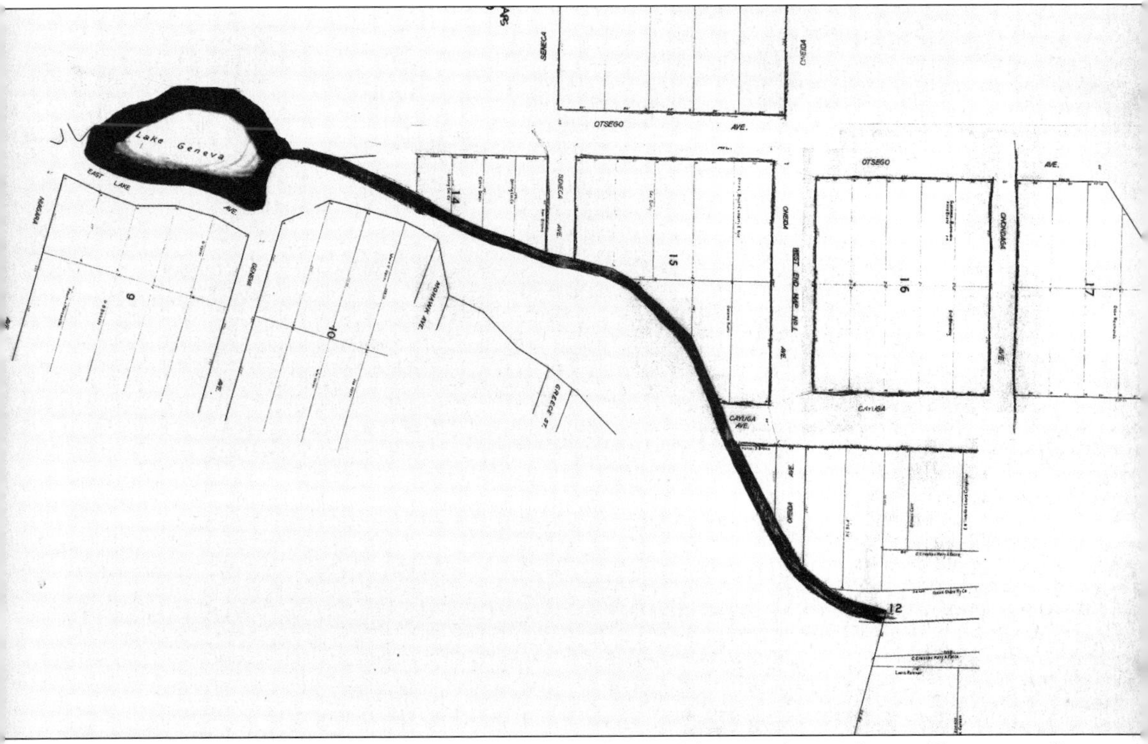

This 1907 map may surprise a great number of residents of the Excelsior, Mission Terrace, and the rest of the Outer Mission (as it is sometimes called), considering that there is a lake on the upper left hand side. Lake Geneva, which is most likely where Geneva Avenue got its name, appears to have been situated in the vicinity of Geneva and Cayuga Avenues. Islais Creek flows out of Lake Geneva to the bay, and when this map is enlarged one can see that this creek flows under the cafeteria of Balboa High School, which accounts for the flooding of the school's cafeteria. Flooding can be prevented if the sump pumps are properly maintained, as is the case with San Francisco's city hall and main library, which use the pumps to keep water out. (Map courtesy of Bonnie Sherek.)

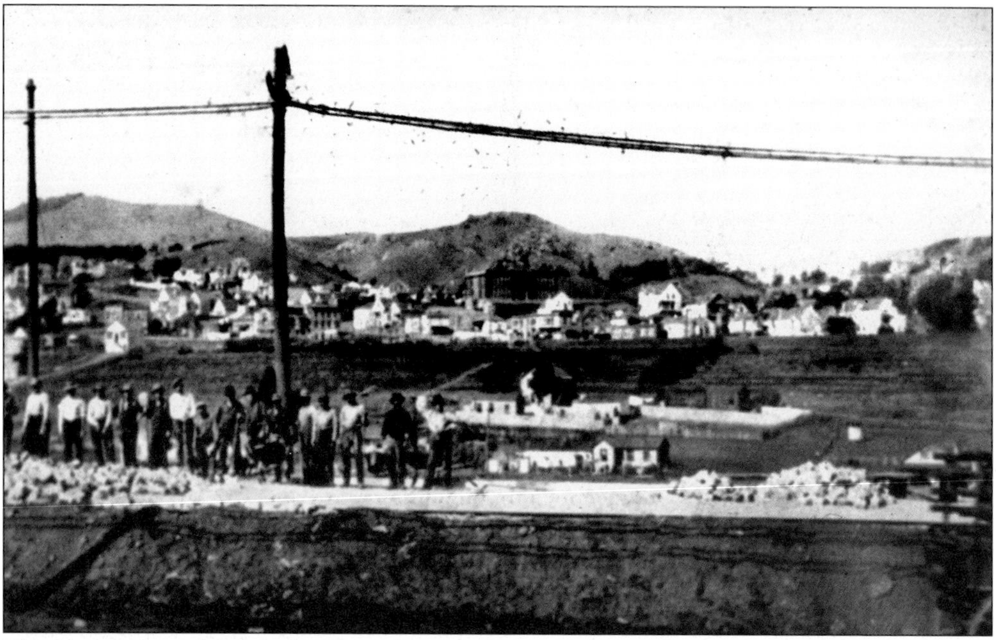

This picture shows hard-working men laying rail tracks for the streetcars to come to the southern part of San Francisco. The residential area has grown much larger, providing one of many reasons to expand the rail system to Daly City. Glen Park School can be seen in the background.

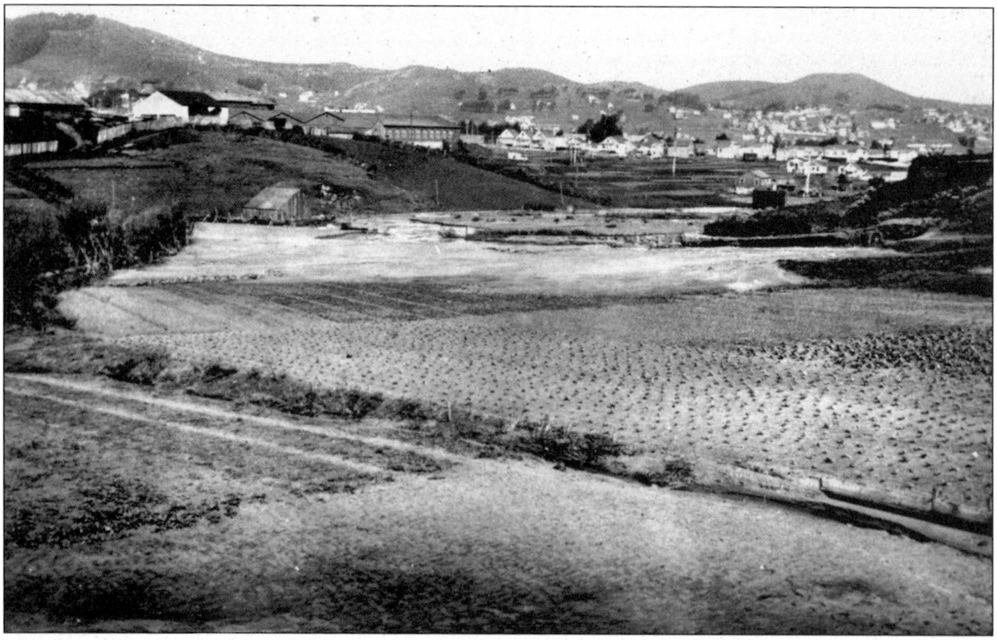

The Excelsior and Mission Terrace areas are in a valley, and this view provides a good idea of the fertile farmland that surrounded that area. This was good farmland that was lost to home building, and history continues to repeat itself as development advances down the peninsula. Glen Park can be seen growing on the upper right; today it is a wonderful area in San Francisco and a major BART (Bay Area Rapid Transit) train stop. The central part of this photo should be just about the location of the Balboa Park Station.

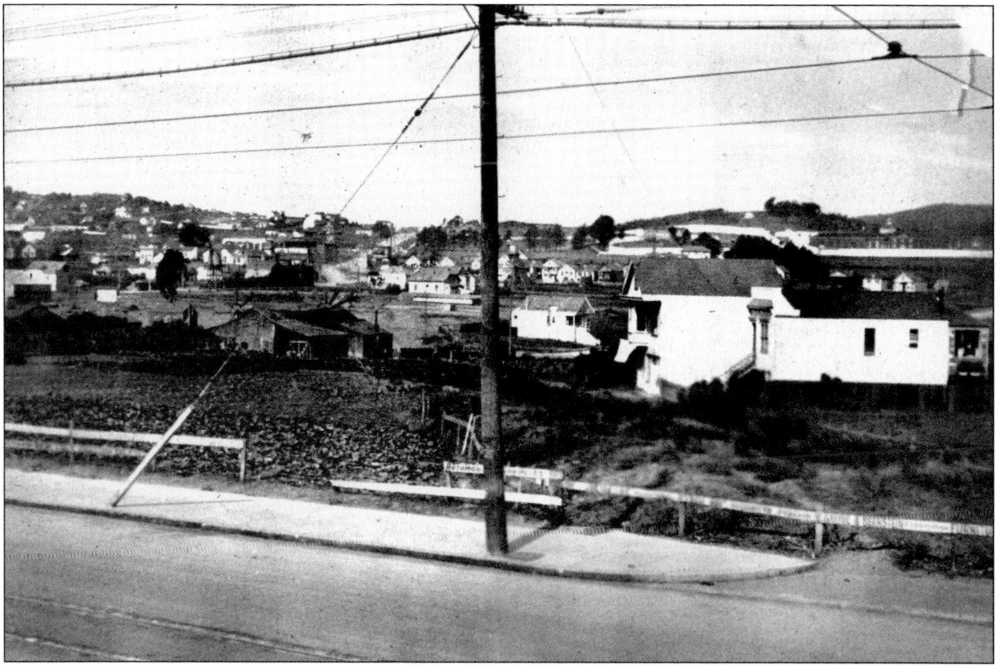

This is a view from Mission Street looking west. It is hard to say if this is a family farm with the owners using their land both to farm and sell vegetables or if it is part farm and some retail. Whatever it may be, note the streetcar tracks (lower left) and the farm area that extends to the sidewalk. The Excelsior District had sidewalks fairly early in its development, and it also is interesting to note that this sidewalk has a curb and is rounded to indicate the ending of a block. Plans for residential neighborhoods obviously were underway at this time.

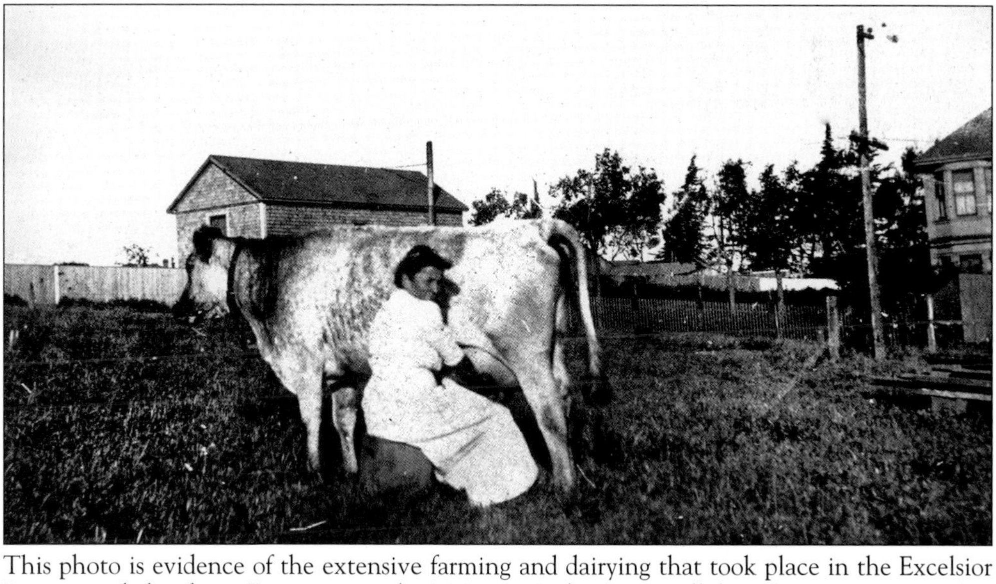

This photo is evidence of the extensive farming and dairying that took place in the Excelsior District and elsewhere. For instance, the McLaren Park area was all dairy farms. Note, too, that the area was sparsely inhabited, as evidenced by this lonely farm house—which nonetheless boasted the famous San Francisco Bay windows. However, the farm wasn't too far out, considering that the power pole near the house showed it had electricity.

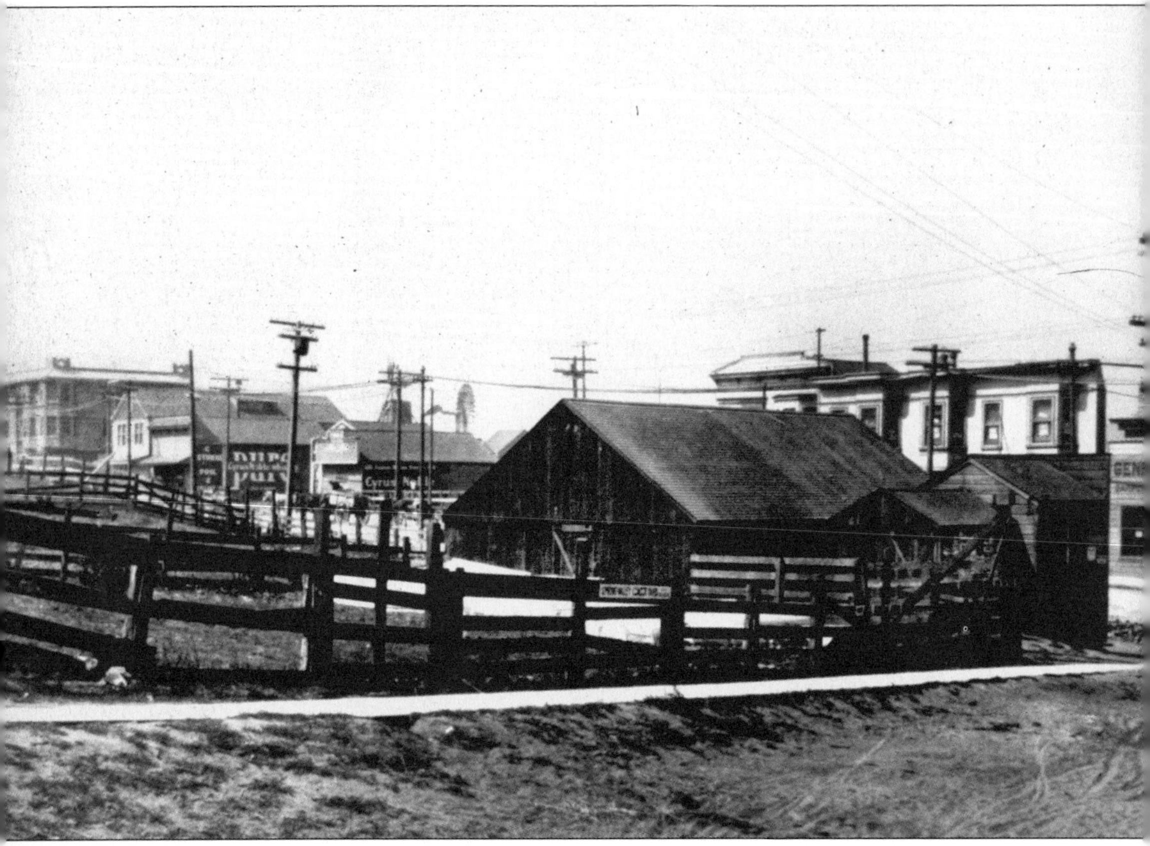

Can you guess the location of this photo? The barn is at a very important intersection in the Excelsior District, while the unpaved area in the lower front is a main intersection today. The street in front of the barn is Mission Street. Left of the barn roof is a windmill, and to the left of the windmill is a water tower that most likely served to store the water pumped by the mill. The bulky building to the far-left center is still in operation at the same location and has not changed much over the years, except for maybe the paint. A bar in that building on the corner of Mission Street is also still in operation. The location? Silver Avenue and Mission Street, known for years as the grand entrance to the Jewish Home for the Elderly. During the writing of this book the entrance has been fenced off.

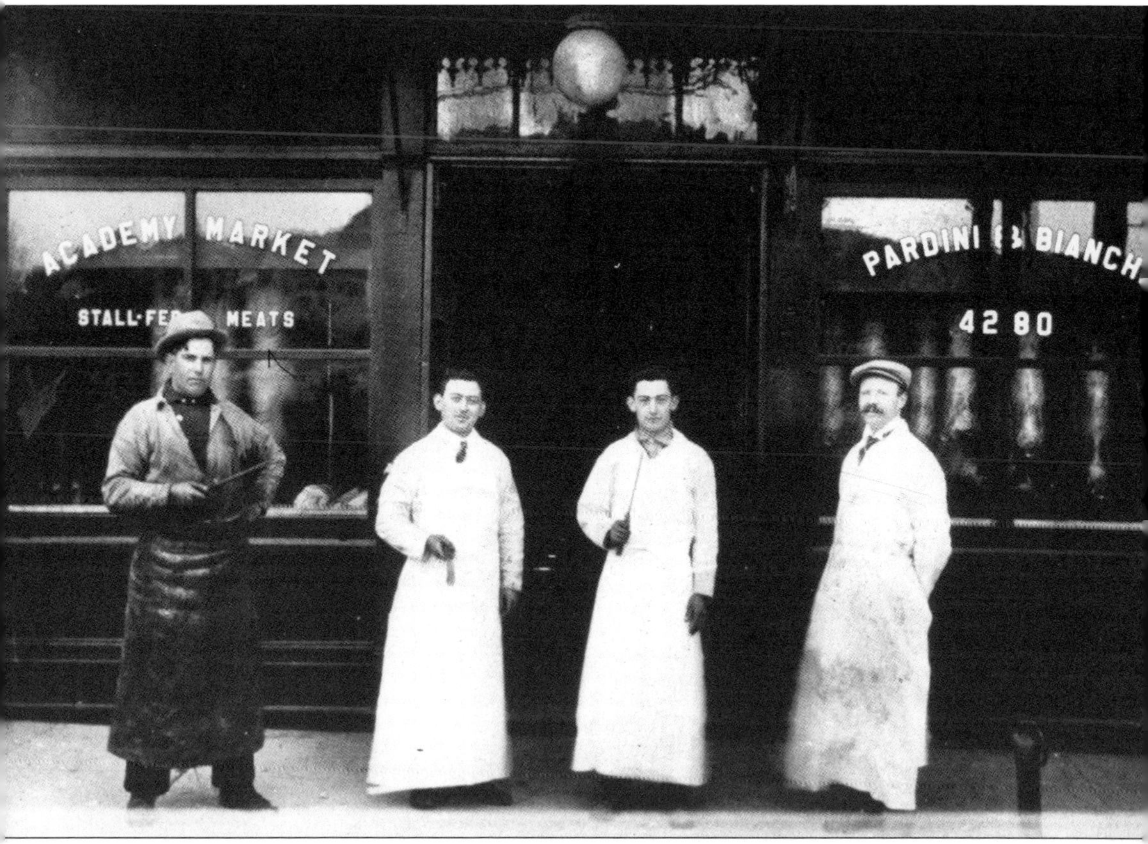

Pardini and Bianchi Academy Market was located at 4280 Mission Street—although you could walk up and down Mission Street for days and not find this address. The best way to describe this location is to say the Pardini and Bianchi Academy Market was directly across from that barn that was the entrance to what is now the Jewish Home for the Elderly at Silver Avenue and Mission Street. Note the whole lambs hanging in the windows, probably without the benefit of refrigeration.

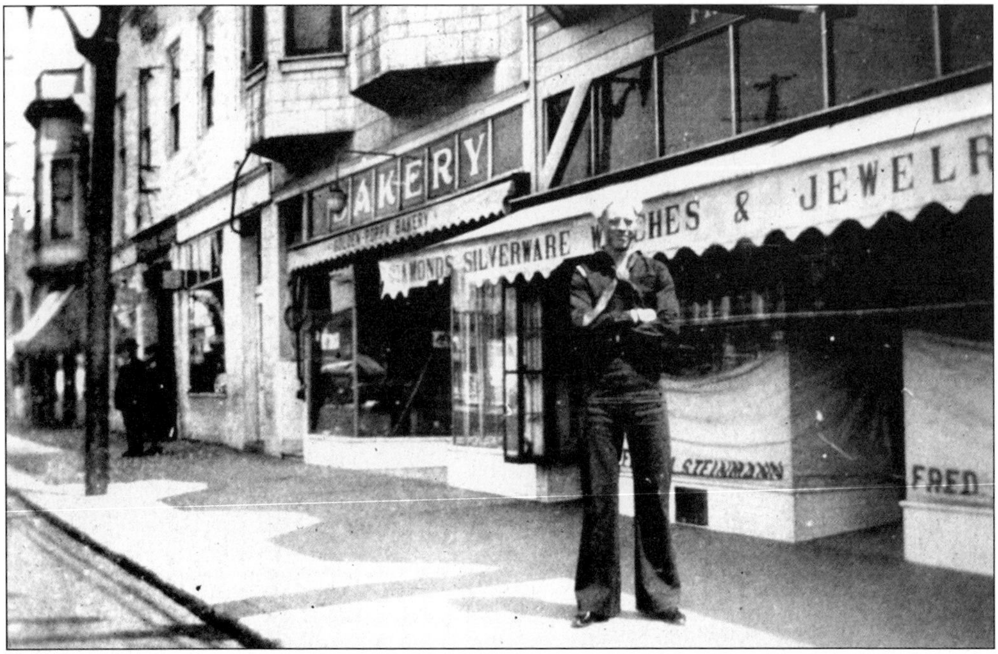

Here we see a sailor in a typical scene during World War II, in the 4500 Block of Mission between Excelsior and Brazil.

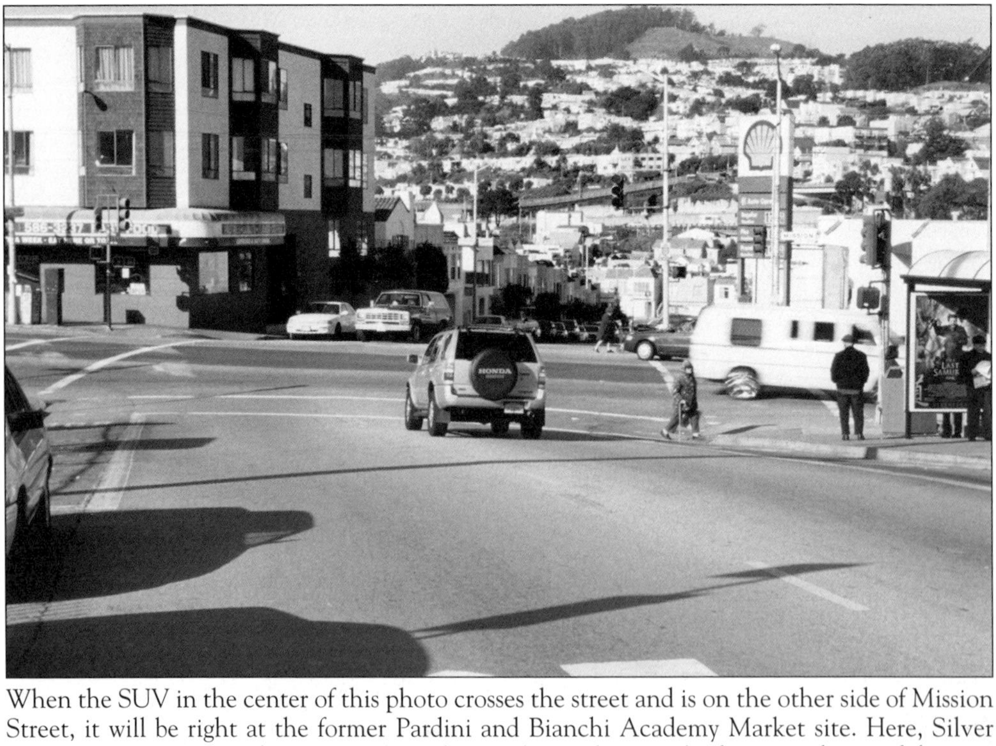

When the SUV in the center of this photo crosses the street and is on the other side of Mission Street, it will be right at the former Pardini and Bianchi Academy Market site. Here, Silver Avenue runs down to Alemany Boulevard. Note how Glenn Park, the central part of the area with the homes, has grown. There are no more farms or vegetable gardens.

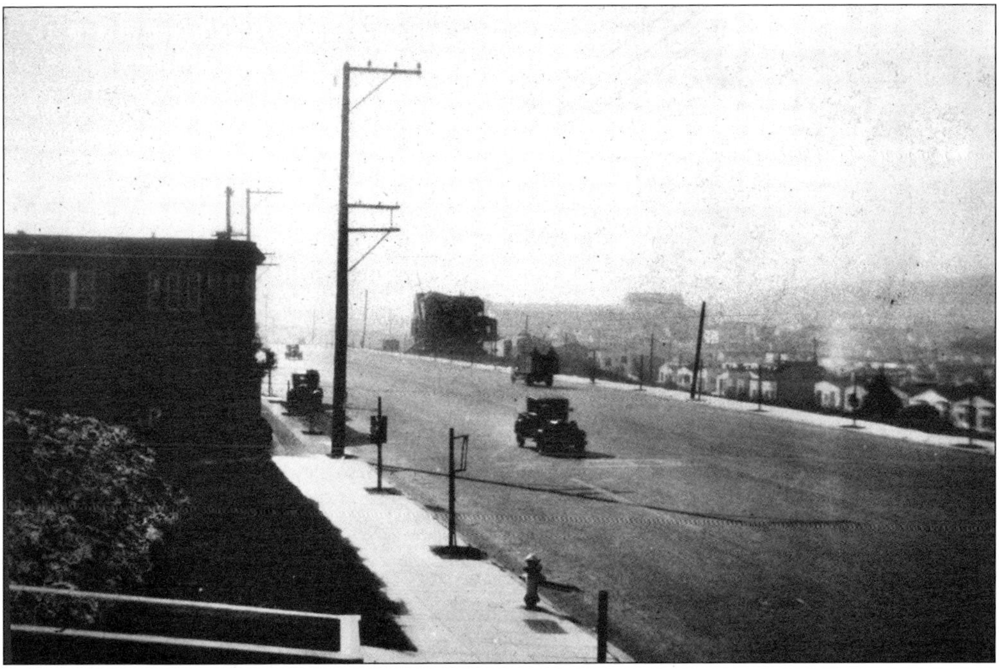

Here, we see some very light traffic (at least compared to today) on Mission Street in the mid-1920s. Below is a view of Mission Street looking south from about Avalon Street.

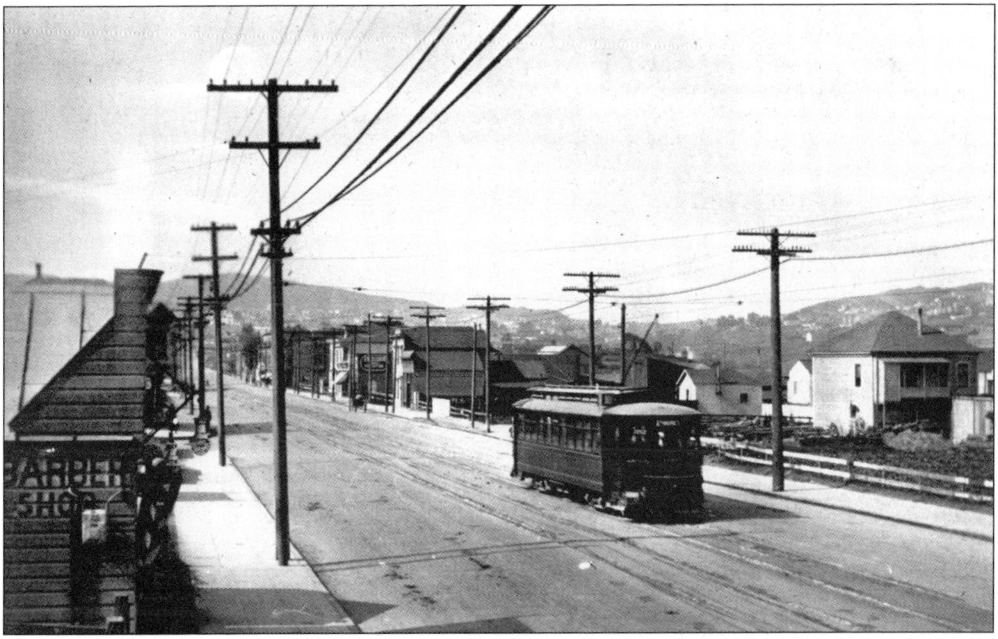

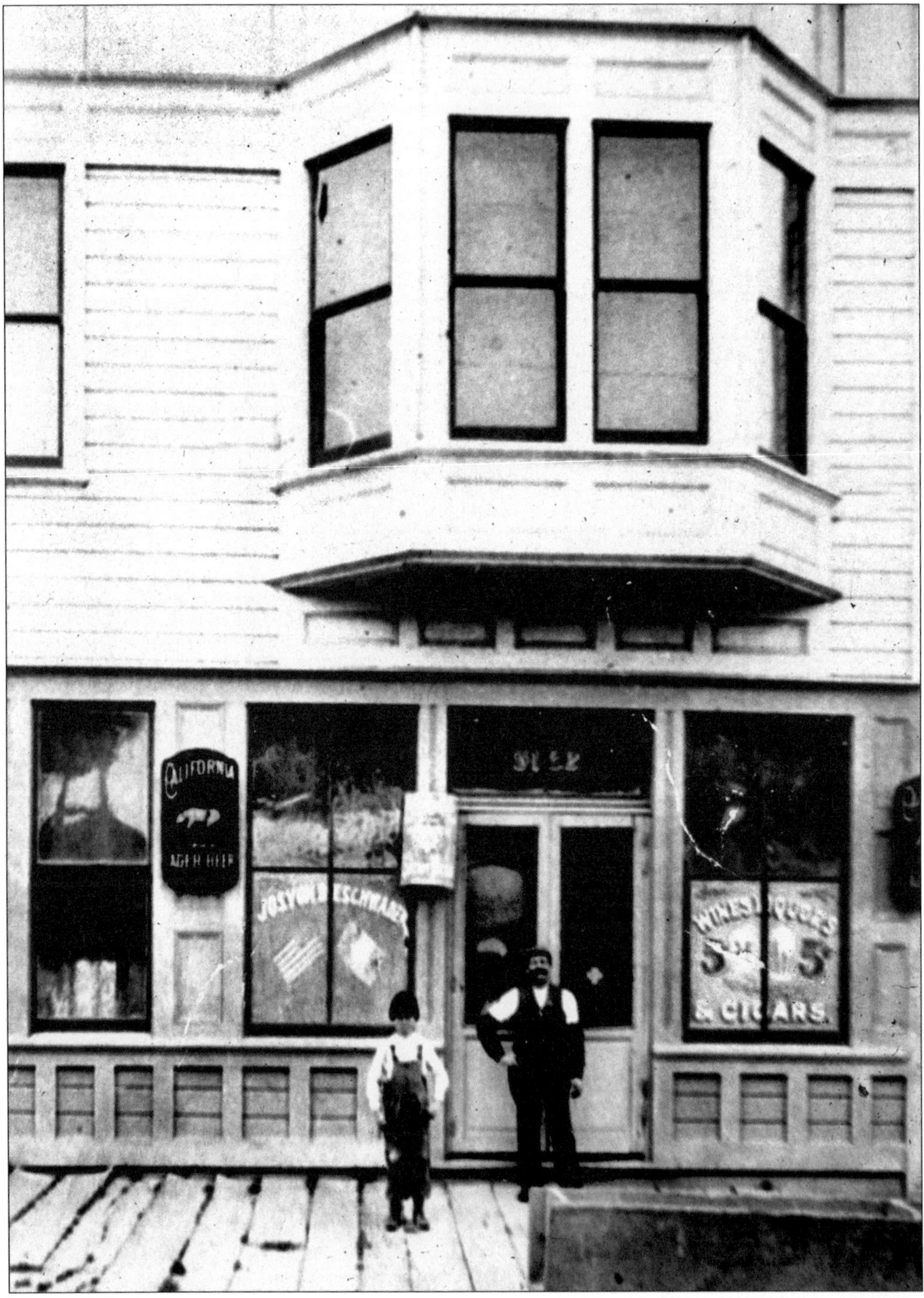

Joyson D. Eschrader is the name on the window to the left of the door at this business. Under the owner's name is an American flag and an Italian flag. Note that the sidewalks are made of well-worn wooden planks while in the lower-right corner is a watering trough for horses. The black sign on the left reads "California Lager Beer" and has the California bear for its symbol. The sign in the right window read "Wine, Liquors & Cigars 5¢."

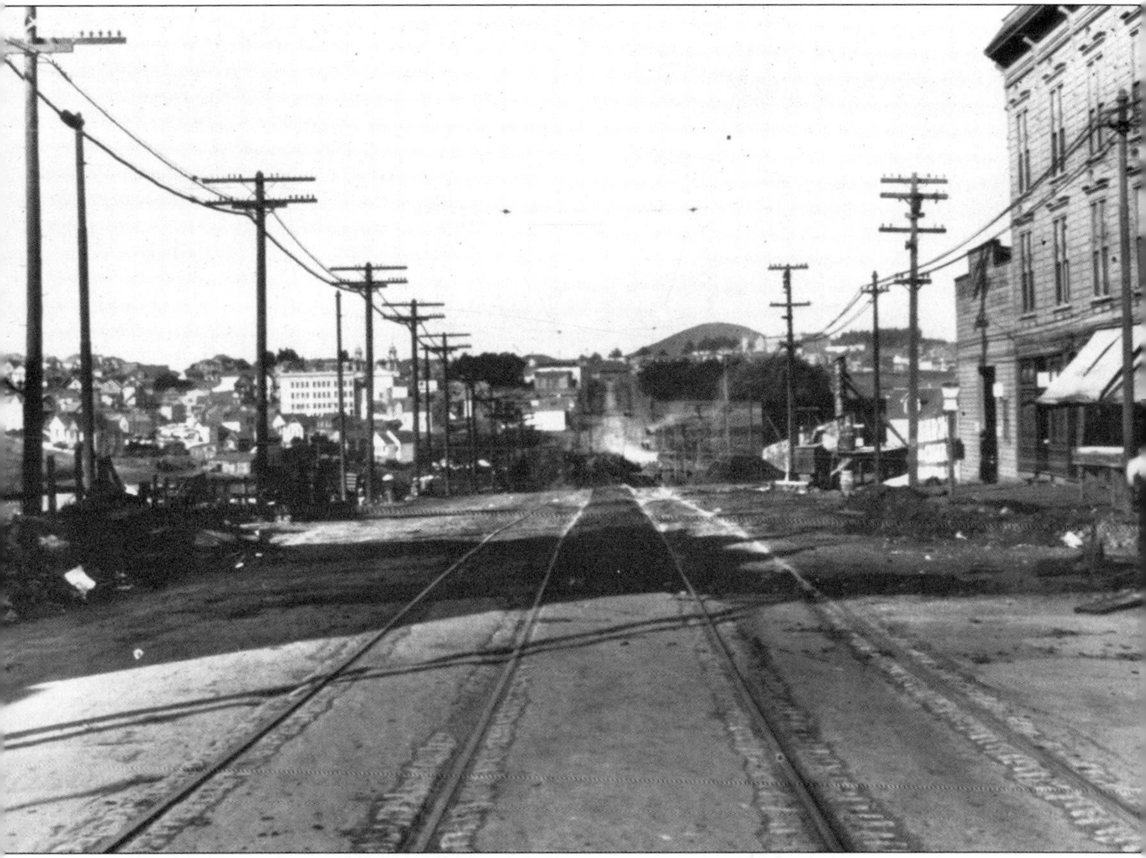

This photo may have been taken around 1915. Note the car tracks in the center leading to Saint John's School on the left. Saint John's was later replaced with a new high school located on Mission Street next to the present YMCA.

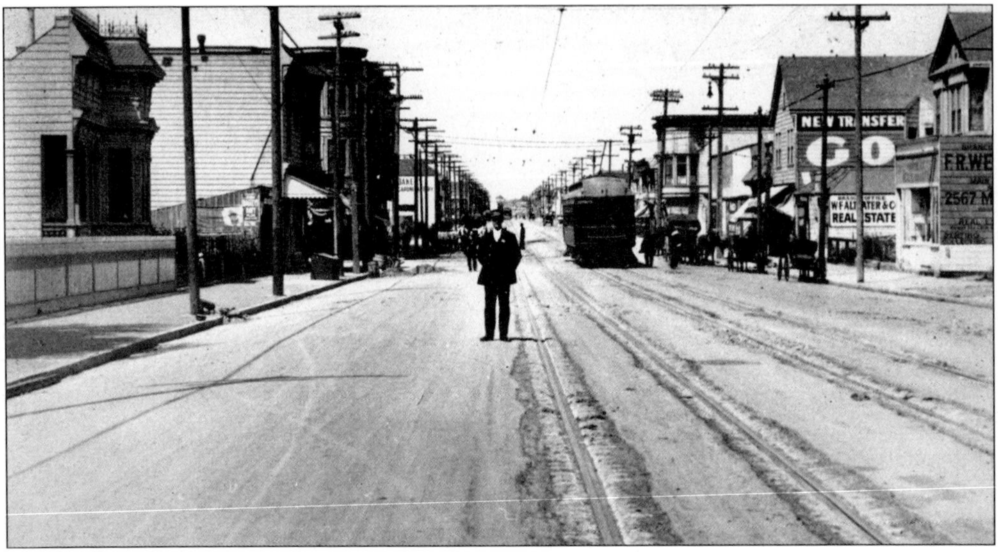

This July 15, 1912 photo shows Mission Street between Onondaga on the left opposite the streetcar looking downtown. Note the building just beyond the one on the right that has the "GO" sign on its side, which boasts the famous San Francisco Bay windows. Those bay windows, and the building, still stand on the corner of Mission Street and Russia Avenue today.

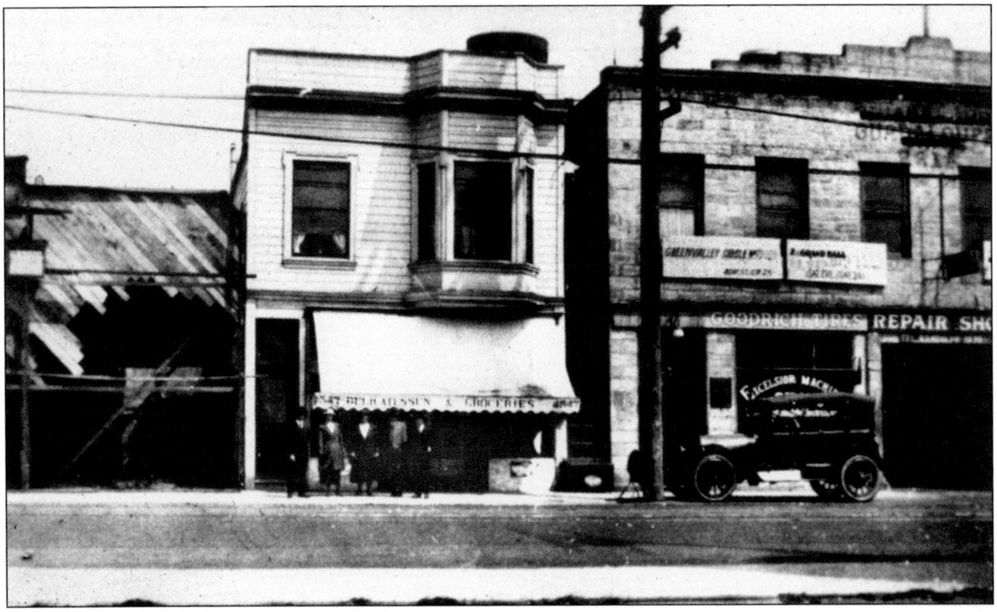

The address of the building with the white awning is 4547 Mission Street, *c.* 1920. The nearly completed building went on to have many uses, including Papageorge's soda fountain and homemade chocolate shop as well as Marina's Italian-style breakfast, lunch, and dinner restaurant, and many Chinese restaurants. The building to the right is Guadalupe Hall, famous for weddings and association receptions and dinners. At one time it was the only social venue in this part of the city and was also the place where the Native Sons and Daughters of the Golden West met. The lower part is now a produce market catering to the Mexican population while at the present time the social hall upstairs is mainly used during the day by senior Filipinos for dances and other events.

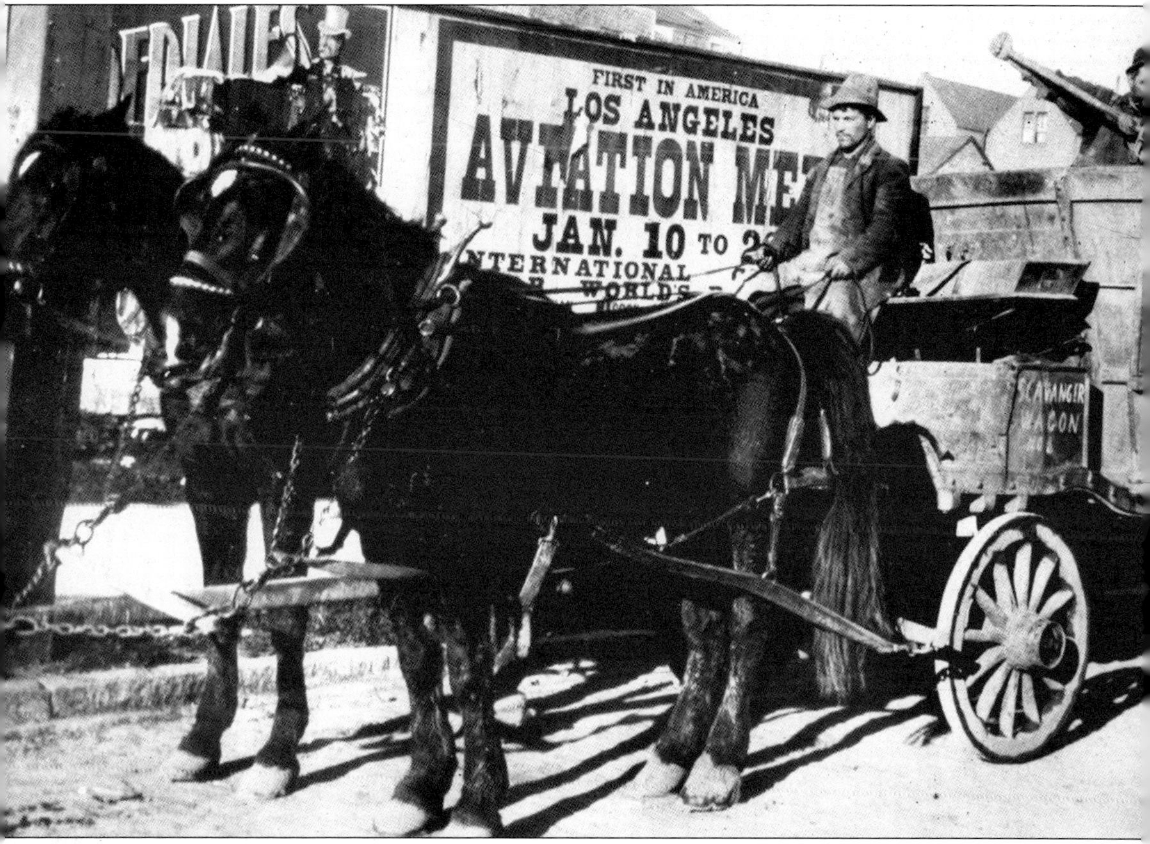

Trash collecting on Mission Street in the Excelsior area involved a two-horsepower, two-manpower wagon, while recycling was undertaken by the "rags bottle sacks man" who would come through the neighborhood in his horse-drawn wagon yelling, "Rags! Bottle! Sacks!" He also collected metal scrap and similar items, giving local children who sold these items to him the means of earning some pocket change. With the Great Depression on, a few pennies or a nickel went a long way and kept the streets clean of trash and junk. Note the advertisement in the background for an aviation meeting in Los Angeles. At this time, aviation was as young as recycling, which is now a billion-dollar business.

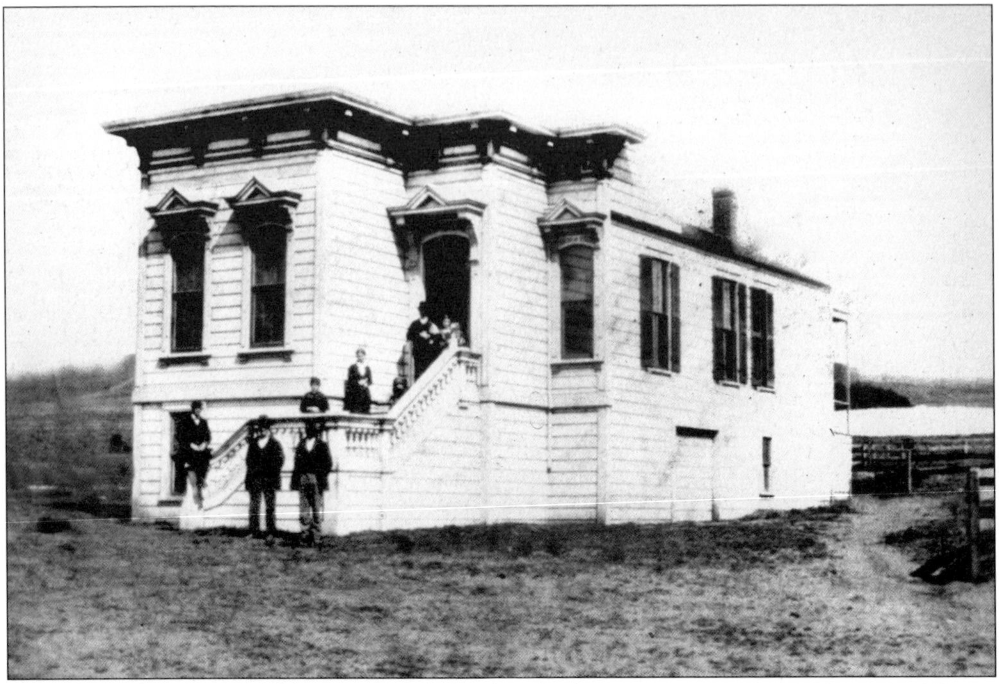

This is the ranch house of the F.R. Smith family. The location was at Vienna Street and Persia Avenue. The family has no exact date of the house's construction, but it was likely around 1880.

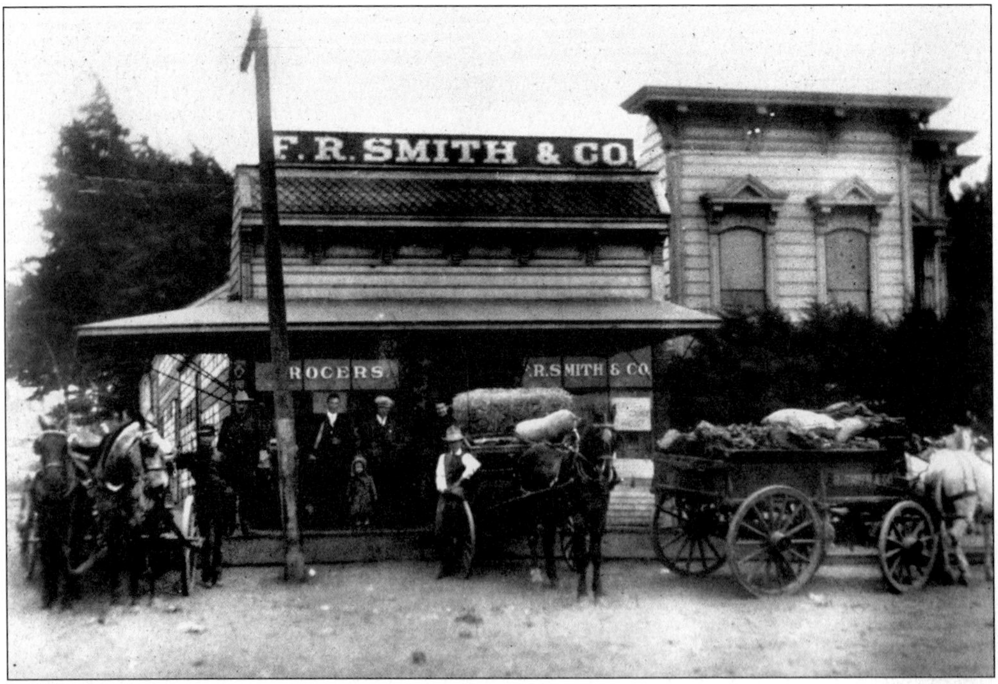

In this photo taken *c.* 1900, the Smith house is partially obscured by trees all around and, of course, by the family's grocery business, which was one of the very few stores on this side of the hill, if not the only one.

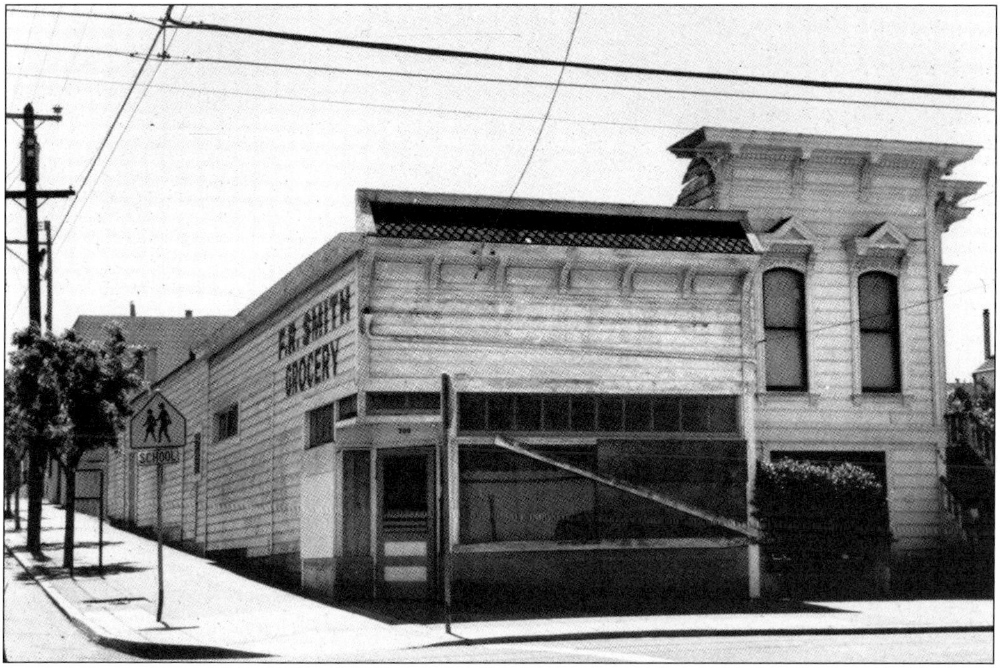

Here is the F.R. Smith house, *c.* 1980. The local members of the Smith family have passed away; those who inherited the house now live in the Midwest. The new owners wanted to demolish it, but a community uproar saved the house. However, the store met its demise.

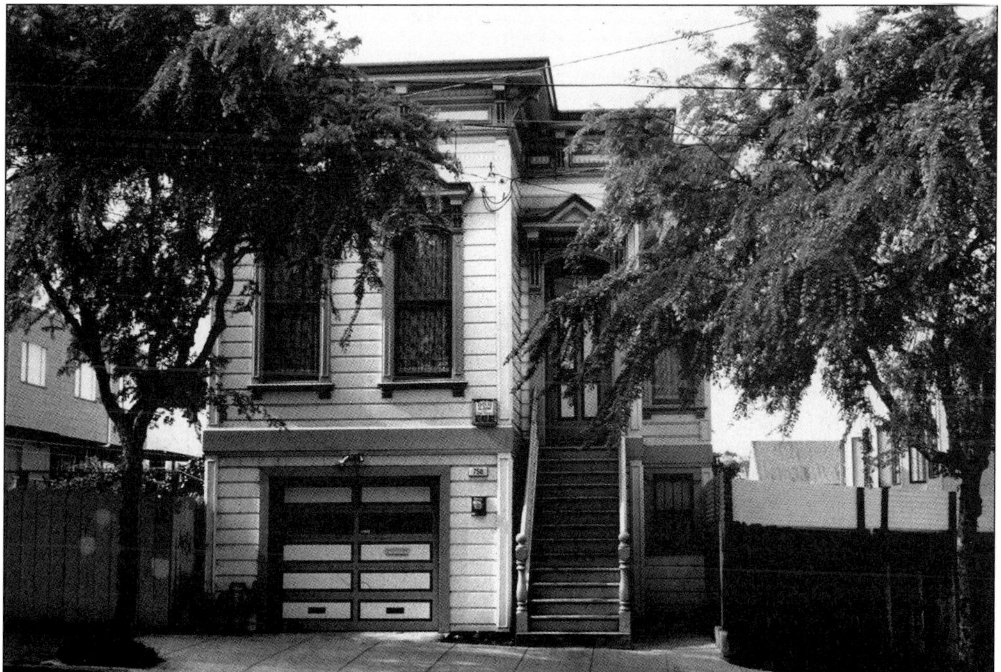
This is the Smith house today It was renovated, turned 45 degrees to face up Persia Avenue, and moved to its present location about 100 feet up Excelsior Avenue, where it now sits.

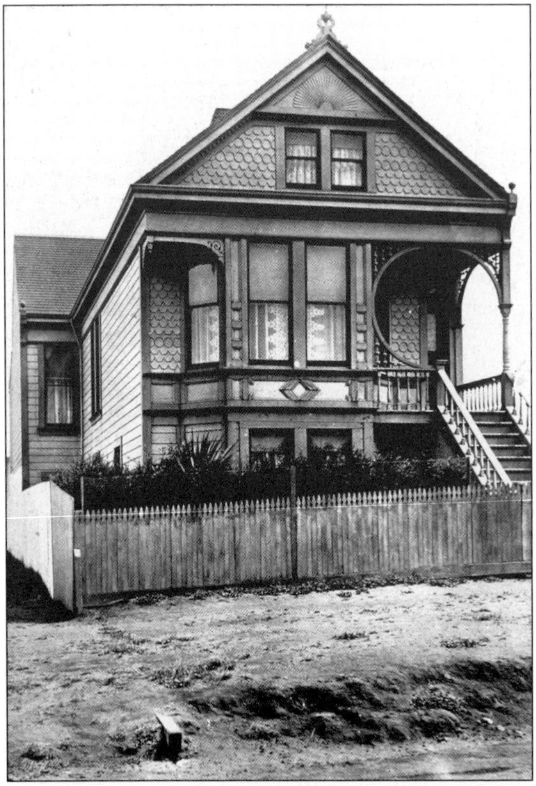

This is one of the many fine Victorian homes that still remain in the Excelsior. It was fairly isolated, with the closest neighbor a block or two away. Notice that there are no telephone poles or electric lines. Also, there was probably a barn in the rear because in the early days this was all farmland up the hillside from Mission Street. There were no automobiles. Horses would have been kept in the barn.

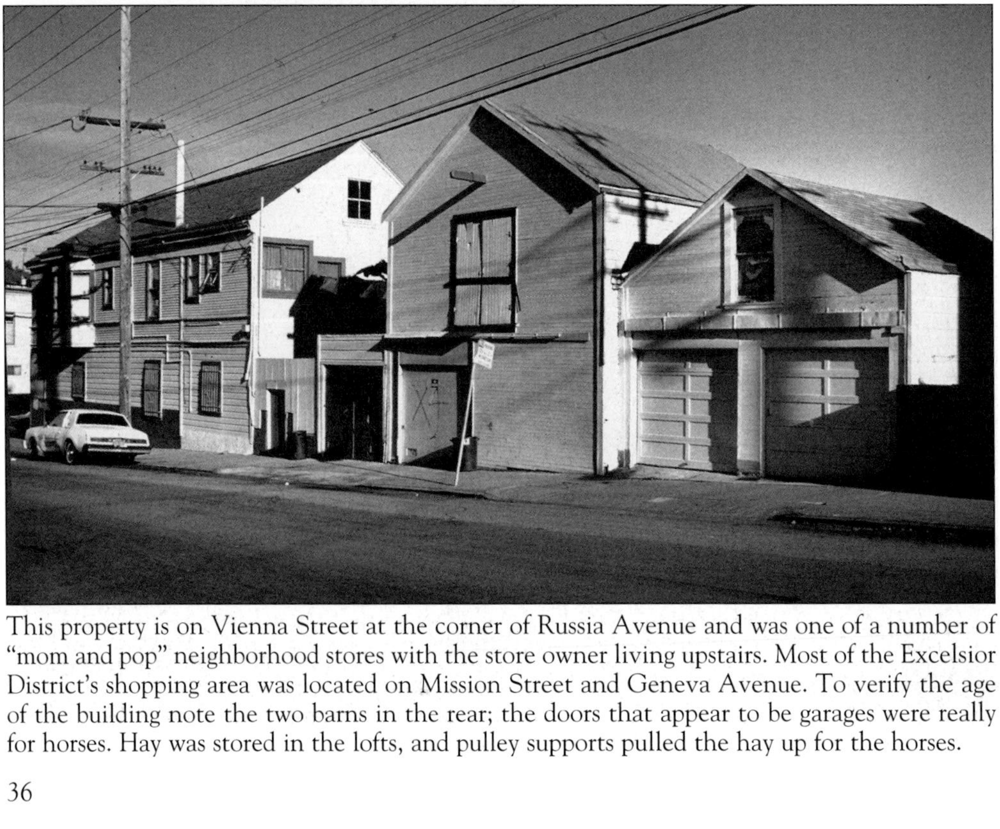

This property is on Vienna Street at the corner of Russia Avenue and was one of a number of "mom and pop" neighborhood stores with the store owner living upstairs. Most of the Excelsior District's shopping area was located on Mission Street and Geneva Avenue. To verify the age of the building note the two barns in the rear; the doors that appear to be garages were really for horses. Hay was stored in the lofts, and pulley supports pulled the hay up for the horses.

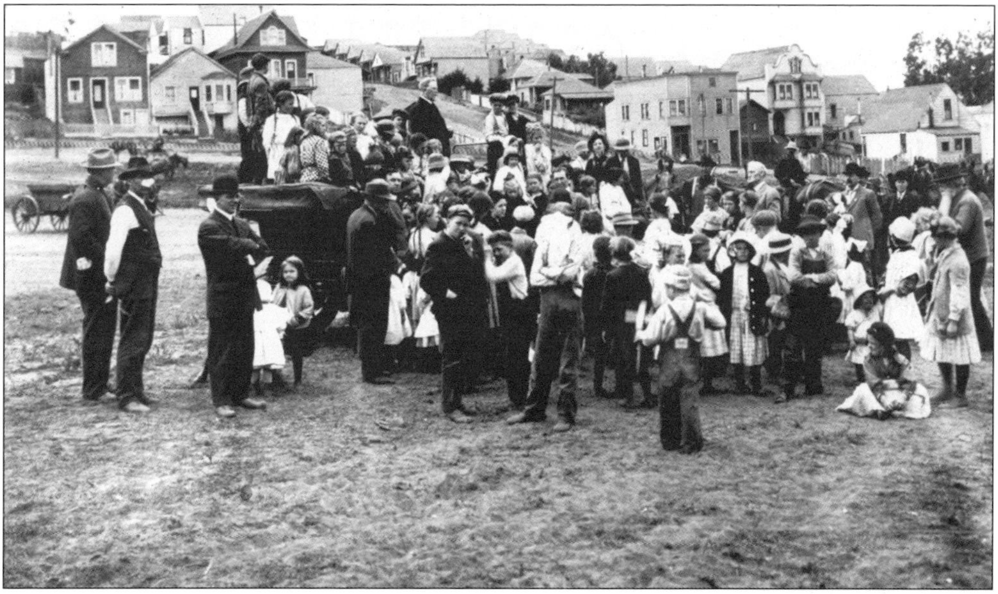

Dedication of the Excelsior Homestead Playground at Russia Avenue and Madrid Street took place on July 30, 1912, and was performed from the back of a convertible sedan by one of the local Catholic priests. Automobiles were few and far between at that time as is evidenced by the old wagon (center left), which represented the more popular mode of transportation at the time. That may be the reason so many kids are in the back of the sedan. The black peaked-roof house at the top left was the home of Nick and Steve Leonadykas. For many years, Nick was a Golden Gate Bridge director. Most of the homes in this photo still stand today.

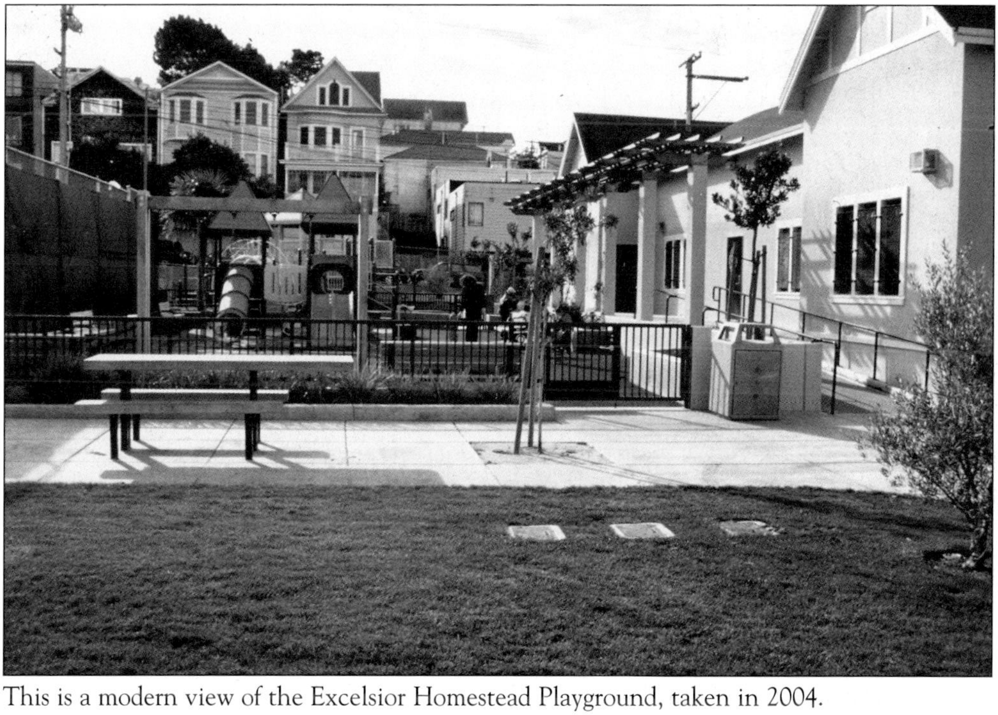

This is a modern view of the Excelsior Homestead Playground, taken in 2004.

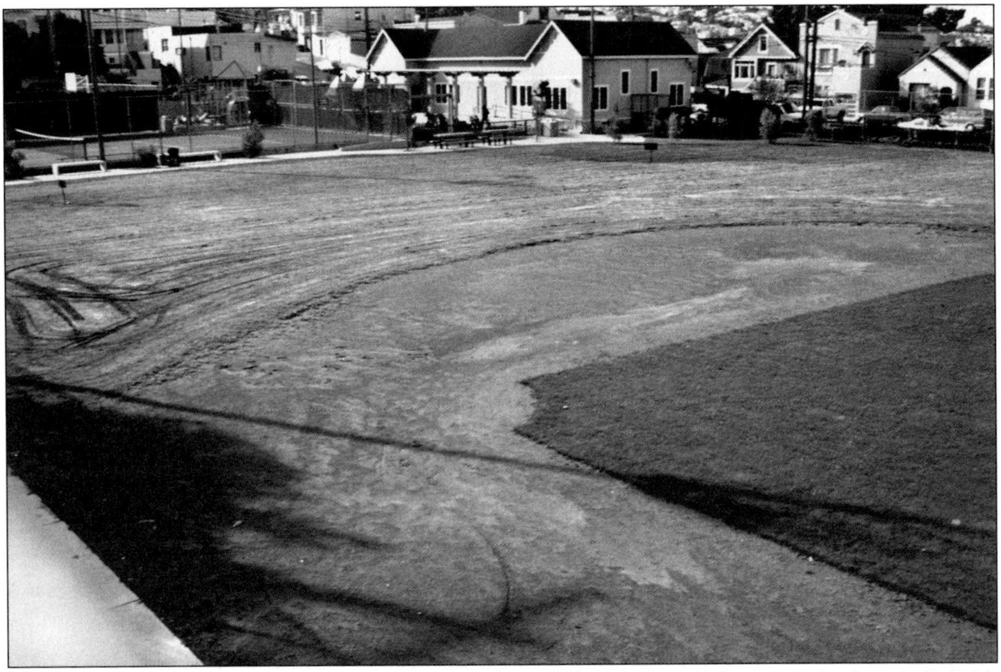

This is an overhead view of the Excelsior Homestead Playground showing the baseball field, tennis courts, basketball court, and play area for the children. The clubhouse is still used for many public classes today.

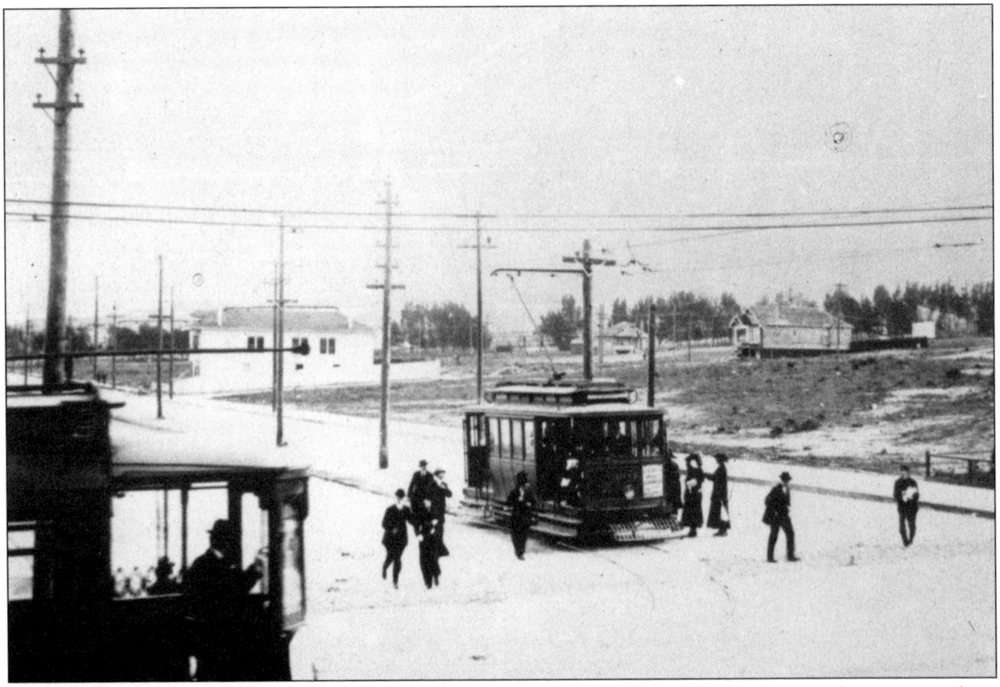

This view of Geneva Avenue was taken from Mission Street, showing a very early streetcar line that ran to the Visitacion Valley area.

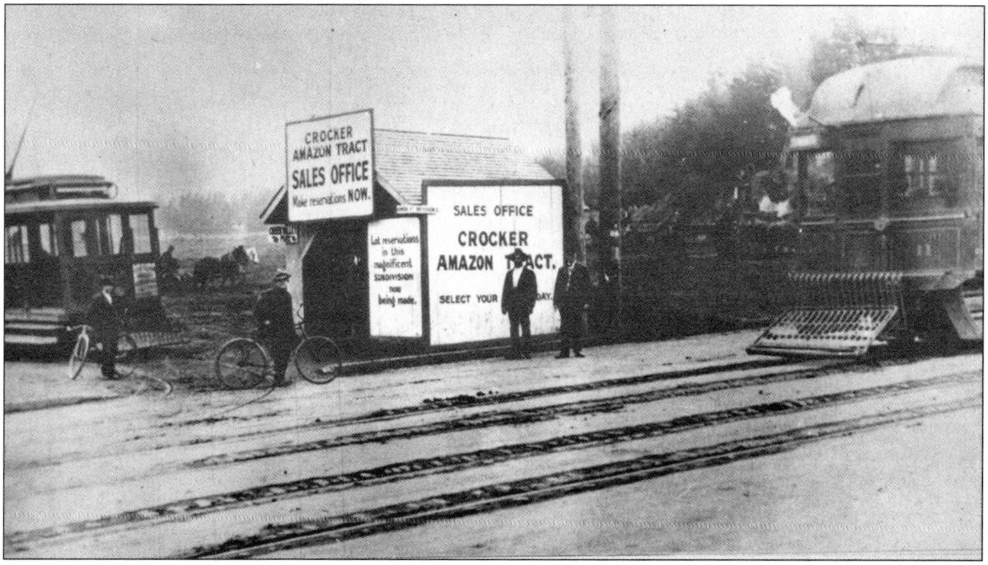

Two streetcars can be seen in this 1912 photo of Geneva and Mission. The area to the rear of the shack is a sales office for a new development. The signs read as follows: "Crocker Amazon Tract Sales Office, select your lot."

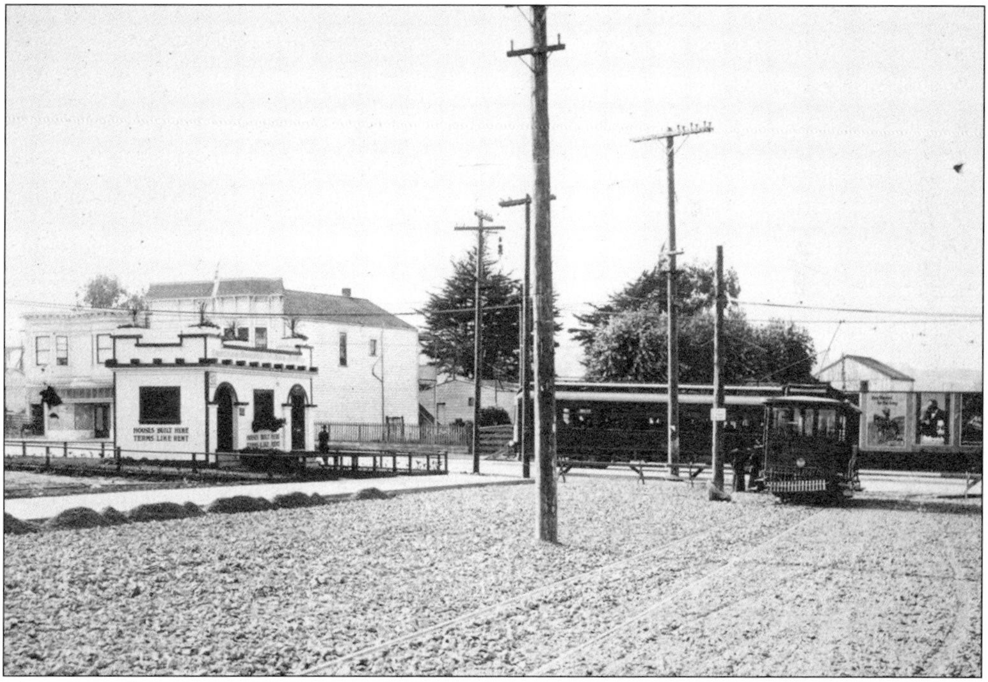

This view of an unpaved Geneva Avenue looks west to Mission Street, an early transfer point for the streetcars. There were many farms in this part of the city, and at this point in time Geneva did not cross Mission Street. Note the small billboard behind the streetcar, on what later became the extension known as Geneva Avenue. It appears business must be good as the Crocker-Amazon track has removed the eyesore shack and built a more presentable office. Even the sidewalk has been cemented in an effort to tidy up. None of the buildings in this photo are standing today.

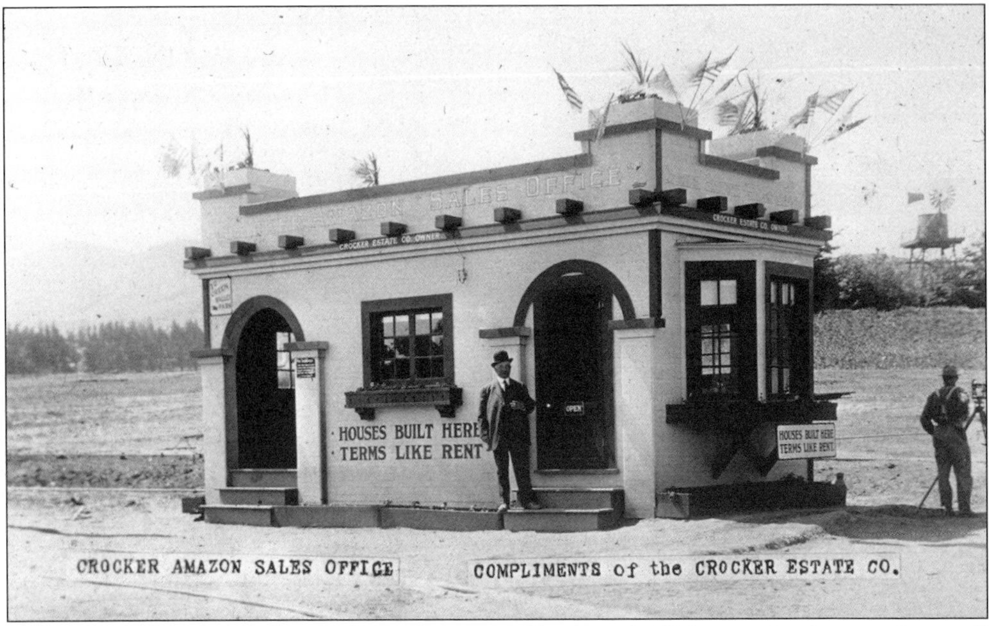

The Crocker Estate Company, shown here possibly around 1920, must be doing rather well considering the upgraded sales office. The manager standing by the doorway with his derby on and his hand in his vest is not Napoleon as he is obviously wearing the wrong hat! The man in the background on the right is ready to survey something. Note the windmill and water tank above the surveyor; this area did and still has water underneath the soil.

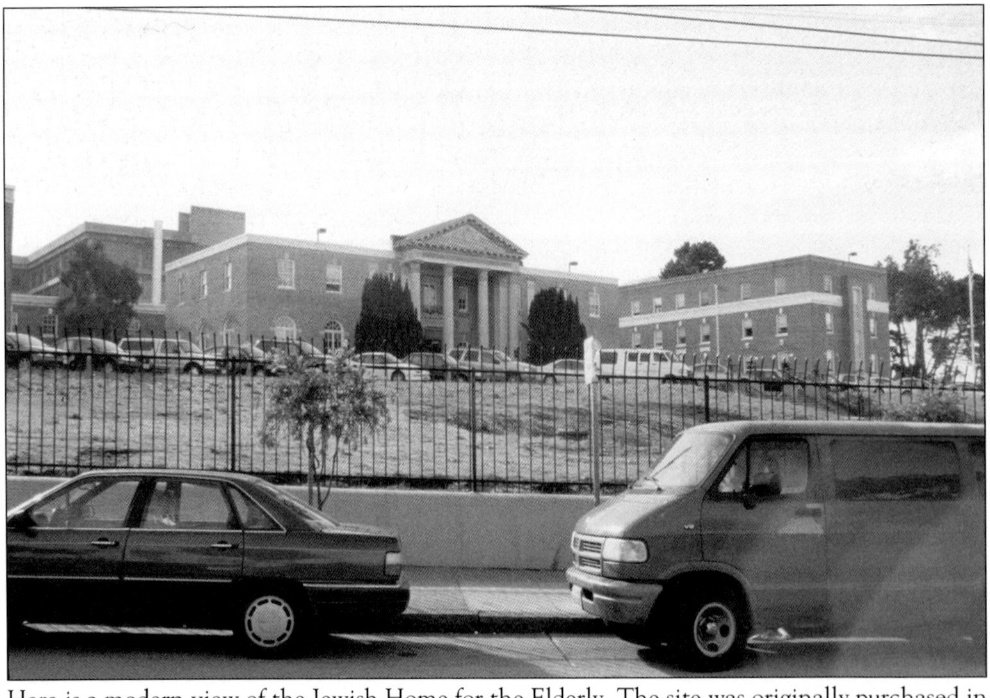

Here is a modern view of the Jewish Home for the Elderly. The site was originally purchased in 1872, and building started in 1890. Today the sprawling complex houses 430 residents.

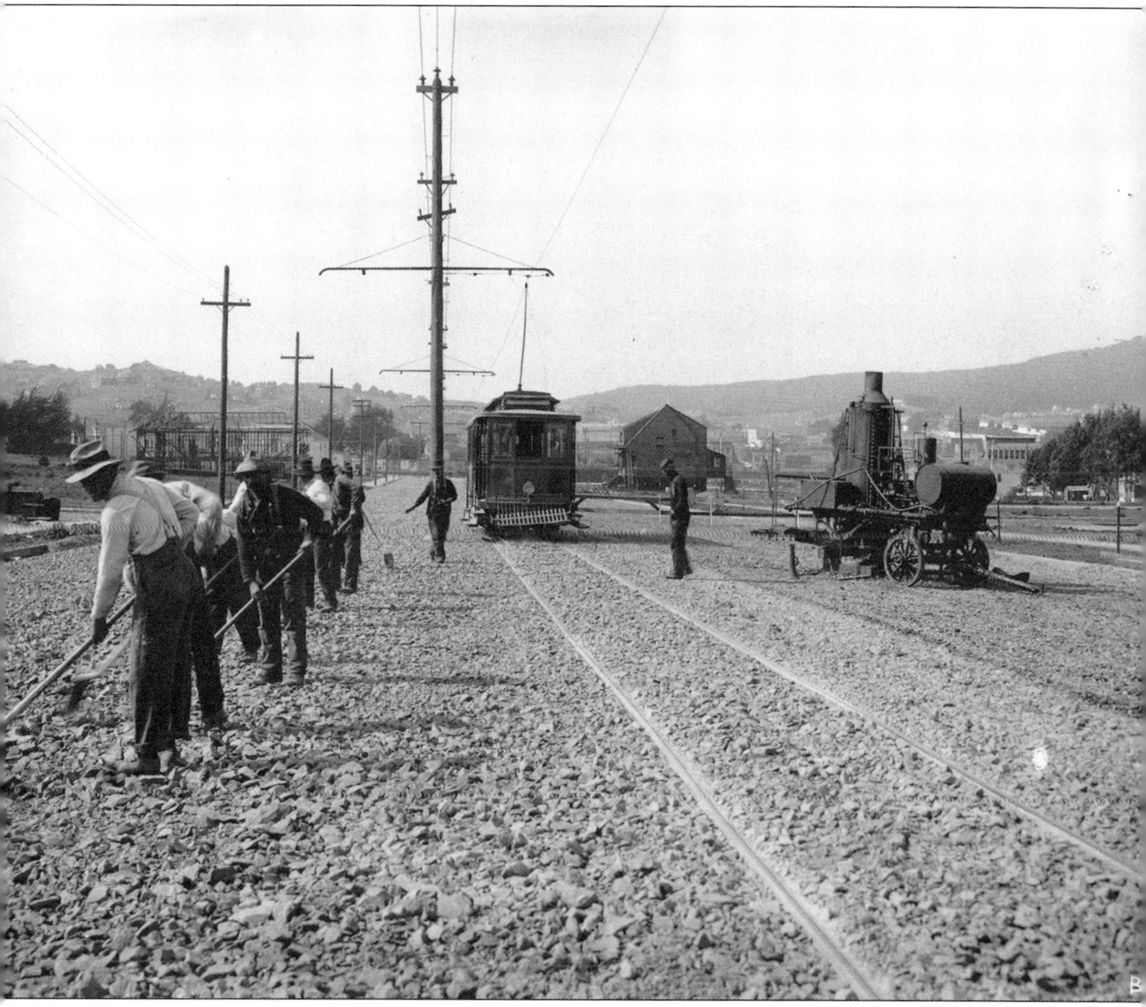

This view of Geneva Avenue looking west in the 1920s shows that things are beginning to happen. Not only are there newer streetcars but more important is the steam donkey to the right of the streetcar. Buildings are beginning to appear as well, mainly on the right side of the photo.

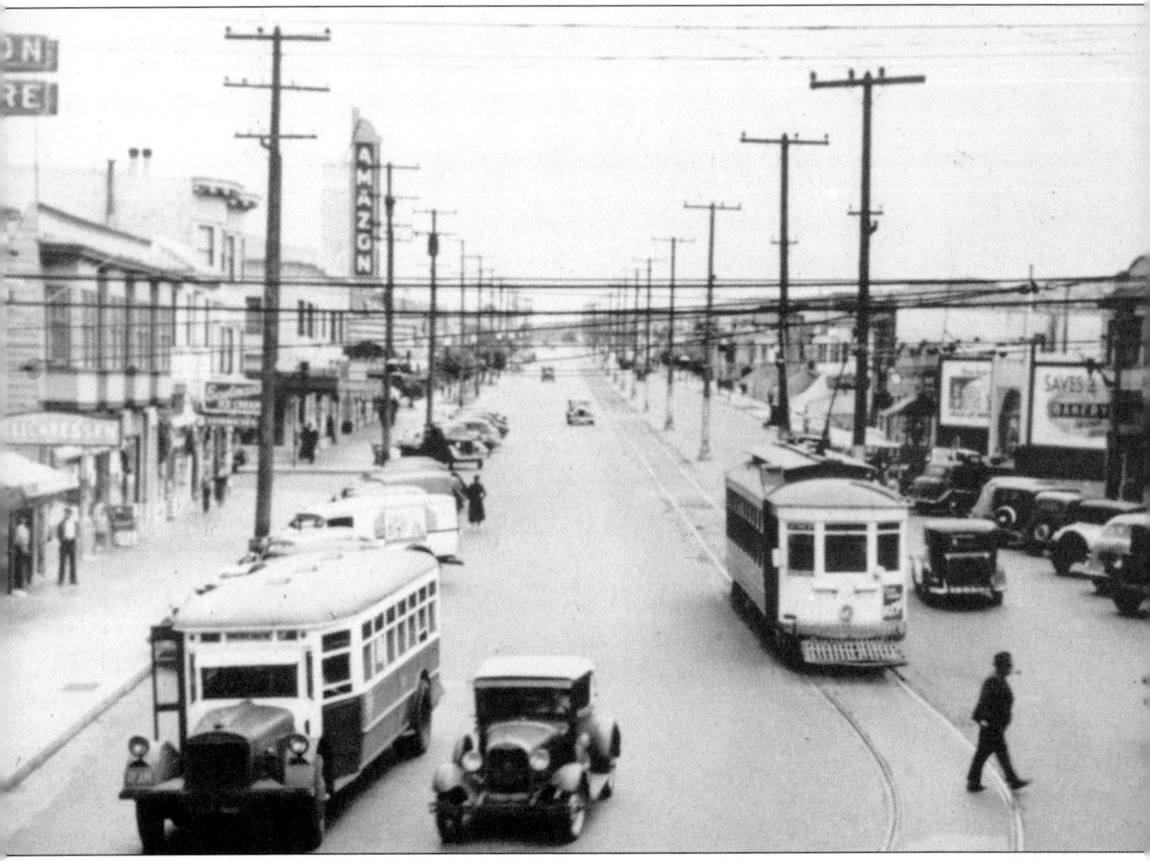

Things are looking good on Geneva Avenue as evidenced by this photo taken from Mission Street looking west sometime in the late 1920s or early 1930s. Note the power lines in the center of the street and the old-fashioned bus, which at one time was called a stage, a term perhaps dating back to the horse-drawn stagecoaches of the past.

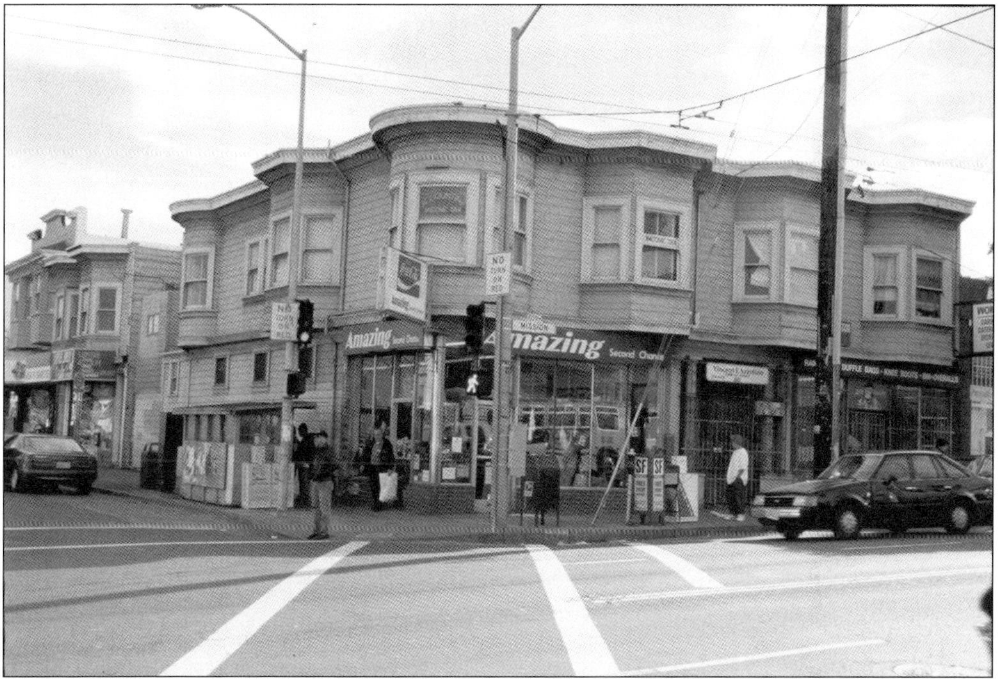

This is Mission Street (right) and Geneva Avenue (left) as they appear today. The building on the corner is the location of Crocker Estate land offices. The entire area today is called Crocker Amazon, suggesting that perhaps they sold at least a few pieces of property.

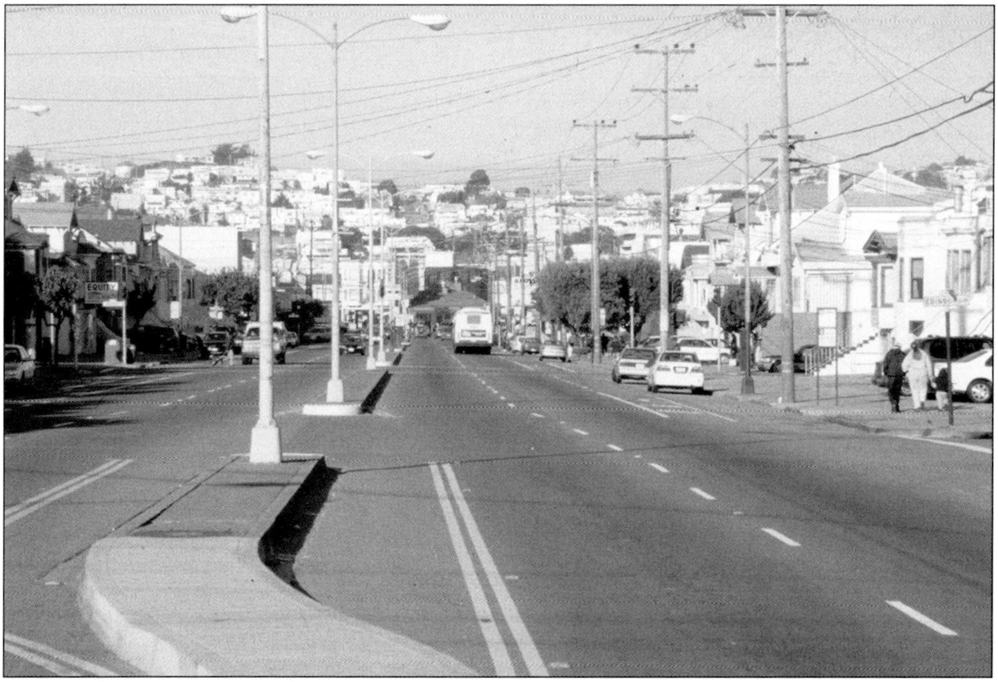

This modern photo was taken from the same location as the gravel-strewn Geneva Avenue seen on page 41, where the steam donkey was located, looking west toward Mission Street. Things certainly have changed!

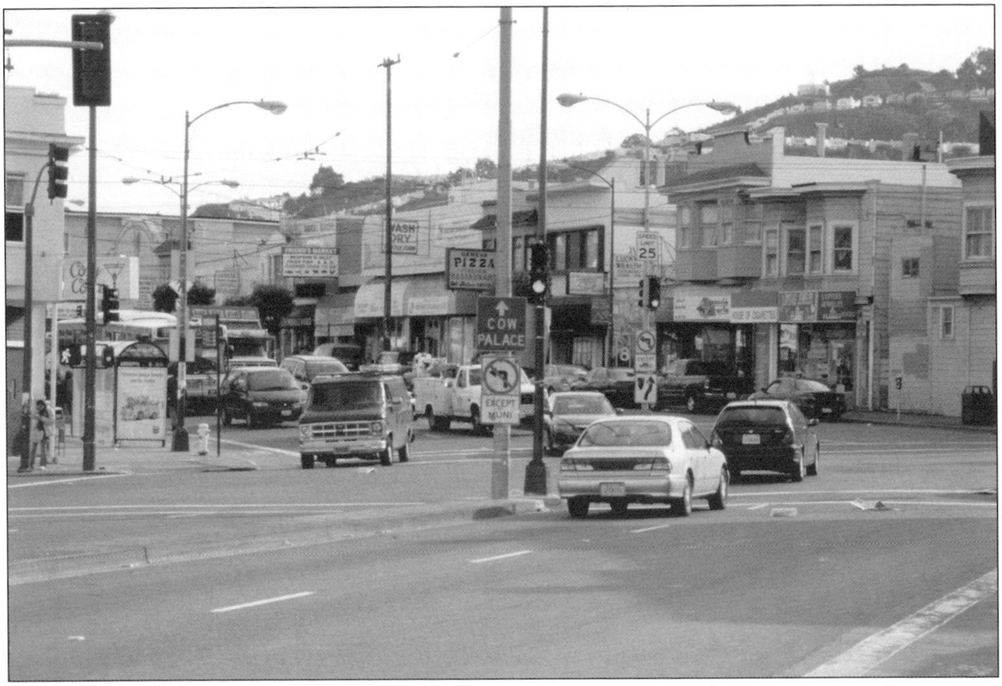

Geneva Avenue at Mission Street is a very busy intersection. It is also a major transfer point in San Francisco.

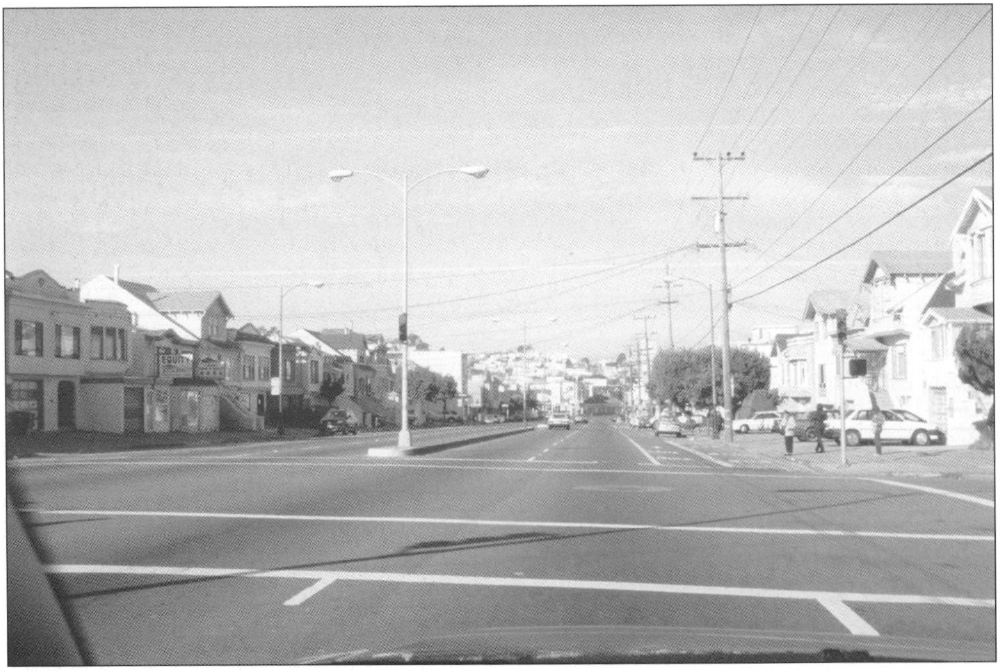

This modern image of Geneva Avenue shows the view looking west towards the ocean.

Two

BUSINESSES AND TRANSPORTATION

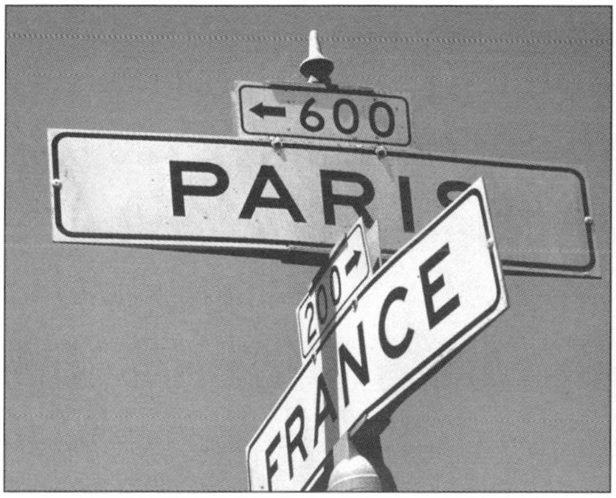

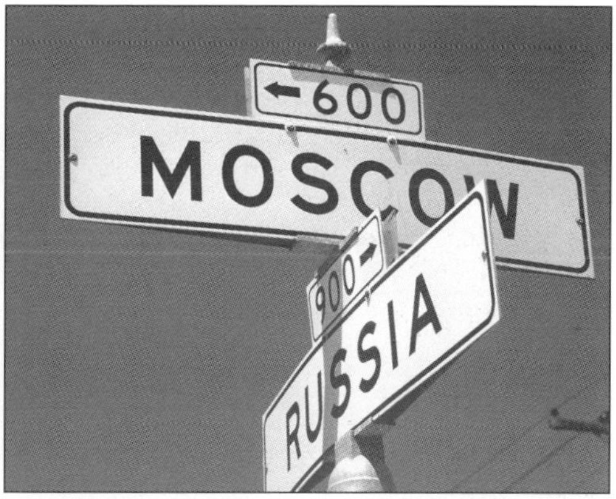

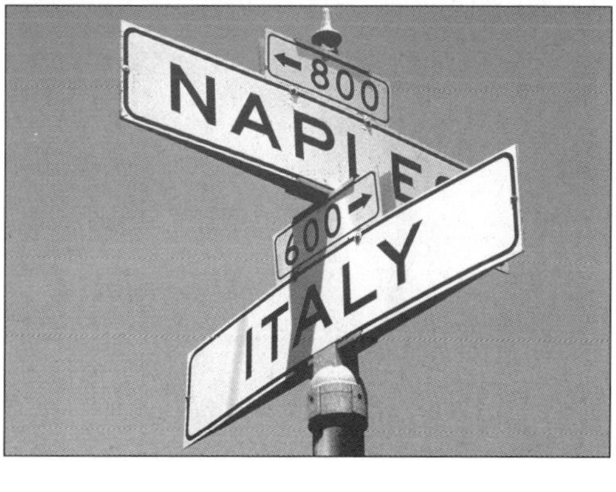

The Excelsior District boasts some very interesting street names. Residents can live in France, Russia, or Italy because all streets running perpendicular to Mission Street are named for countries, while the streets parallel to Mission are the capitals of countries.

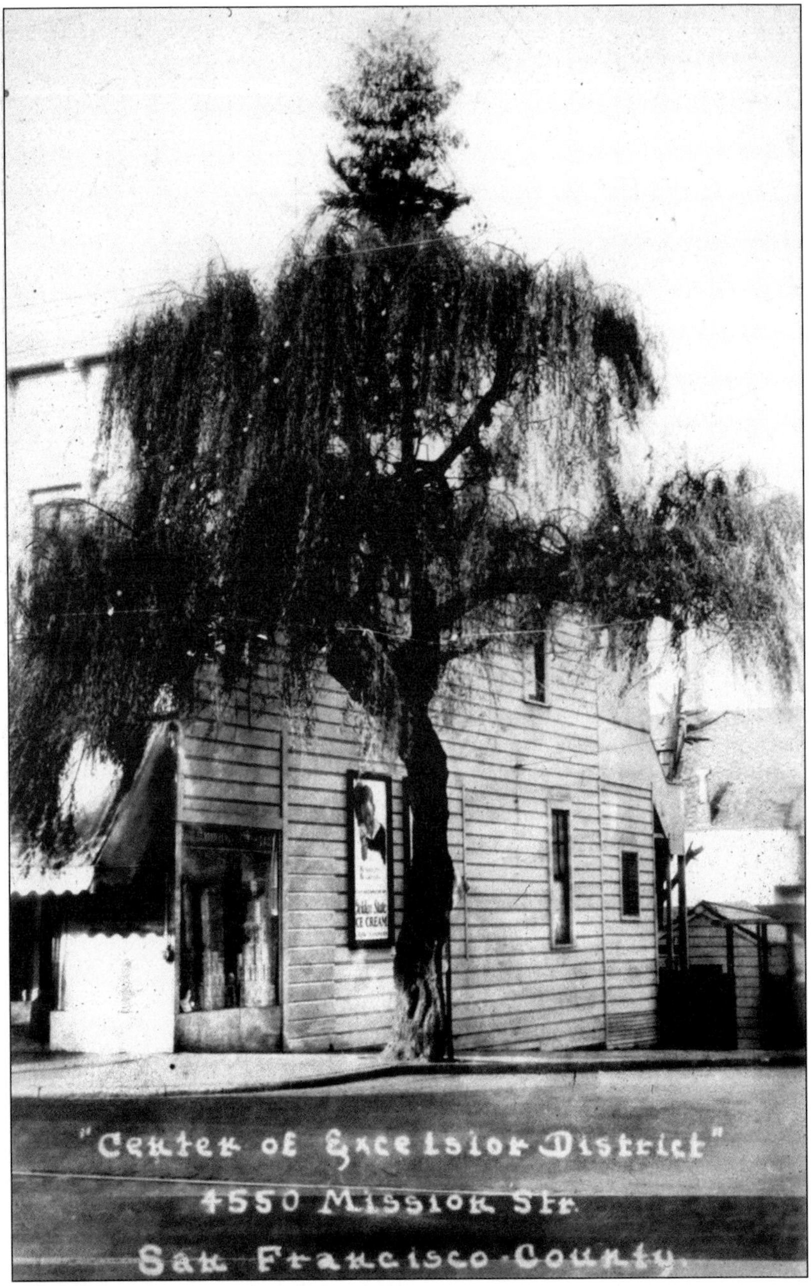

This is one of those sad things that happen during so-called progress: this tree on Mission and Harrington Streets was cut down because it wasn't fashionable anymore. Weeping willow trees require a lot of water, which is why they generally grow near rivers or lakes—or, in this case, across the street from Alfonso Ferrera's hardware store, which had a well in the basement for water for the apartments in the building, indicating that there was plenty of ground water to help the willow thrive. The building to the left of the tree was the Liberty Ravioli and Spaghetti factory. The building was eventually torn down and replaced by several large stores. The store on this corner was the second largest Woolworth's store in San Francisco. A close look at the tree may reveal Christmas tree lights as it served as the neighborhood's Christmas tree.

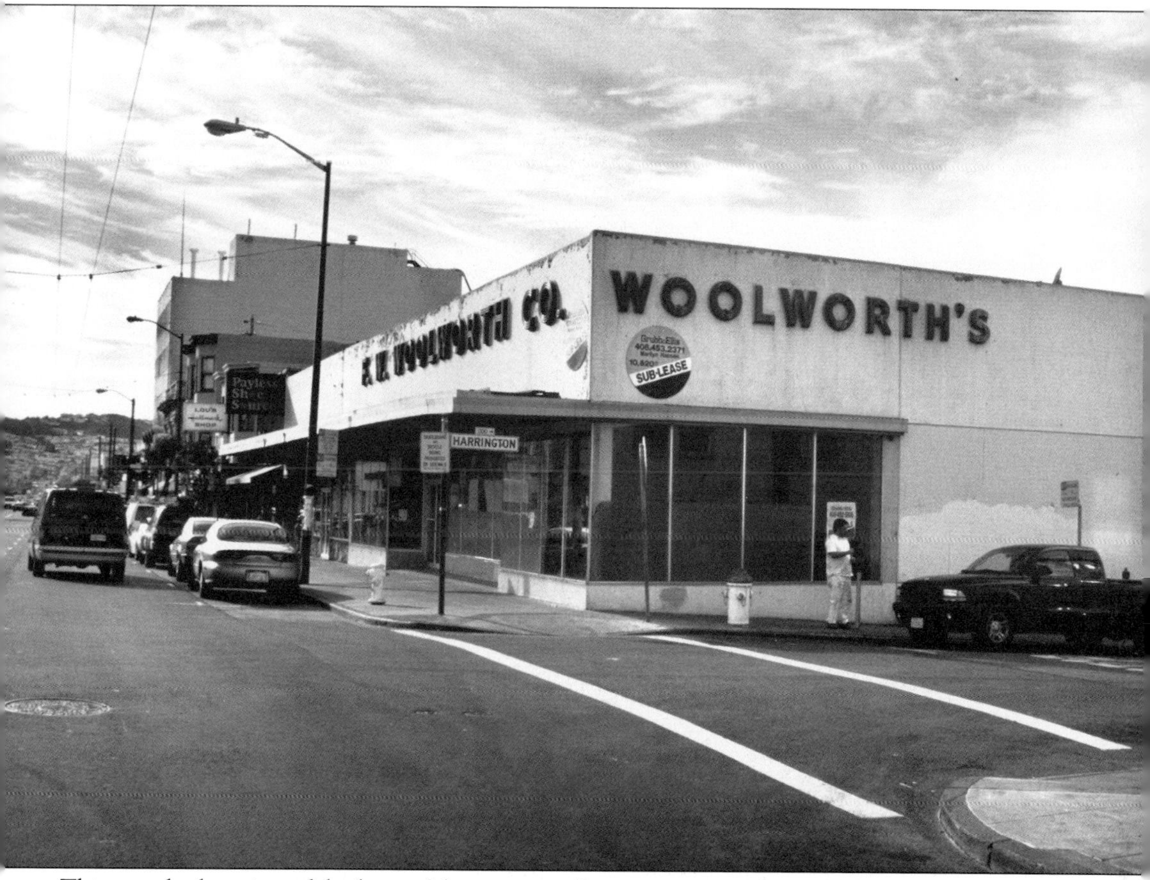

This was the location of the beautiful weeping willow tree seen in the previous page. It was also the site of the second largest Woolworth's store in San Francisco.

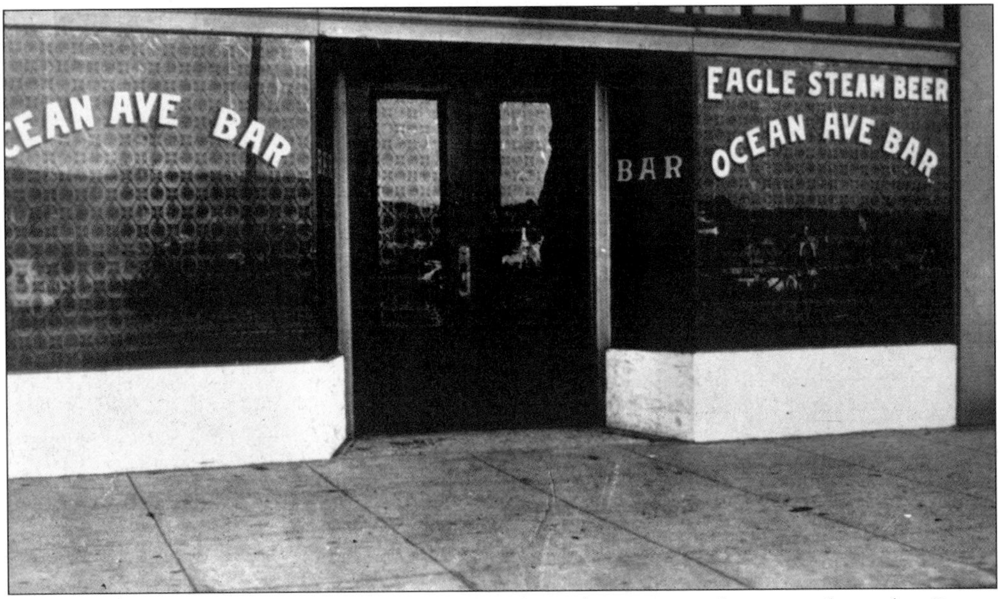

The Eagle Steam Beer Brewery was located a short distance up the street from the Ocean Avenue Bar, at Mission and Seneca one block east of Geneva Avenue.

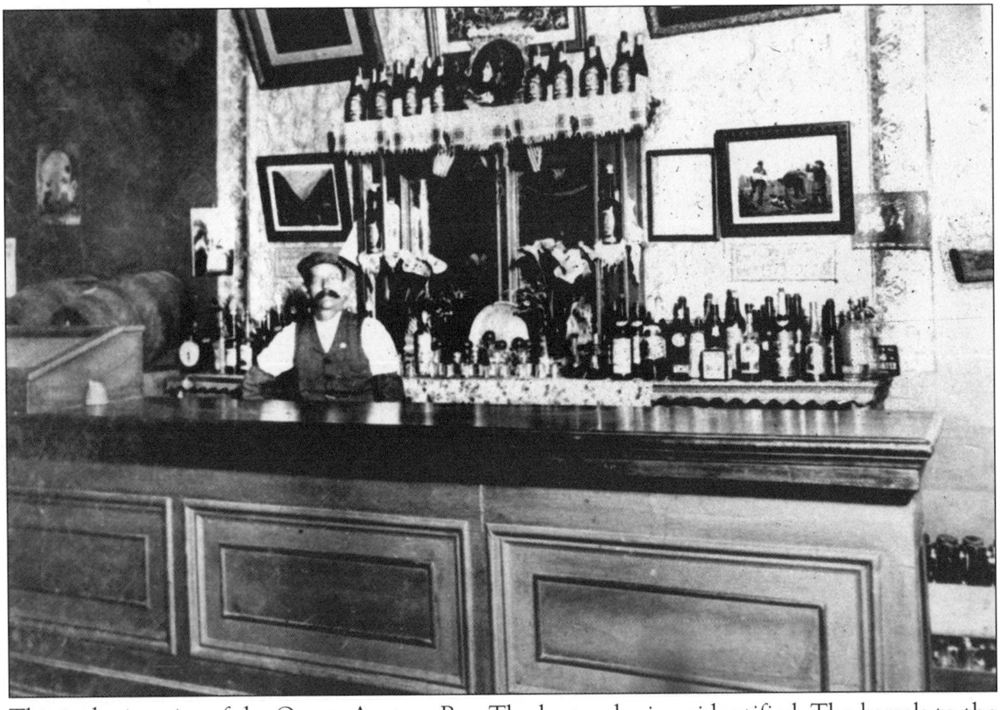

This is the interior of the Ocean Avenue Bar. The bartender is unidentified. The barrels to the left against the wall could contain either wine or beer, although wine seems more likely as steam beer was dispensed from the barrel by being pumped to a spigot.

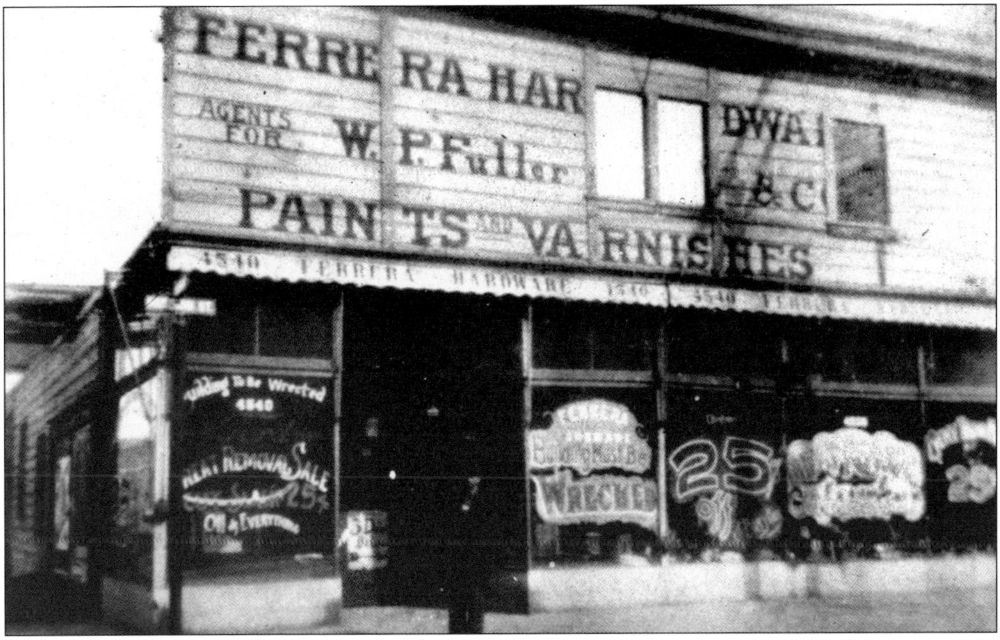

This is the very first Ferrera Hardware store in the Excelsior District. At the time, the area was called the Excelsior Homestead. Alfonso Ferrera and his brother, Tony, owned businesses on Mission Street, with Alfonso running Ferrera Hardware and Tony running Ferrera Electric and Hardware. (Photo by Alfonso Ferrera.)

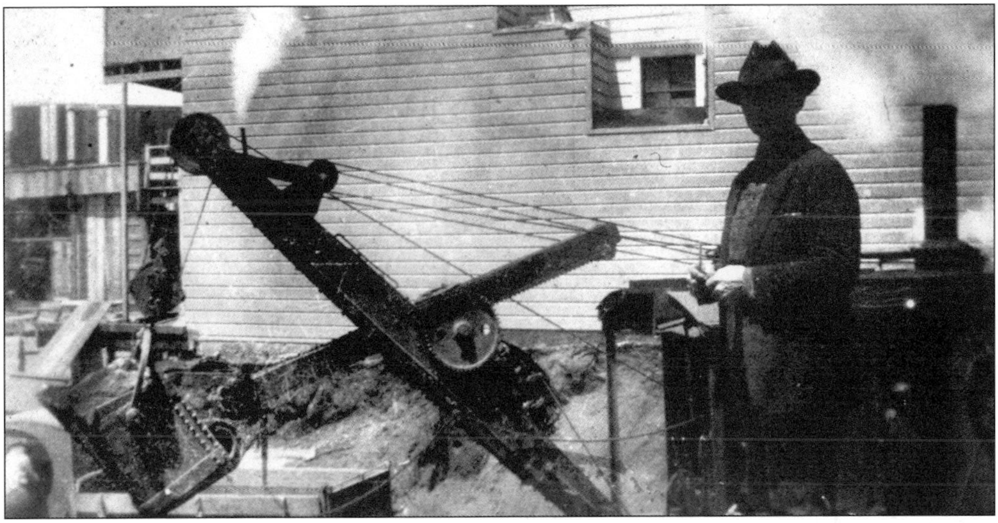

The author's uncle, Alfonso Ferrera, supervises the digging of a basement in the new Ferrera building carrying his signature trademark, a Toscana Marca Petri cigar. A tobacco drying room was located right down the street at Italy and Mission where Italian immigrants rolled cigars after the tobacco leaves were marinated in a grappa grape-based distilled spirit. When planning and building his new store, which was begun in 1928 and finished in 1929, Alfonso proved a far-sighted man and ahead of his time. Because the building had three floors above the ground for apartments and medical offices, Alfonso had a basement dug with parking stalls for each apartment and freshwater wells for the tenants. Until the city made him cap it, it was one of the last freshwater wells in San Francisco.

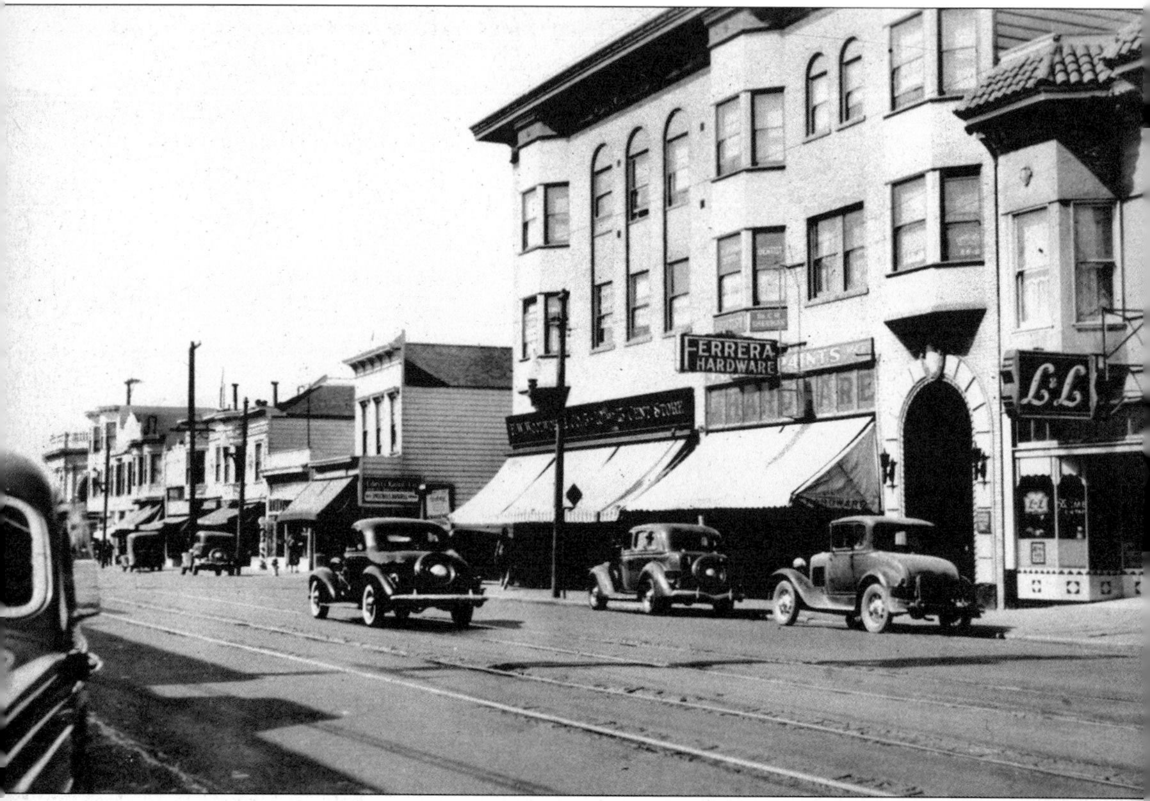

The new Ferrera building on Mission and Harrington Streets included Ferrera Hardware and the second largest Woolworth's Department Store in San Francisco. Later, when the old Liberty Ravioli factory on the corner of Harrington was torn down and a larger building erected in its place, Woolworth's moved across the street to this larger location and Alfonso enlarged the hardware store to use the entire ground floor.

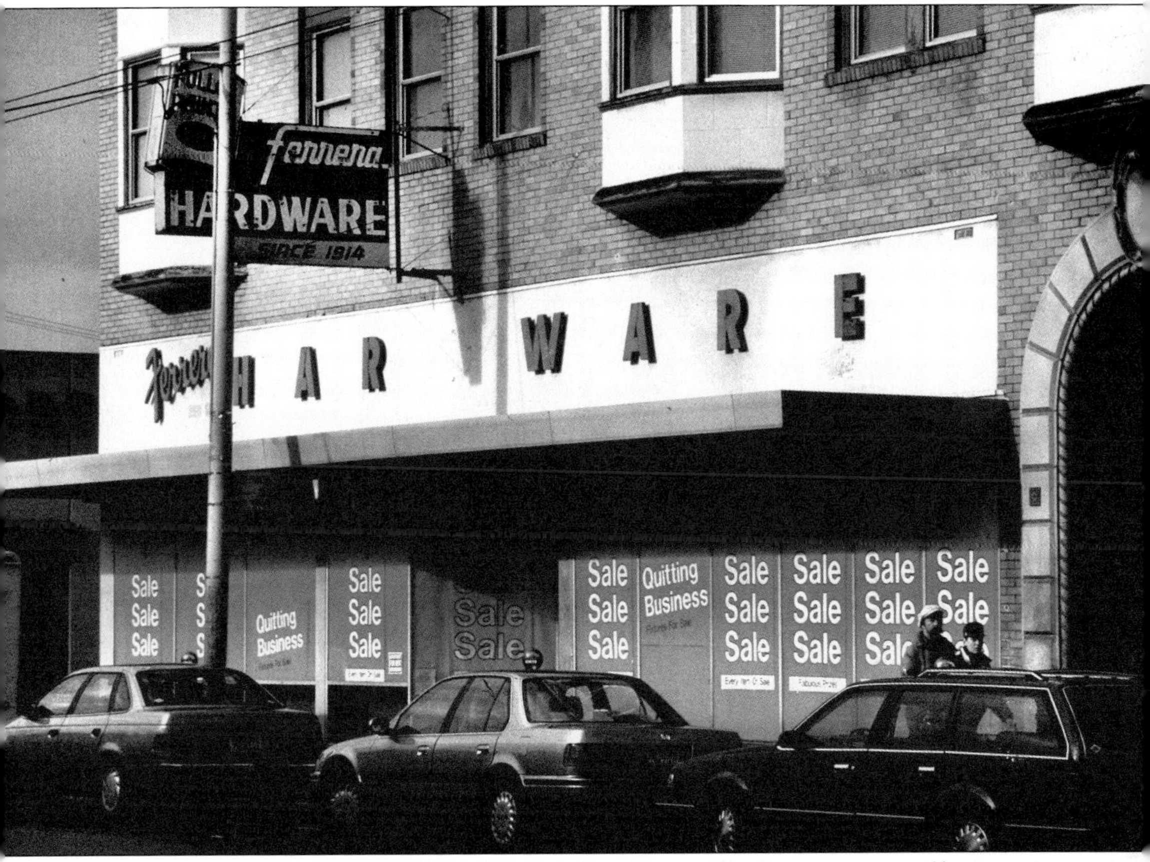

One more Excelsior institution falls by the wayside as Ferrera Hardware goes out of business in 1992. When Alfonso Ferrera passed away, his son, Emil, and Frank Ferrera continued with the business until Emil sold his half to his brother Frank Ferrera in 1987. When Frank passed away, his son Richard took over before closing Ferrera Hardware in 1992. The property was then rented to Kragen's Auto Supply.

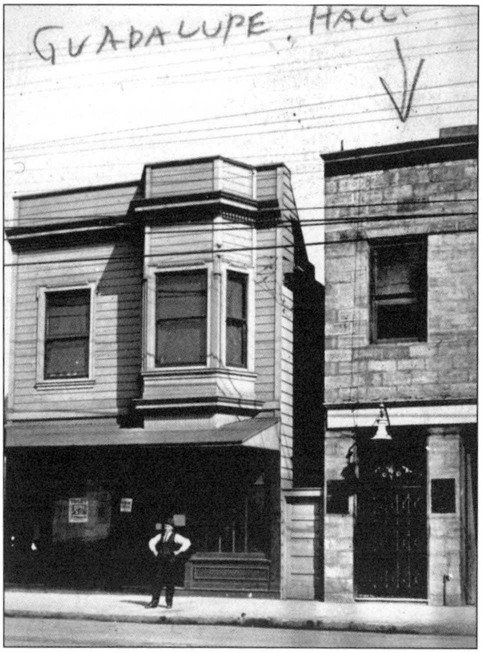

The 4500 block of Mission Street in the Excelsior included this flat or apartment above the store, which was the home of the Mineri family for many years. The building to the right is Guadalupe Hall, which was used by many organizations for lodge meetings, parties, and numerous weddings.

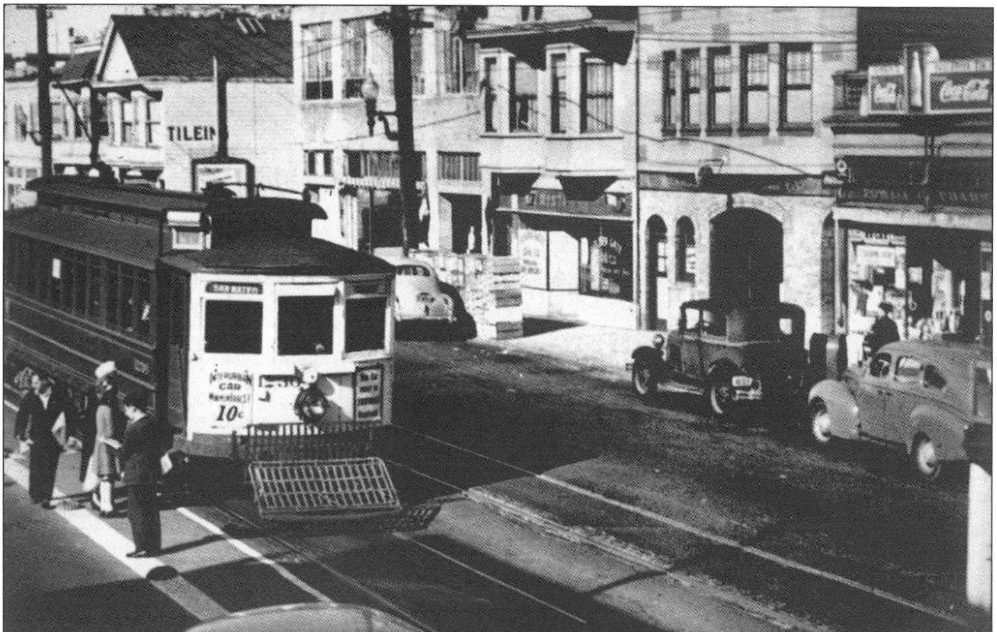

This is one of the first deluxe inter-urban streetcars. The famous No. 40 would park at the end of Fifth Street, which dead-ended at Market Street, and it was common for people to walk to that car stop and pay the extra fare of 10¢, double the regular fare of 5¢, just to ride it. However, this high fare would take a passenger only to the county line, where an additional fare was required—although then you would have a great ride to San Mateo. Note the car door on the left, which closed completely to keep the bad weather out of the car, making for a more comfortable ride. The interior was luxurious, with seats of richly upholstered green leather and hardware of polished brass.

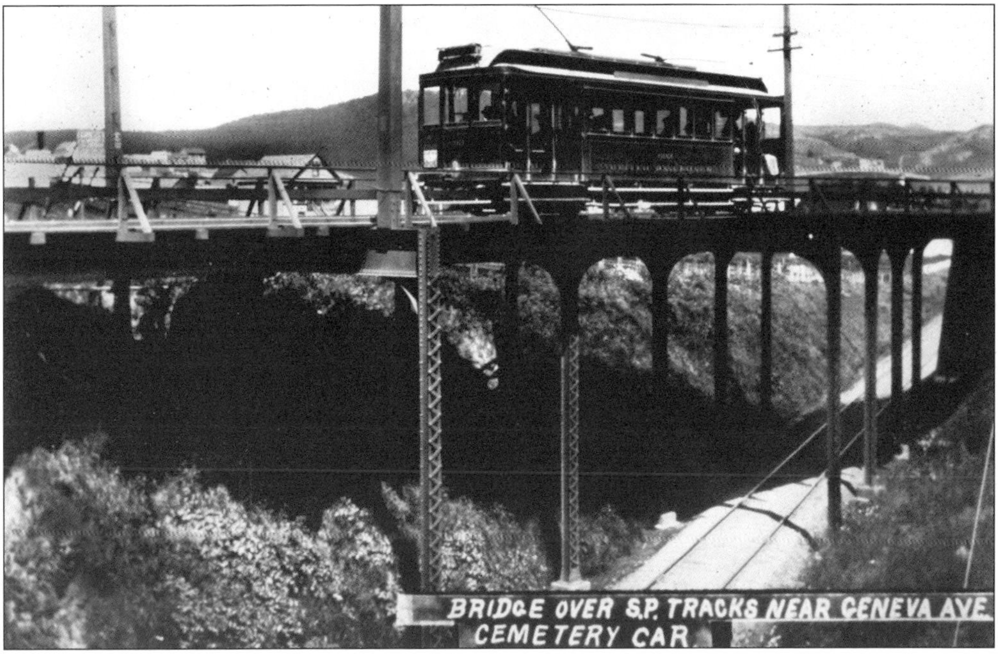

This image shows the bridge over the Southern Pacific tracks near Geneva Avenue. This car is one of several cemetery cars in the system. These were special cars used for funerals in nearby Colma. The cars could pick up the entire family, friends, and casket, and the whole gathering could make the trip in comfort and faster than a regular funeral hearse.

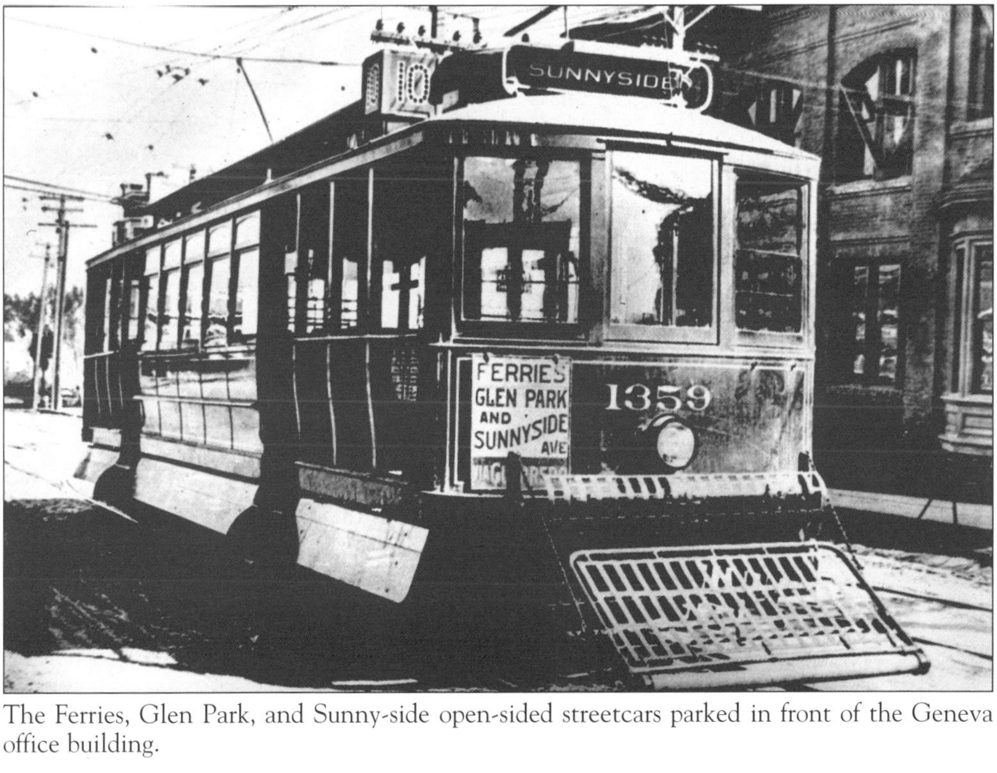

The Ferries, Glen Park, and Sunny-side open-sided streetcars parked in front of the Geneva office building.

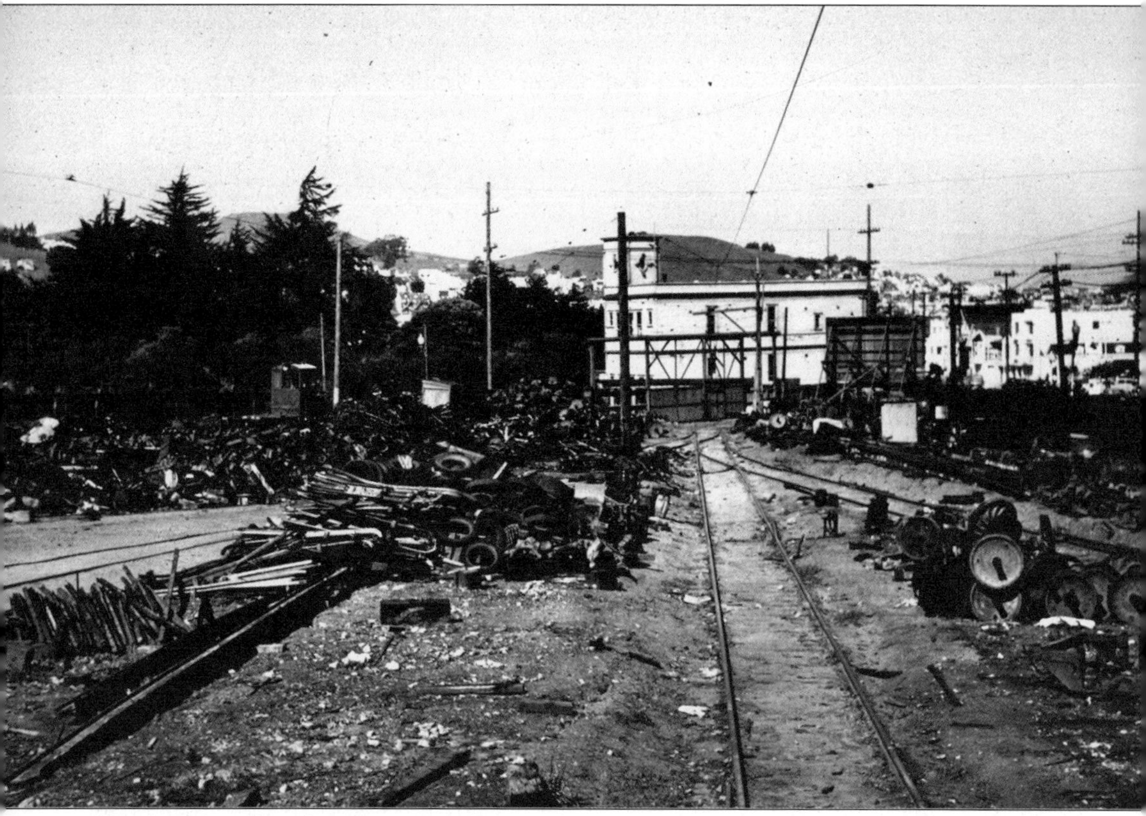

This former junkyard is the Curtis E. Green Light Rail Center today. Looking east, the light-colored building toward the right is a former fire station located in Balboa Park at the corner of San Jose and Ocean Avenue. The big trees to the left are the cypress trees of Balboa Park. The area in the foreground served as the junkyard for the area's streetcar repair station. Today this same location is a beautiful building that encloses the repairing area for both streetcars and buses and is adjacent to the Balboa BART Station.

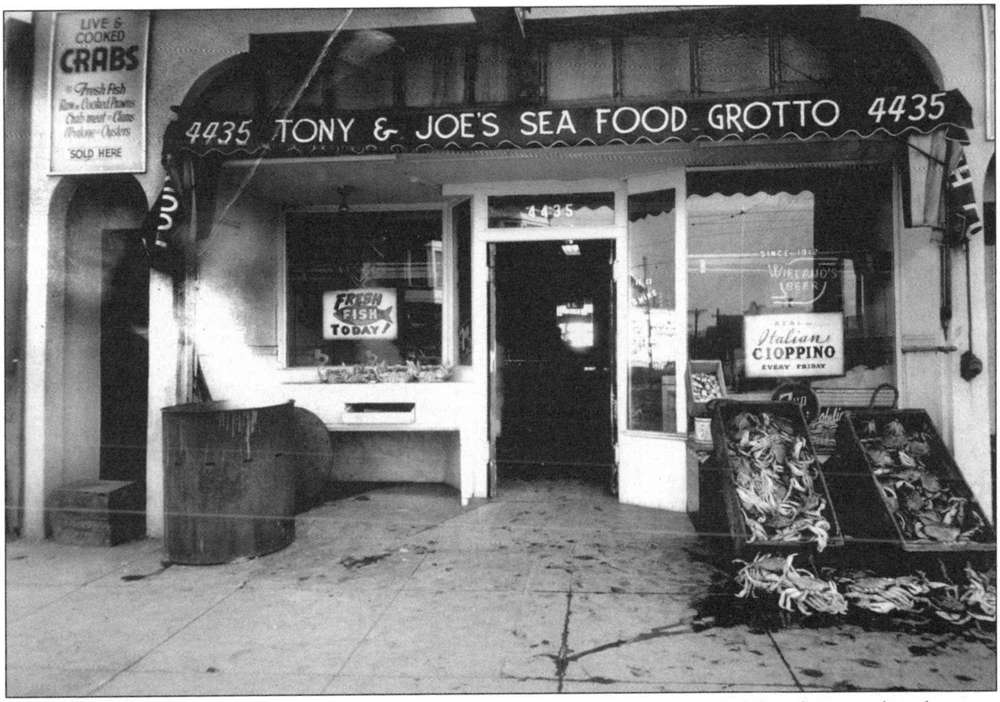

Tony and Joe's Sea Food Grotto at 4435 Mission Street was founded by the two brothers in 1946. Today it is called Joe's Fish Grotto. Like the famed Fisherman's Wharf, Tony and Joe's kept big boxes of crabs on the sidewalk, a tradition that came from the coastal area of Italy.

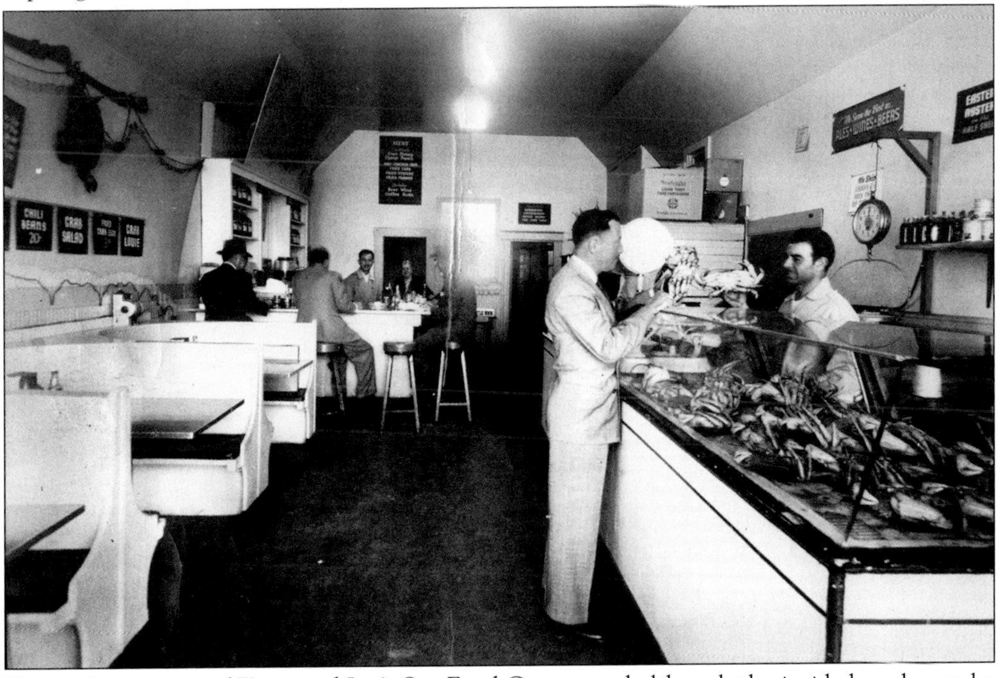

This is the interior of Tony and Joe's Sea Food Grotto, and although the inside has changed a lot from the original, the restaurant still serves both white and red clam chowder and some of the best seafood in San Francisco.

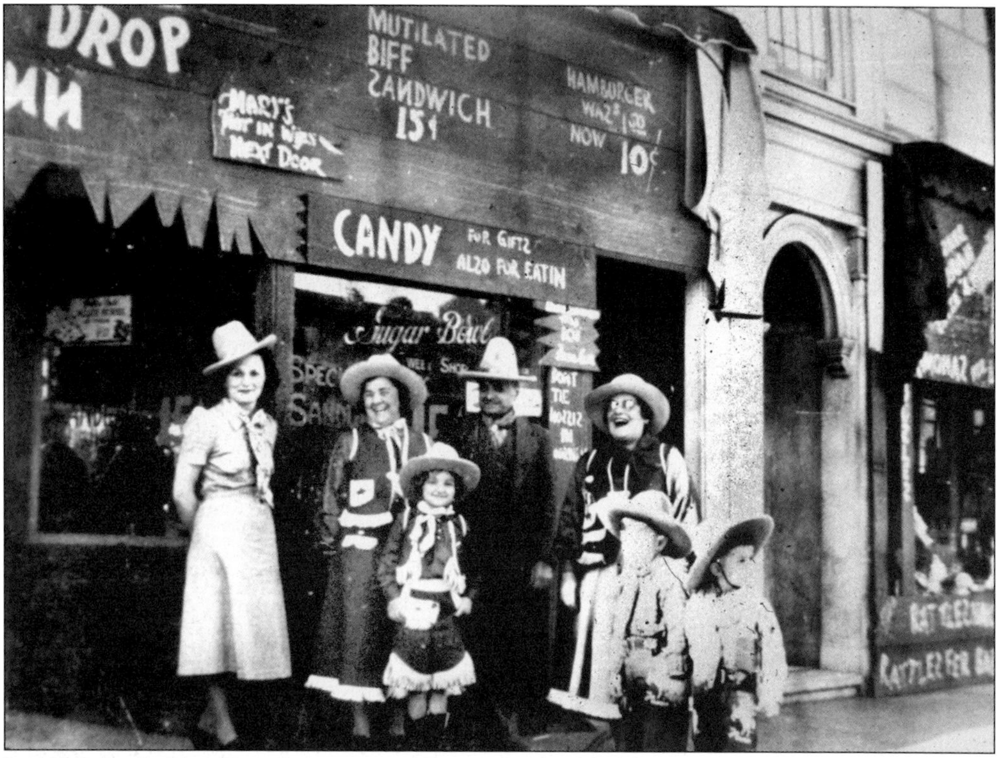

In 1939 the Golden Gate International Exposition was held in San Francisco to celebrate the completion of the world's two largest bridges of their kind. The world's largest manmade island, Treasure Island, was built specifically for the celebration. The theme was a Southwestern fiesta and merchants were requested to install false fronts on their businesses to give them an "Old West" feeling. The city asked that all people dress in Western or Mexican attire. The little store behind the people in this picture is the Sugar Bowl Coffee Shop and Creamery, located at 4568 Mission Street opposite Excelsior Avenue.

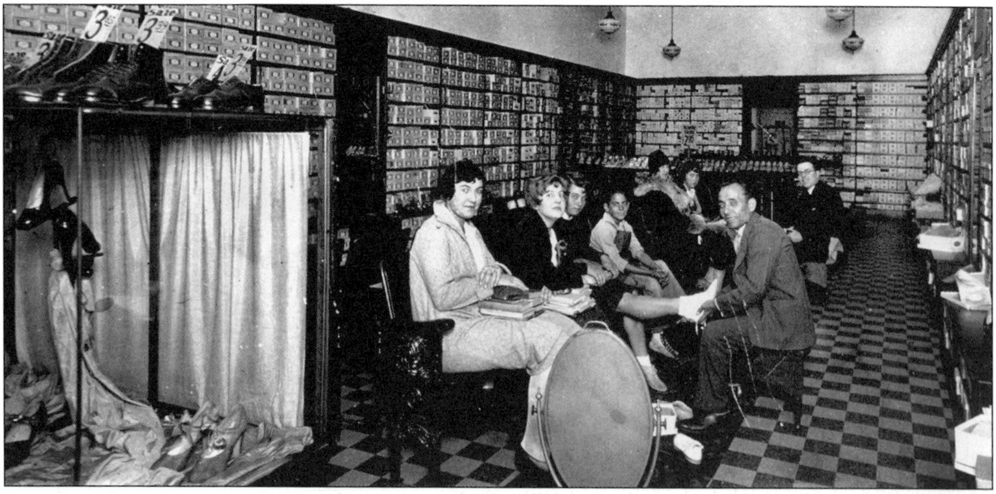

Farrah's Shoe Store was located at 4576 Mission Street. It was one store away from Farrah's Department Store at 4558 Mission Street, which belonged to Mr. Farrah's brother. The department store's slogan was "We can outfit you from cradle to the grave."

The bank on the corner of Mission Street and Ocean Avenue is the American Trust Company, which later merged with Wells Fargo. After the merger the building was remodeled and enlarged to extend 25 feet down Ocean Avenue, forcing the Excelsior Branch Library to be moved to the 4400 block of Mission Street. The streetcar tracks on Mission Street are now gone as well.

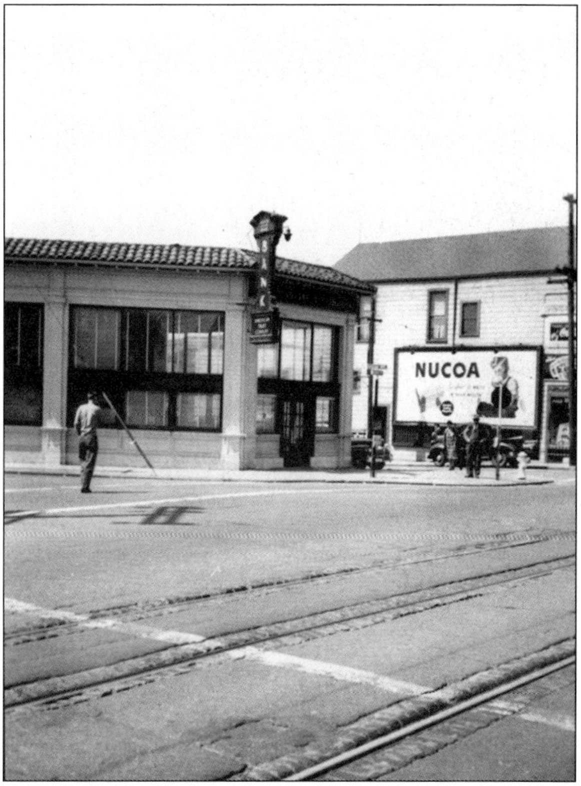

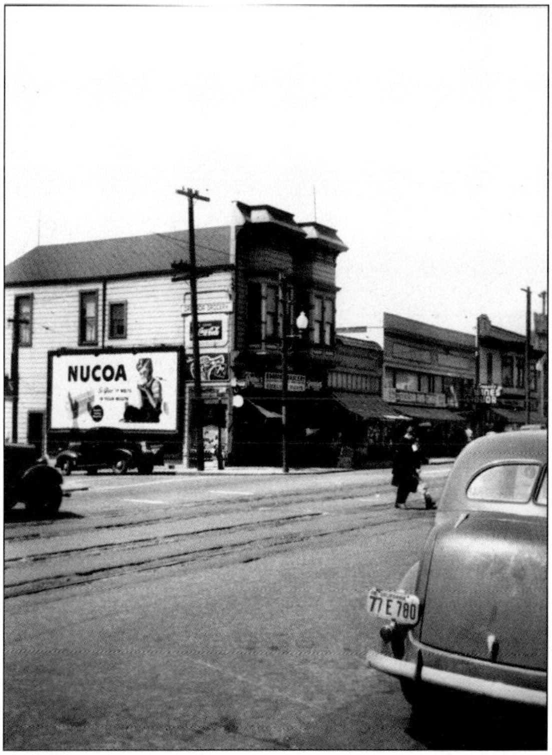

This crosswalk at the corner of Mission Street and Ocean Avenue where the American Trust Company bank stood was badly in need of a stop sign. There were three deaths at this intersection before the city installed the stoplights requested by the local merchants association. Note the man crossing the street without the benefit of crosswalk markings of any kind or even a stop sign. The two buildings on the corner are now gone after they were combined into a bank.

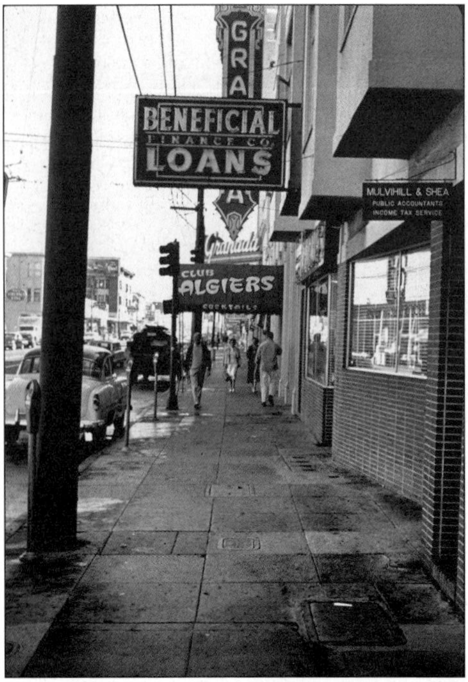

This photo is of the same location, taken a few years later. Jebe's Camera Shop has moved one block east to 4619 Mission Street opposite Alfonso Ferrera's hardware store. Beneficial Finance Company has taken the place of Tony Ferrera Hardware, which moved south to 4711 Mission Street. The Algiers bar was a cozy place to relax and have a drink.

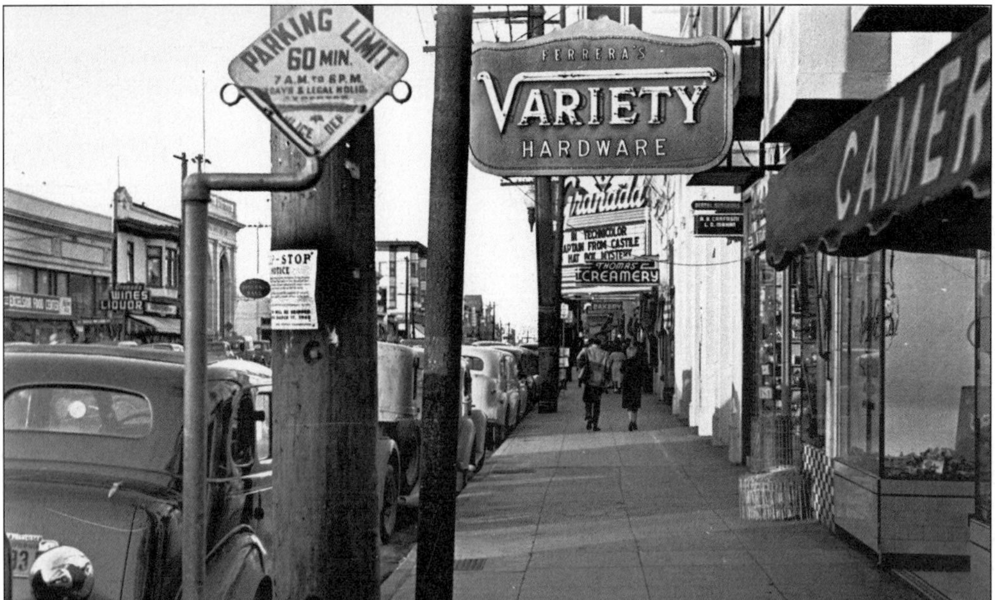

This photo was taken around 1949 and shows Mission Street opposite Ocean Avenue with the author's camera shop beside Ferrera Variety and Hardware at 4615 Mission (owned by the author's father-in-law, Anton "Tony" Ferrera). Tony and his brother Alfonso were partners in 1914 and later went their own way. Tony started Ferrera Electric and Hardware and Alfonso opened Ferrera Hardware at 4500 Mission Street—the tall building between the two poles in the center of this photo. Down the street stood the well-known Thomas Creamery sandwich shop and then the Granada Theater, which showed a double feature with a newsreel, cartoon, and, on weekends, an episode from the *Flash Gordon* or *Dick Tracy* series, all for 25¢.

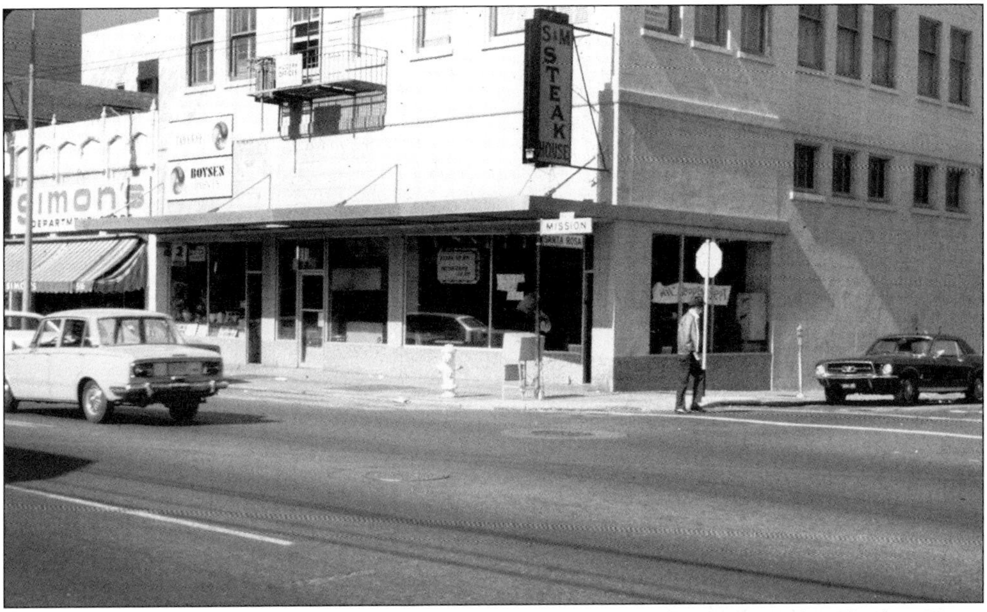

The corner of Mission Street and Santa Rosa Avenue is a good place to eat. The Chicken Coop has good food at great prices, including rotisserie chicken, baked ham, corned beef and cabbage, veal cutlets, and fish on Fridays. The entire operation is a mom and pop, Hofbrau-style establishment where you always feel welcome.

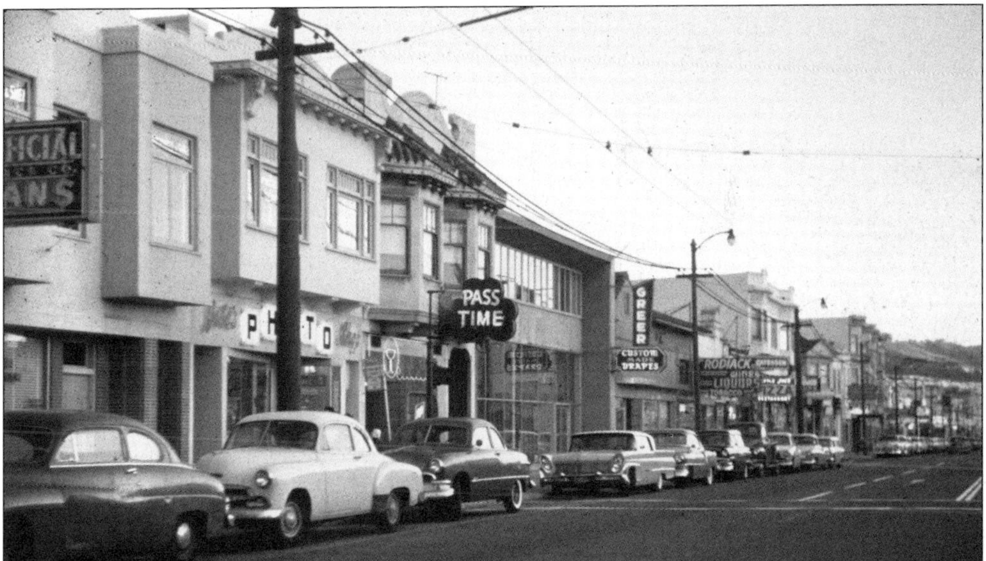

This photo of the intersection of Mission Street and Ocean Avenue shows that the Beneficial Finance Company (left) has taken over the former Hardware and Electric Company site. By then Tony Ferrera had moved to the next block at 4711 Mission, which is now a Chinese bakery and restaurant know as Kowloon. Then comes Jebe's Camera Shop next to the Past Time Bar (formerly Willie Keane's), and the Greer Drapery Company in the large flat-fronted building designed and owned by the well-known architect Mario Campi, who also designed Corpus Christi Church. Roadiack's Liquor and other businesses are visible to the corner of Persia Avenue.

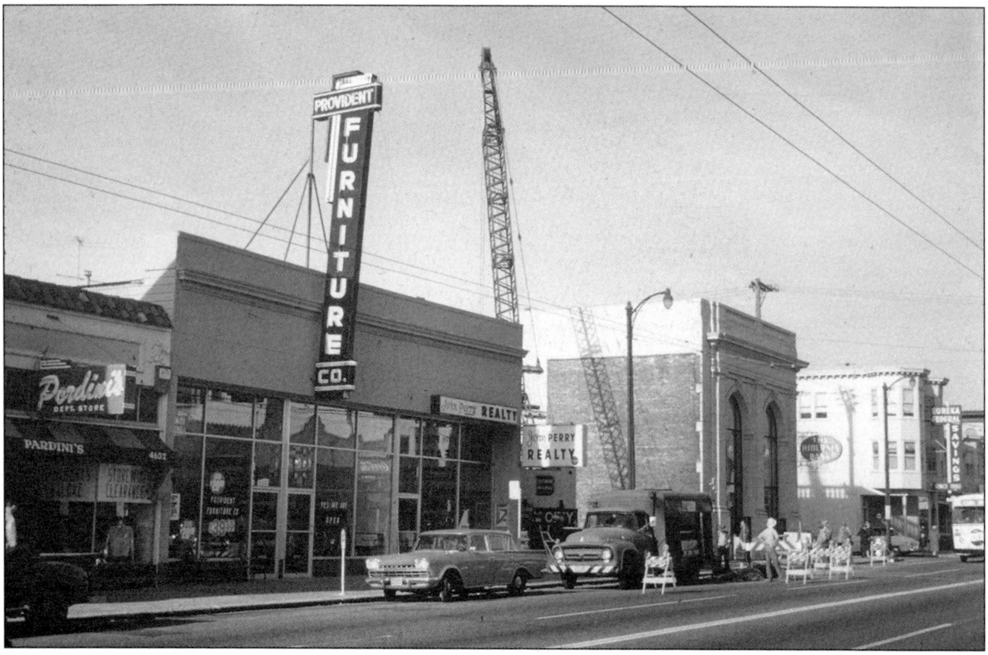

This location is between San Juan Avenue and Norton Streets, which at the time was home to Padinis' clothing store, Provident Furniture Company, and Time Realty, owned by one of the best real estate agents in the entire Outer Mission, John "Pipes" McClosky. The construction site is slated for the new home of Eureka Savings and Loan, which is currently located at the far right. Today the beautiful granite Hibernia Bank building occupies this location.

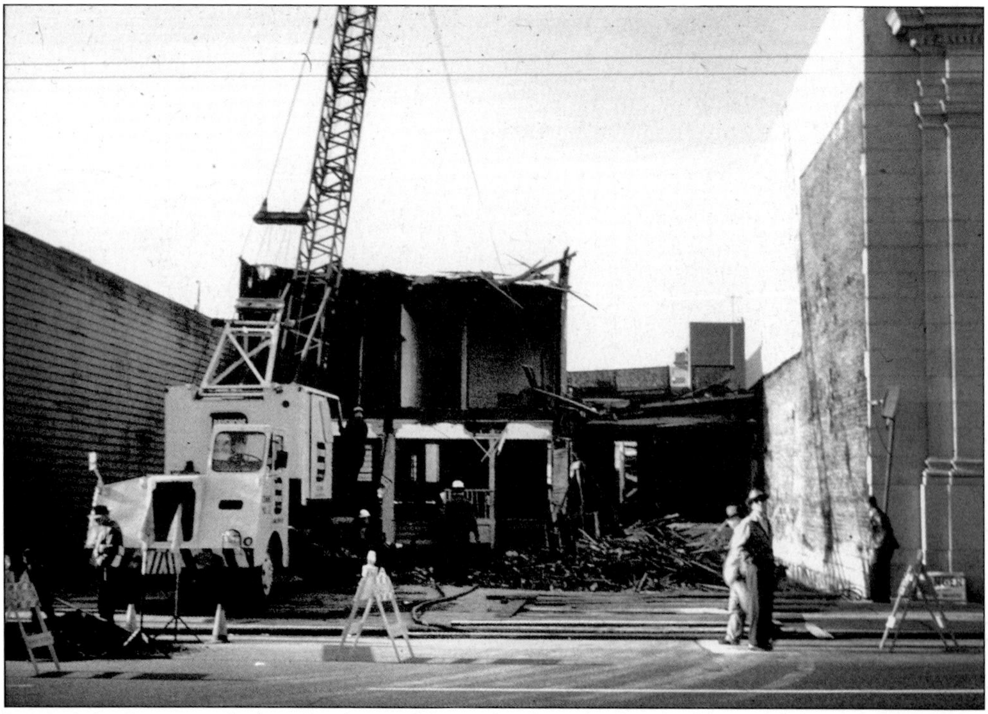

It won't be long now before this beautiful new bank and office building will be complete.

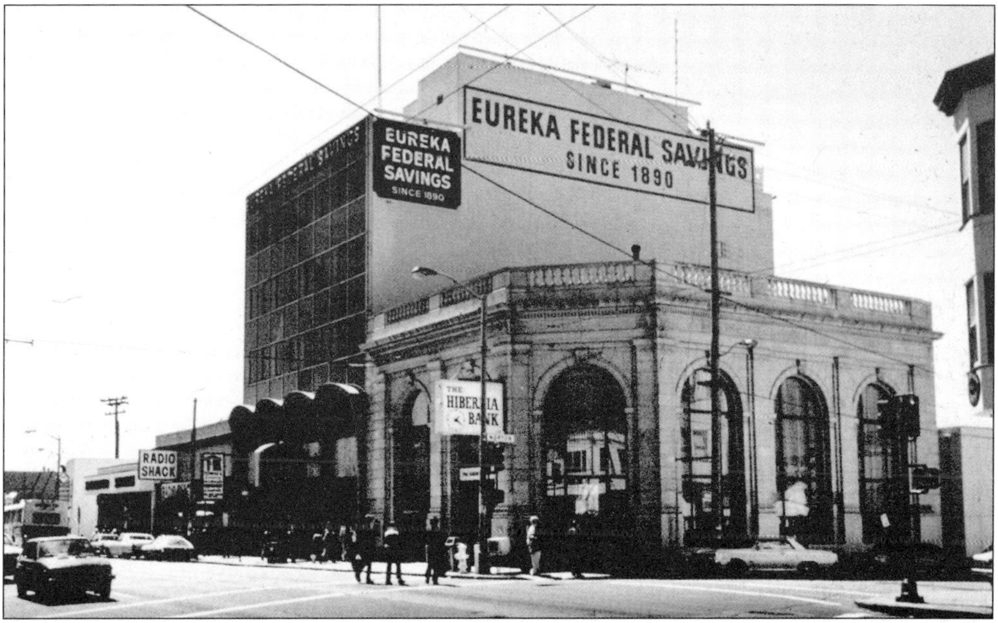

Eureka Federal Savings has been completed and stands five stores high. During the construction other changes have occurred in the immediate area, including the installation of a plastic sign with a clock for the Hibernia Bank, which seems out of place on the classy building. Time Realty has closed because John McClosky passed away and is now a Radio Shack. Mr. Pardini retired and his clothing store is now the location of another bank.

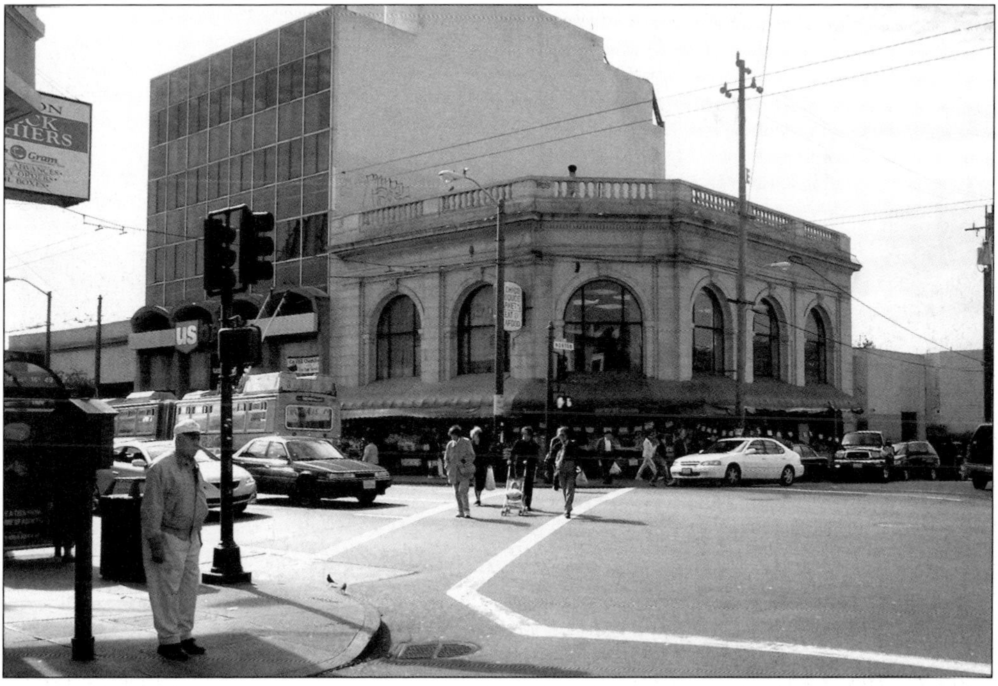

Changes have also come to the area surrounding the Hibernia Bank building. Electric traffic lights and a painted crosswalk have been added, and the sidewalk ends up in one of the Bay Area's most elegant Granite produce markets.

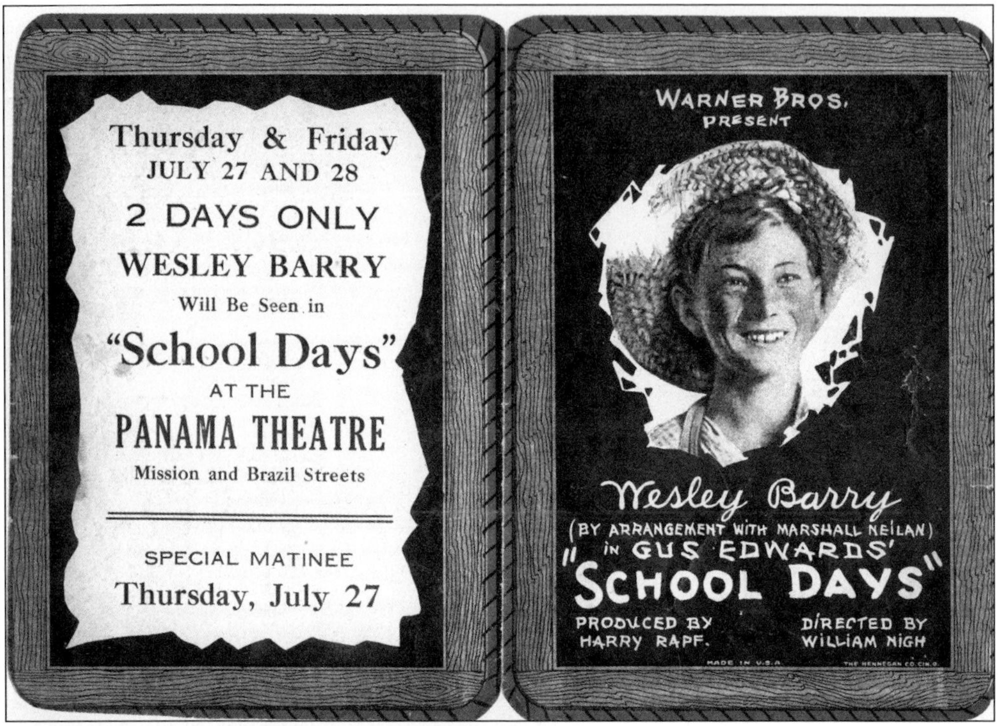

Theaters have finally made it to the Excelsior and Outer Mission areas. The Panama at Mission and Brazil Streets is showing Wesley Barry in Gus Edward's *School Days* for two days only. (Original playbill from author's collection.)

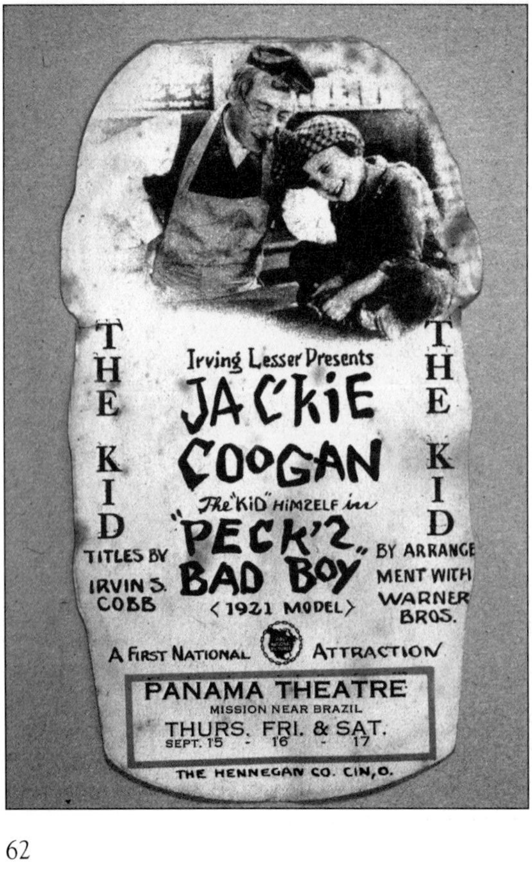

Jackie Coogan starred in *Peck's Bad Boy*, which played at the Panama Theatre on Mission Street near Brazil on Thursday the 15th, Friday the 16th, and Saturday the 17th. The playbill does not include the month or year, although the movie was released in 1921. Note that this was a silent film with titles by Irving S. Cobb. (Original playbill from author's collection.)

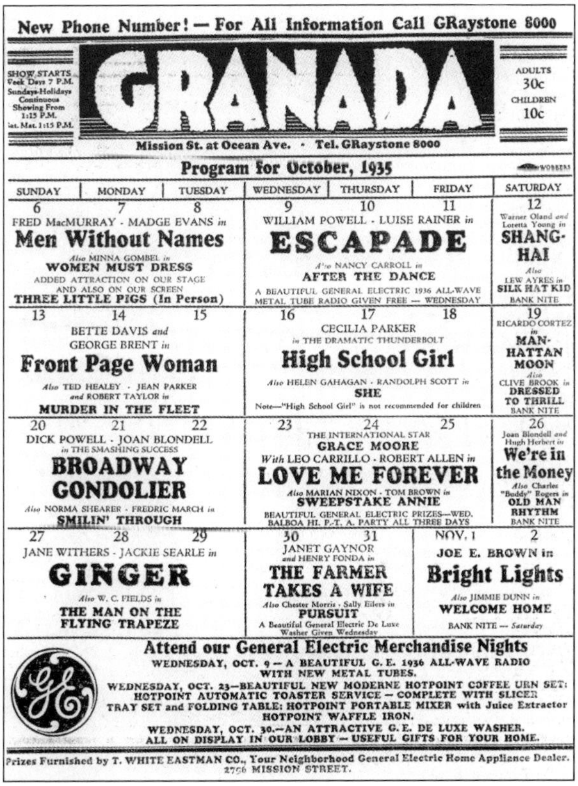
New Phone Number! — For All Information Call GRaystone 8000

SHOW STARTS
Week Days 7 P.M.
Sundays-Holidays
Continuous
Showing From
1:15 P.M.
Sat. Mat. 1:15 P.M.

GRANADA

ADULTS
30c
CHILDREN
10c

Mission St. at Ocean Ave. · Tel. GRaystone 8000

Program for October, 1935

WOBBERS

SUNDAY | MONDAY | TUESDAY | WEDNESDAY | THURSDAY | FRIDAY | SATURDAY

6 7 8
FRED MacMURRAY - MADGE EVANS *in*
Men Without Names
Also MINNA GOMBEL *in*
WOMEN MUST DRESS
ADDED ATTRACTION ON OUR STAGE
AND ALSO ON OUR SCREEN
THREE LITTLE PIGS (In Person)

9 10 11
WILLIAM POWELL - LUISE RAINER *in*
ESCAPADE
Also NANCY CARROLL *in*
AFTER THE DANCE
A BEAUTIFUL GENERAL ELECTRIC 1936 ALL-WAVE
METAL TUBE RADIO GIVEN FREE — WEDNESDAY

12
Warner Oland *and*
Loretta Young *in*
SHANG-HAI
Also
LEW AYRES *in*
SILK HAT KID
BANK NITE

13 14 15
BETTE DAVIS *and*
GEORGE BRENT *in*
Front Page Woman
Also TED HEALEY - JEAN PARKER
and ROBERT TAYLOR *in*
MURDER IN THE FLEET

16 17 18
CECILIA PARKER
in THE DRAMATIC THUNDERBOLT
High School Girl
Also HELEN GAHAGAN - RANDOLPH SCOTT *in*
SHE
Note—"High School Girl" is not recommended for children

19
RICARDO CORTEZ
in
MAN-HATTAN MOON
Also
CLIVE BROOK *in*
DRESSED TO THRILL
BANK NITE

20 21 22
DICK POWELL - JOAN BLONDELL
in THE SMASHING SUCCESS
BROADWAY GONDOLIER
Also NORMA SHEARER - FREDRIC MARCH *in*
SMILIN' THROUGH

23 24 25
THE INTERNATIONAL STAR
GRACE MOORE
With LEO CARRILLO - ROBERT ALLEN *in*
LOVE ME FOREVER
Also MARIAN NIXON - TOM BROWN *in*
SWEEPSTAKE ANNIE
BEAUTIFUL GENERAL ELECTRIC PRIZES—WED.
BALBOA HI. P.-T. A. PARTY ALL THREE DAYS

26
Joan Blondell *and*
Hugh Herbert *in*
We're in the Money
Also Charles
"Buddy" Rogers *in*
OLD MAN RHYTHM
BANK NITE

27 28 29
JANE WITHERS - JACKIE SEARLE *in*
GINGER
Also W. C. FIELDS *in*
THE MAN ON THE FLYING TRAPEZE

30 31
JANET GAYNOR
and HENRY FONDA *in*
THE FARMER TAKES A WIFE
Also Chester Morris - Sally Eilers *in*
PURSUIT
A Beautiful General Electric De Luxe
Washer Given Wednesday

NOV. 1 2
JOE E. BROWN in
Bright Lights
Also JIMMIE DUNN *in*
WELCOME HOME
BANK NITE — *Saturday*

Attend our General Electric Merchandise Nights
WEDNESDAY, OCT. 9 — A BEAUTIFUL G. E. 1936 ALL-WAVE RADIO
WITH NEW METAL TUBES.
WEDNESDAY, OCT. 23—BEAUTIFUL NEW MODERNE HOTPOINT COFFEE URN SET:
HOTPOINT AUTOMATIC TOASTER SERVICE — COMPLETE WITH SLICER
TRAY SET and FOLDING TABLE: HOTPOINT PORTABLE MIXER with Juice Extractor
HOTPOINT WAFFLE IRON.
WEDNESDAY, OCT. 30.—AN ATTRACTIVE G. E. DE LUXE WASHER.
ALL ON DISPLAY IN OUR LOBBY — USEFUL GIFTS FOR YOUR HOME.

Prizes Furnished by T. WHITE EASTMAN CO., Your Neighborhood General Electric Home Appliance Dealer.
2756 MISSION STREET.

Below is the Granada Theater on Mission Street between Brazil and Persia Avenues. The previous playbills stated that there was a Panama at Mission and Brazil Streets. The Panama may have been very close to where the Granada is today. When this theatre was built they may have called it Panama, but the Granada vertical sign and maybe the marquee was moved from Market Street (it was likely from the Paramount originally). Notice in this photo Geneva Excelsior Lions Club was putting on a show for all of the neighborhood children.

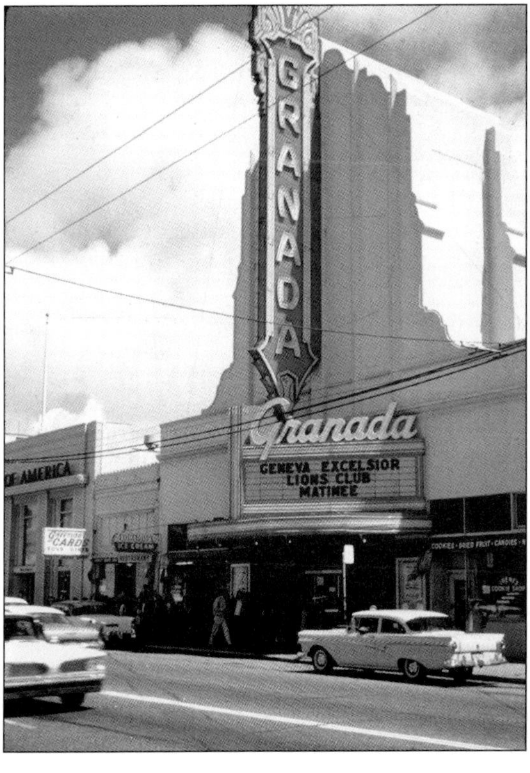

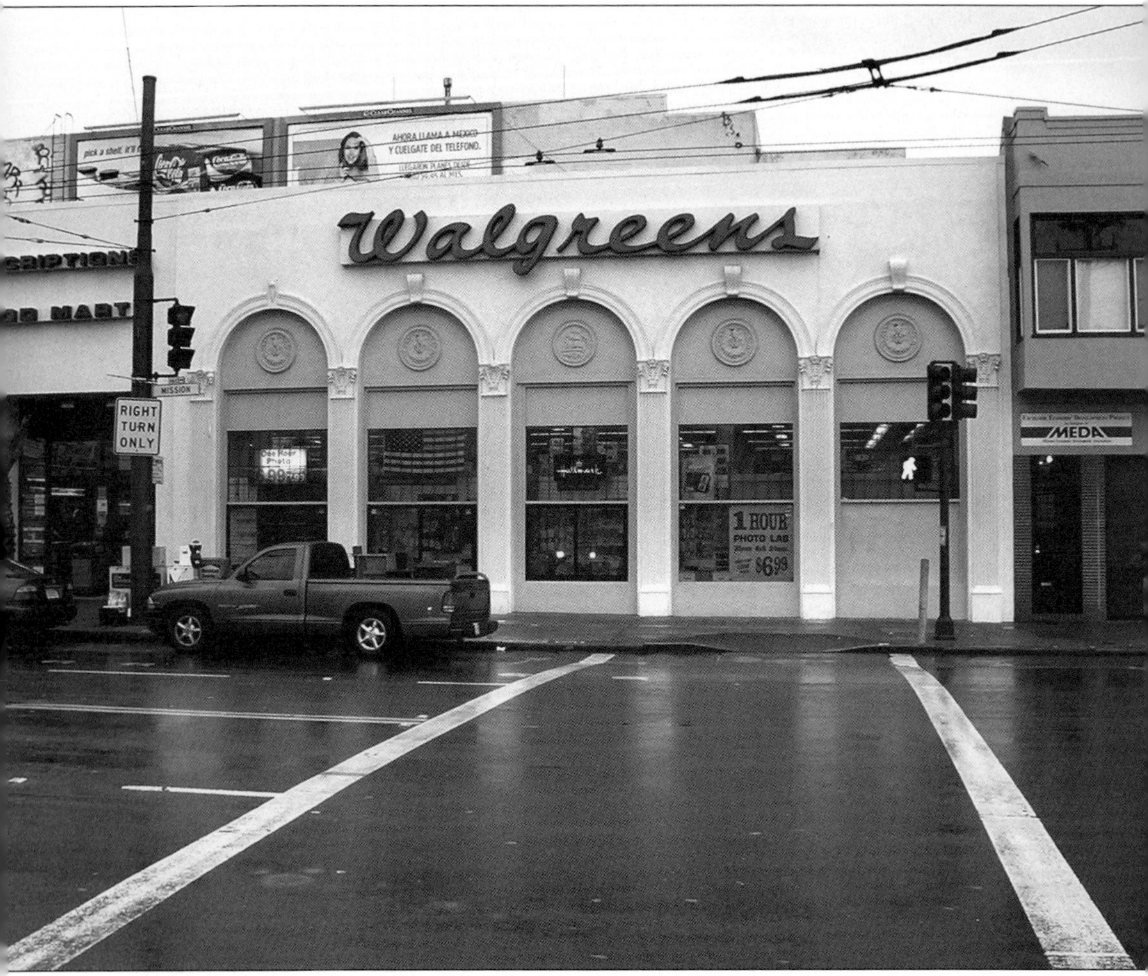

This Walgreens store on Mission Street opposite Ocean Avenue was originally the Excelsior Bank of America. The building in the rear with the billboards is the former auditorium at the Granada Theatre. According to a former executive at the Bank of America, the Excelsior branch had the largest savings accounts of any bank west of Chicago in the 1940s and 1950s, an interesting anecdote since this was a blue collar neighborhood. The medallions in the arches are the seals of the Bank of America; the main seal is an image of the ship *San Carlos*, the first Spanish ship (and most likely the first ship ever) to enter the San Francisco Bay, on August 5, 1775.

Sorrento Italian delicatessen is the last Italian deli in the Excelsior. Old timers remember Mario Bruzzoni's deli, which later changed to Zufi's Italian deli, and Lucca's deli, all located on Mission Street on a stretch between Excelsior and Brazil. There was also a German deli on Mission near Persia Avenue, operated by the Schnur/Krumpt family, famous for its pickles, potato salad, sausages, sauerkraut, and potato chips in bulk. The Sorrento Italian deli's shelves were stocked with imported Italian canned goods, the finest Italian olive oil and olives, fresh tagliarini and ravioli, dried codfish known as bacala, festooned with hanging salamis, and a multitude of Italian cold-cuts and cheeses. Every store on a corner in the neighborhood bore the name of the family that ran it, and the owners didn't commute to work but lived behind their stores. Long after closing, locals still remember Augostino's Grocery, Balma's Grocery Store, Icardi's Grocery, Zenone's Grocery, Greco's Grocery, Flageolet's Butcher Shop with Bob and Al Antraccoli, Becutti's Beauty Salon, Andrieni's Shoe Repair, and Humphrey's Donuts. Next to Sorrento is the Granada Italian Restaurant, which has never changed.

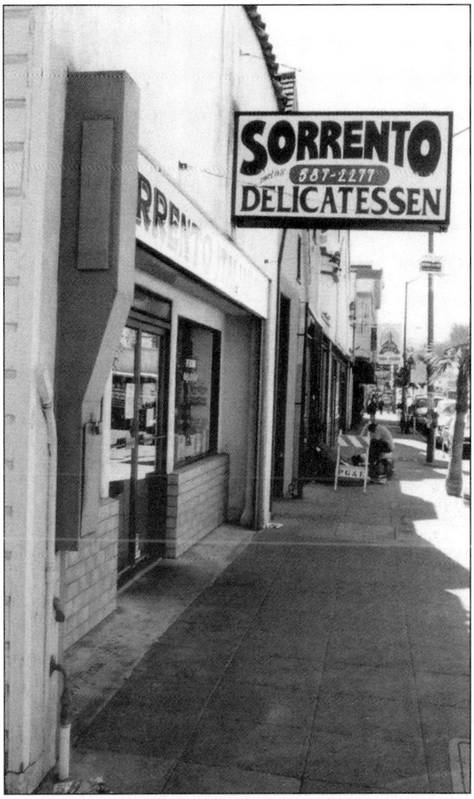

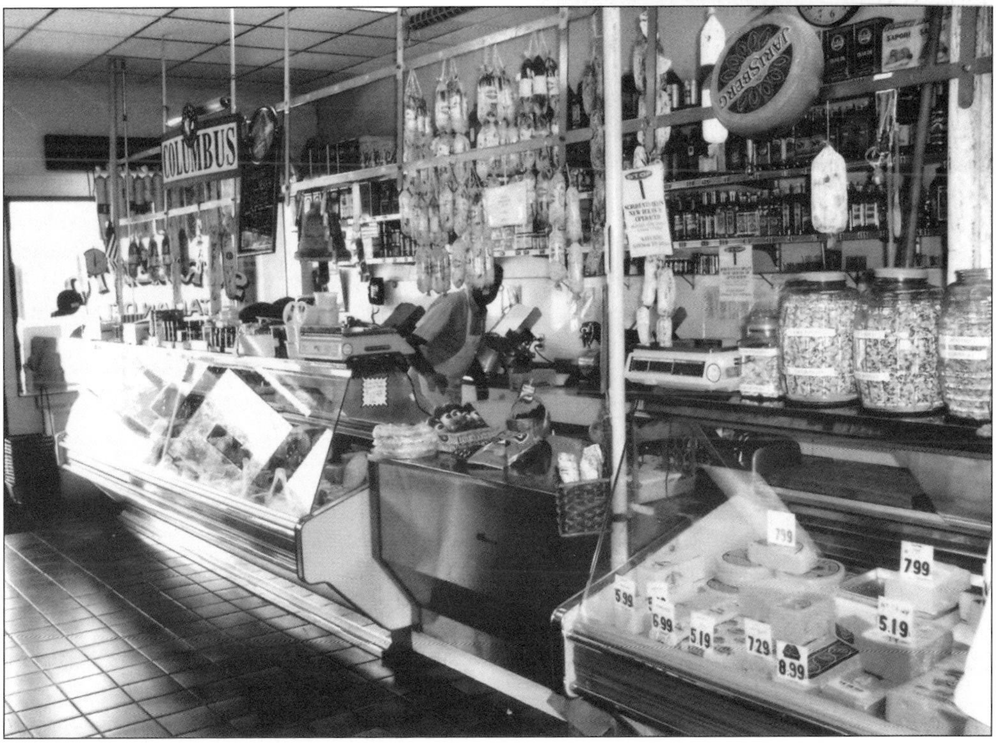

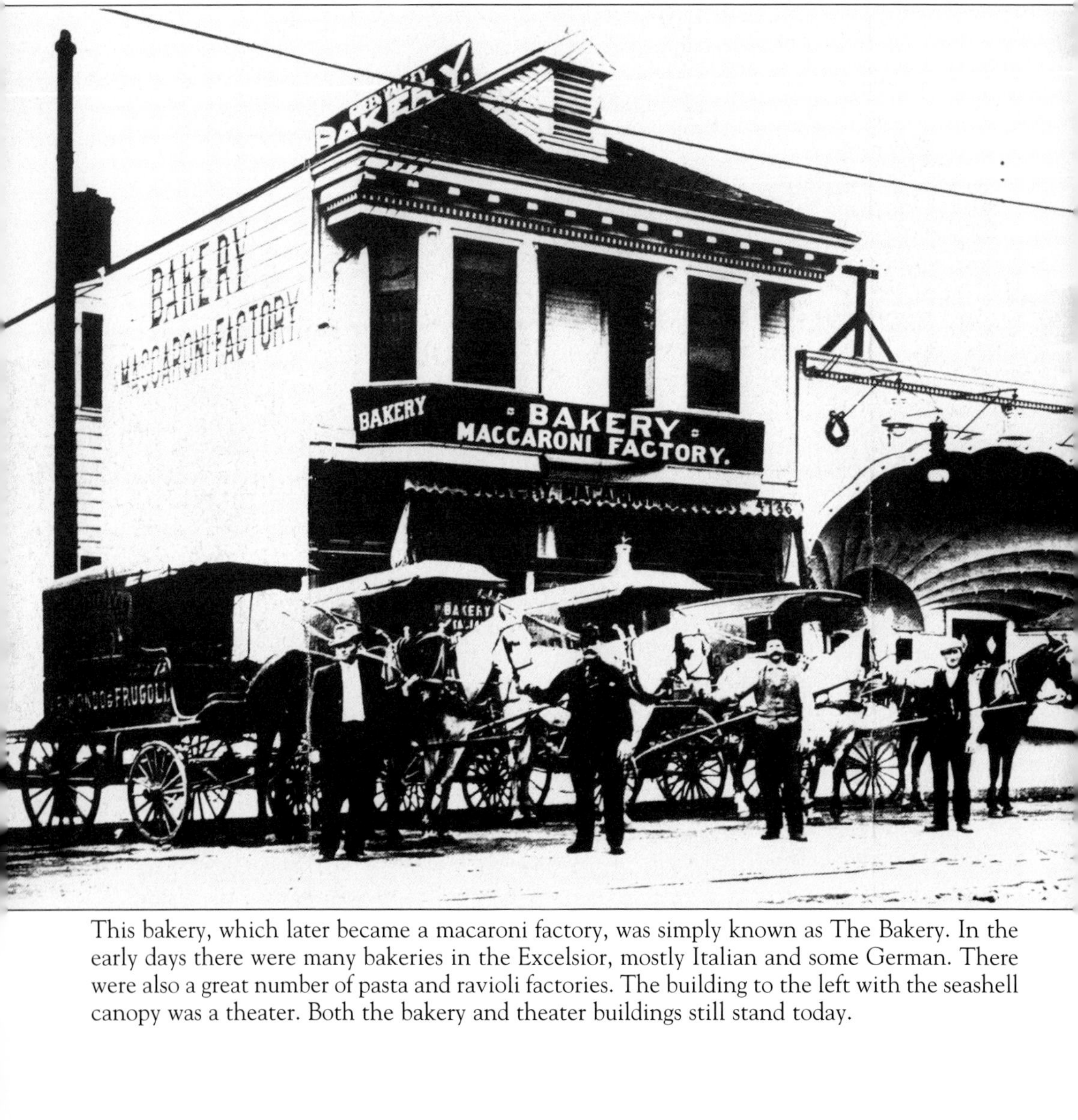

This bakery, which later became a macaroni factory, was simply known as The Bakery. In the early days there were many bakeries in the Excelsior, mostly Italian and some German. There were also a great number of pasta and ravioli factories. The building to the left with the seashell canopy was a theater. Both the bakery and theater buildings still stand today.

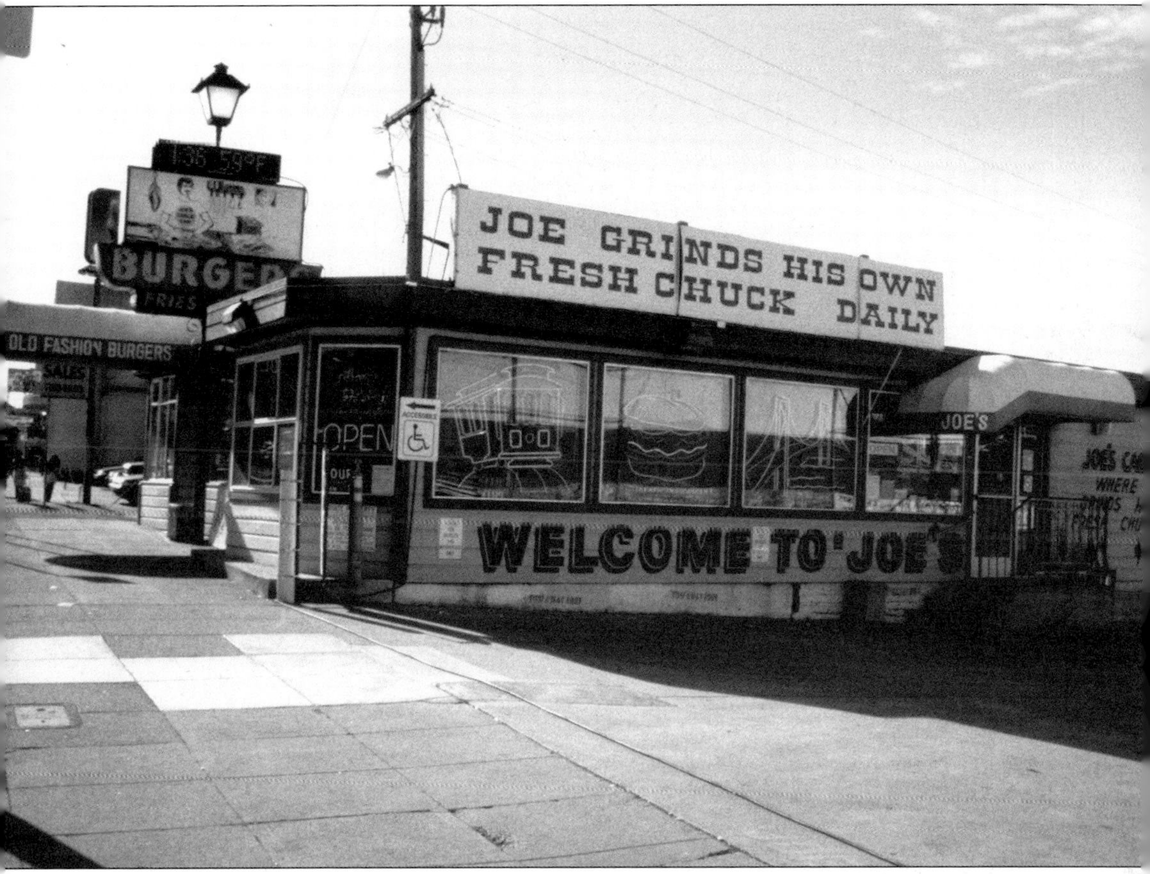

Joe grinds his own fresh chuck daily, using the best quality beef for Joe's Hamburgers on Mission Street across from the Jewish Home near Silver Avenue. Joe offers 18 different kinds of hamburgers and has won many awards. One of his most famous customers was Don Johnson of the TV series *Nash Bridges*. Joe's has for many years ranked as a San Francisco's classic.

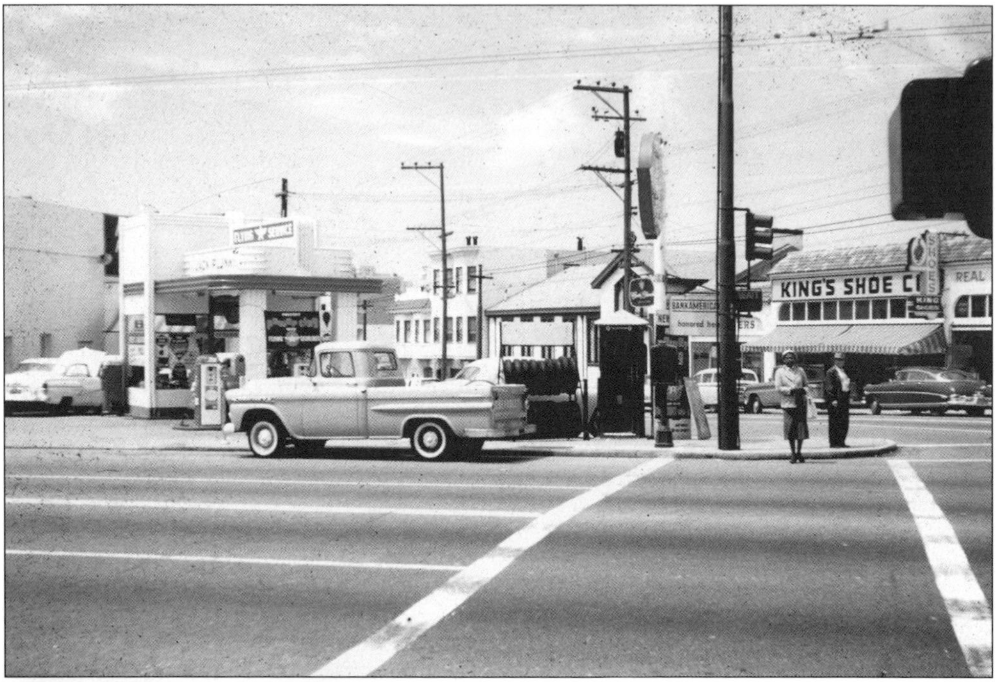

The Flying A service station at the intersection of Mission Street and Orange Avenue was a busy location in the mid-1950s. On the right is Kings Shoe Company, owned and operated by Mike Thompson, and the Ocean Avenue Presbyterian Church, designed by acclaimed architect Julia Morgan.

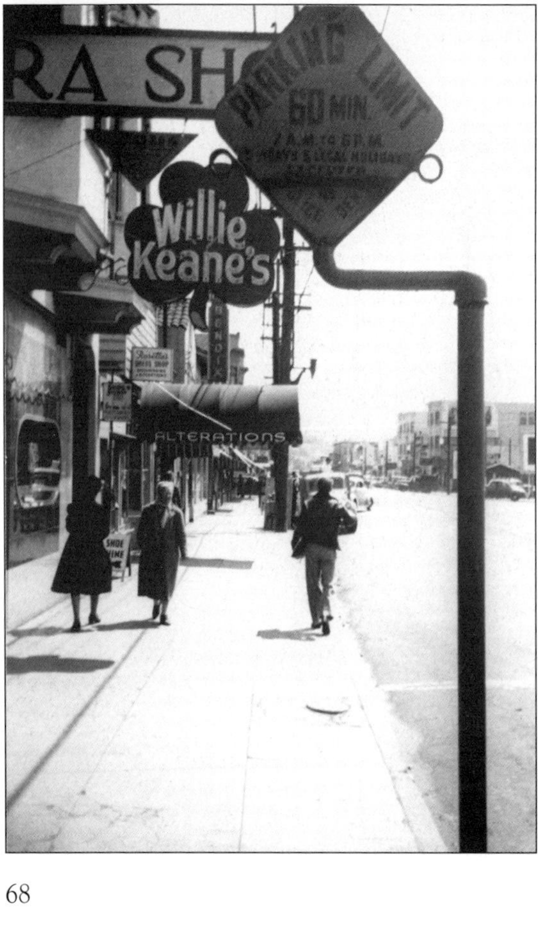

Willie Keane's bar stood next to Jebe's Camera Shop. At one time Willie Keane was one of Lew Powell's aspiring boxers; Powell was the lightweight boxing champion of California in 1906.

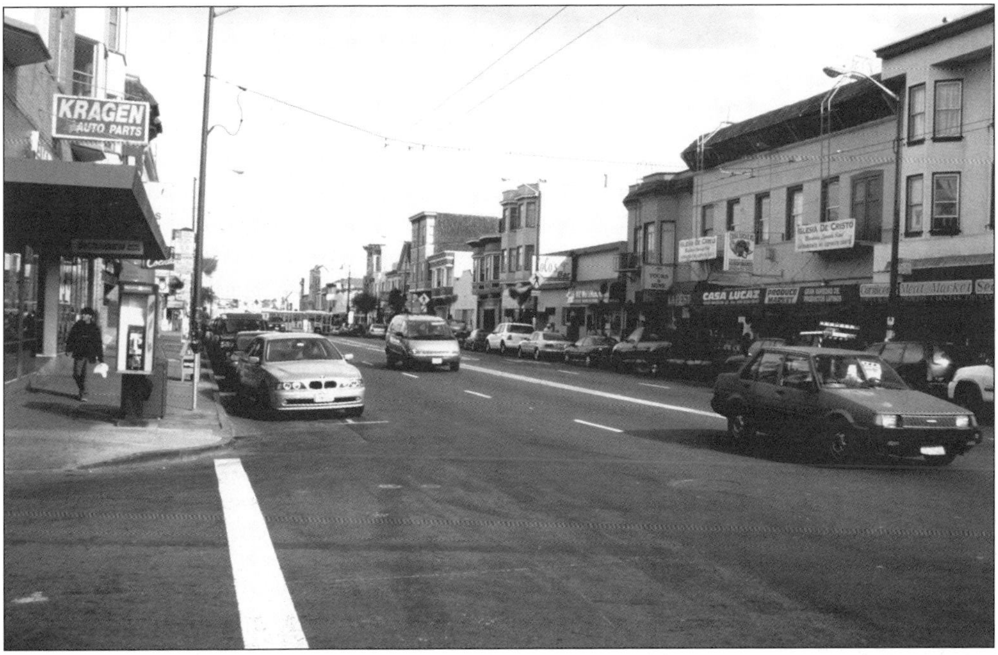

Kragen's Auto Supply is well established in the Ferrera Building at Mission and Harrington Streets in this photo, taken sometime after 1992. Note the lack of streetcar tracks. The area is now serviced by electric buses or trackless trolleys. The large gray building on the right is Casa Lucas, a large Latino fresh produce market.

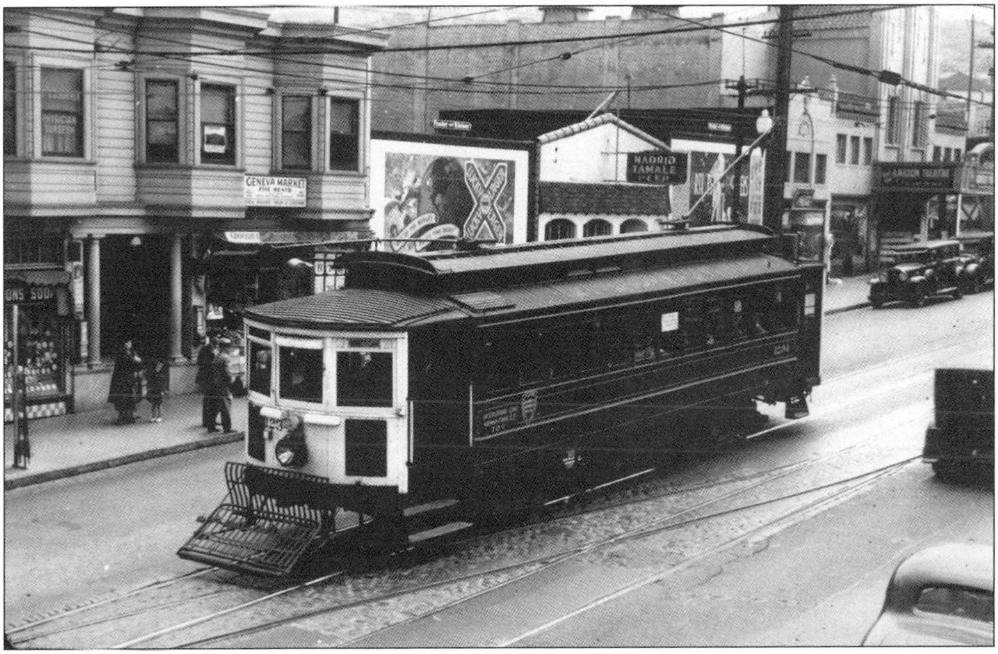

The No. 40 streetcar is at Mission Street about to cross Geneva Avenue in this *c.* 1930s photo. The white building directly behind the streetcar is the Tamale restaurant. The tall building on the far right is the State Theatre. The area had several theaters located very close to each other, with the Amazon on Geneva Avenue and the State Theater in the upper right of this picture.

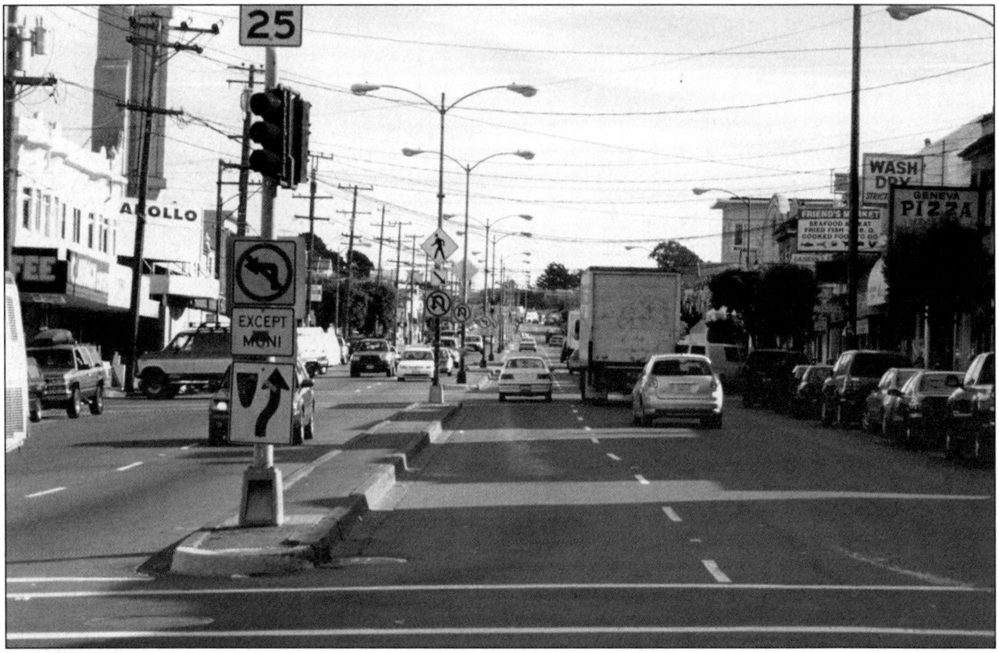

The Apollo at Mission and Geneva was originally known as the Amazon Theater. After the Amazon closed it was reopened as the Apollo, but it was not very successful either. It was later converted to a church, but that venture also was unsuccessful. In fact, the whole block that comprised Geneva Avenue between Paris and London Streets began to get a little rundown after Al and Harriet Kleinback closed their Hilda's Bakery, which attracted many people to the area. The Apollo complex was recently purchased by a group of enterprising businessmen and is being remodeled with new facades and new stores save for the cobbler on the corner of Persia Avenue. The theater is being gutted and will house apartments and offices while the ground floor will become a Walgreens store.

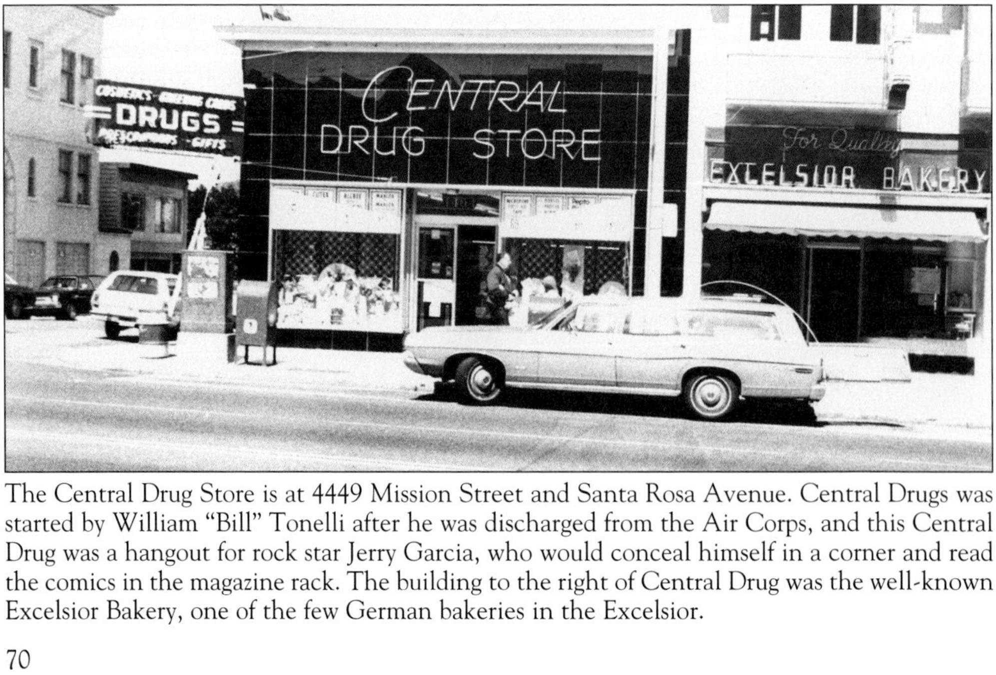

The Central Drug Store is at 4449 Mission Street and Santa Rosa Avenue. Central Drugs was started by William "Bill" Tonelli after he was discharged from the Air Corps, and this Central Drug was a hangout for rock star Jerry Garcia, who would conceal himself in a corner and read the comics in the magazine rack. The building to the right of Central Drug was the well-known Excelsior Bakery, one of the few German bakeries in the Excelsior.

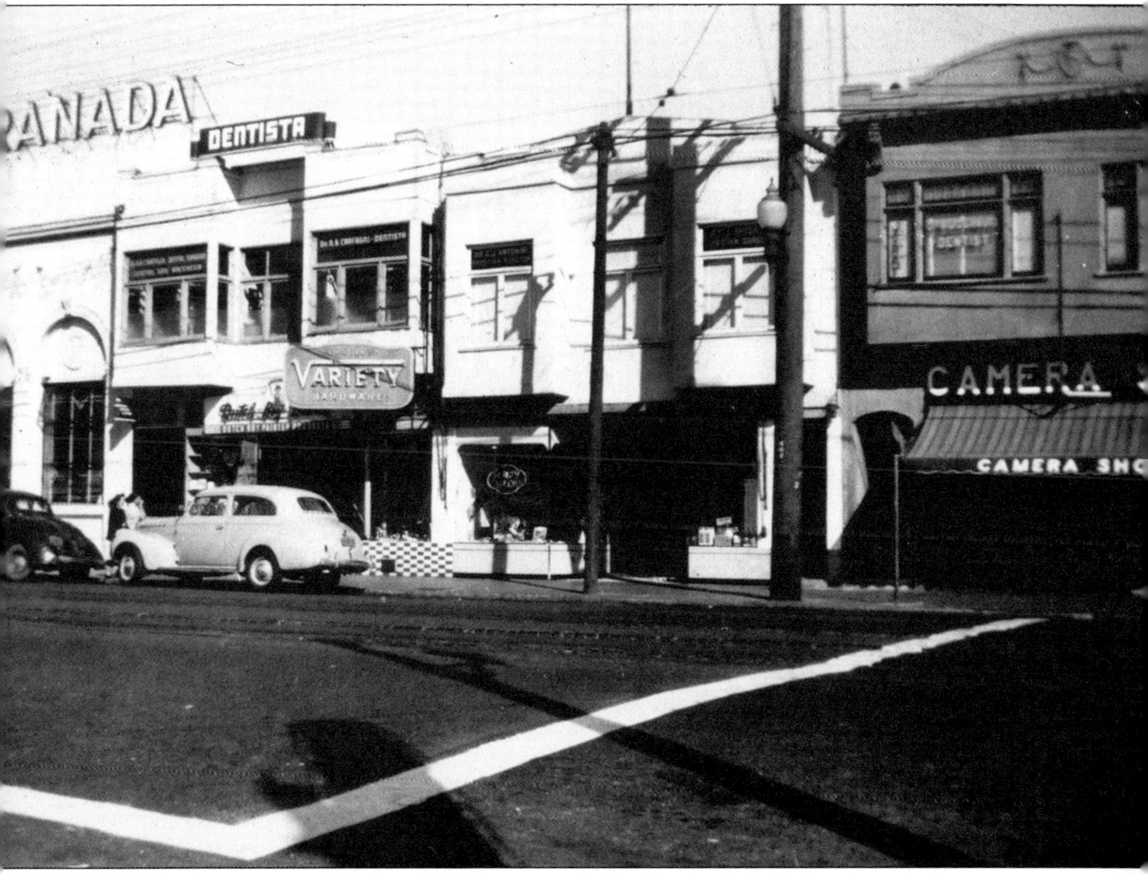

This *c.* 1948 photo was taken on Mission Street at Geneva Avenue looking east into the Excelsior. The Granada Theater is still open, and the building on the left is the well-known Casbah, an ornate drinking establishment with an Arabian theme. The space above Ferrera Variety was the office of the internationally known dentist, Dr. Carfagni. Patients came from as far as South America for his expertise. To the right of Dr. Carfagni's office was the CPA firm of Mulvahill and Shea, and above Jebe's Camera Shop was another dentist, Dr. Cirruti.

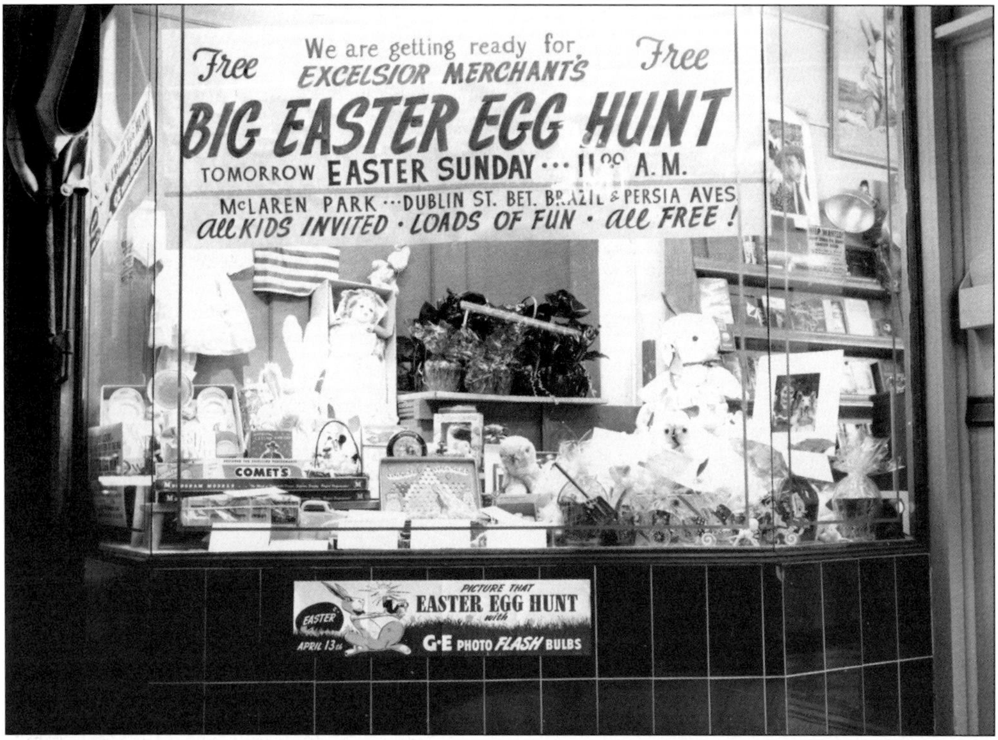

The Excelsior Merchants Association has always been very active in local events for major holidays. This display from Jebe's Camera Shop displays the goods and prizes for the annual Easter egg hunt, held in McLaren Park on Dublin Street between Persia Avenue and Brazil.

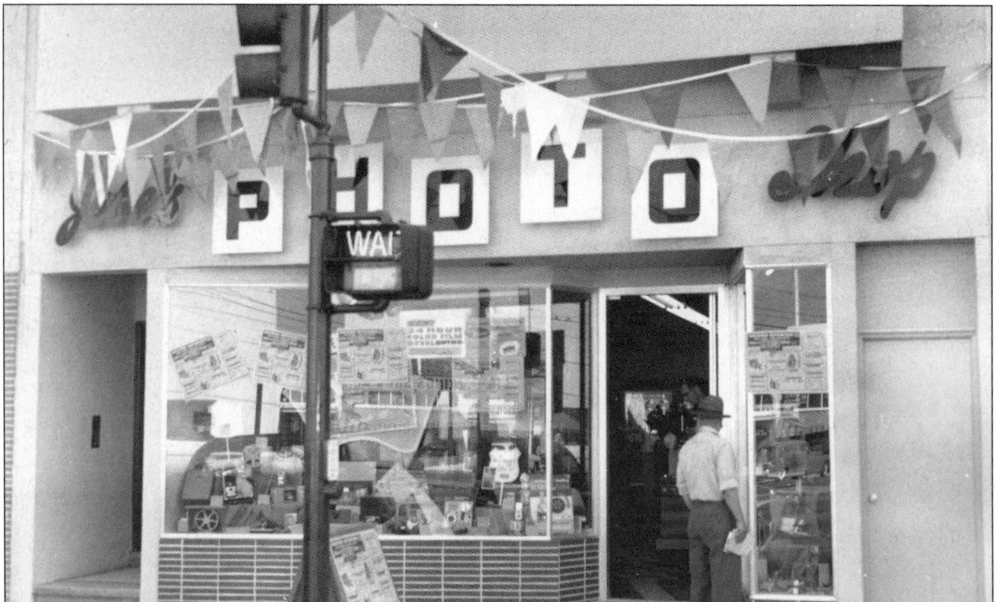

The store at 4561 Mission Street opposite Ocean Avenue is one of the many specialty businesses in the Excelsior District. Jebe's Camera Shop is the only shop of its kind within five miles in any direction.

Three
SCHOOLS AND CHURCHES

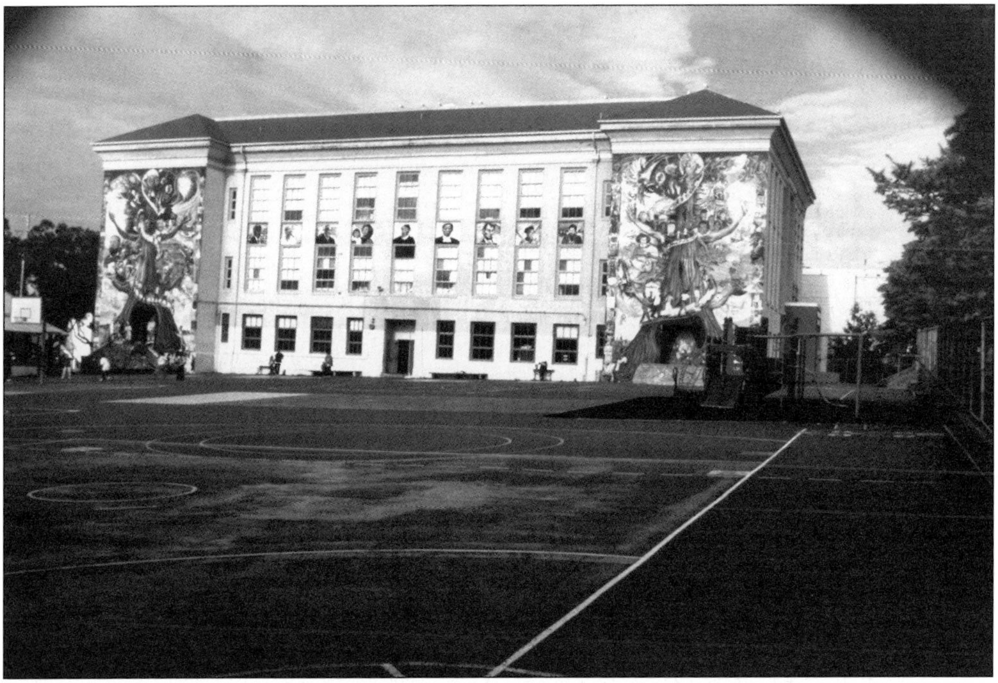

Cleveland Grammar School was one of the "feeder" schools to Balboa High School. Often students switched to Monroe in order to participate in Monroe's industrial arts and homemaking program for eighth-grade students. Cleveland is located on Persia Avenue at Vienna and Naples Streets. Note the murals on the right and left wings of the building and the pictures of famous people on the third floor.

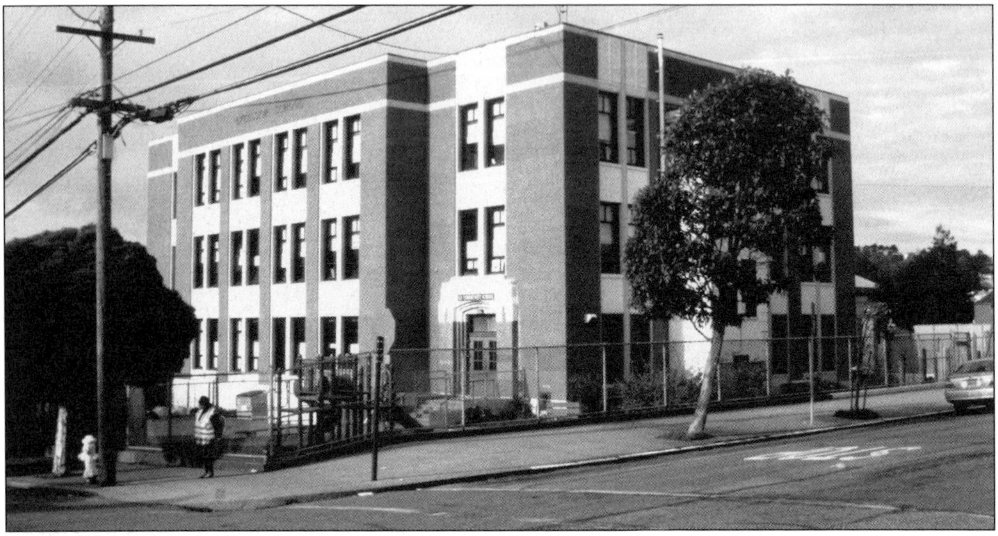

Excelsior Elementary School is located at Excelsior Avenue and London and Paris Streets. This photo was from the Paris Street side showing the school's frontage. Most of the neighborhood students started kindergarten at Excelsior and then moved up the street one block to Monroe Grammar School for the fourth through eighth grade.

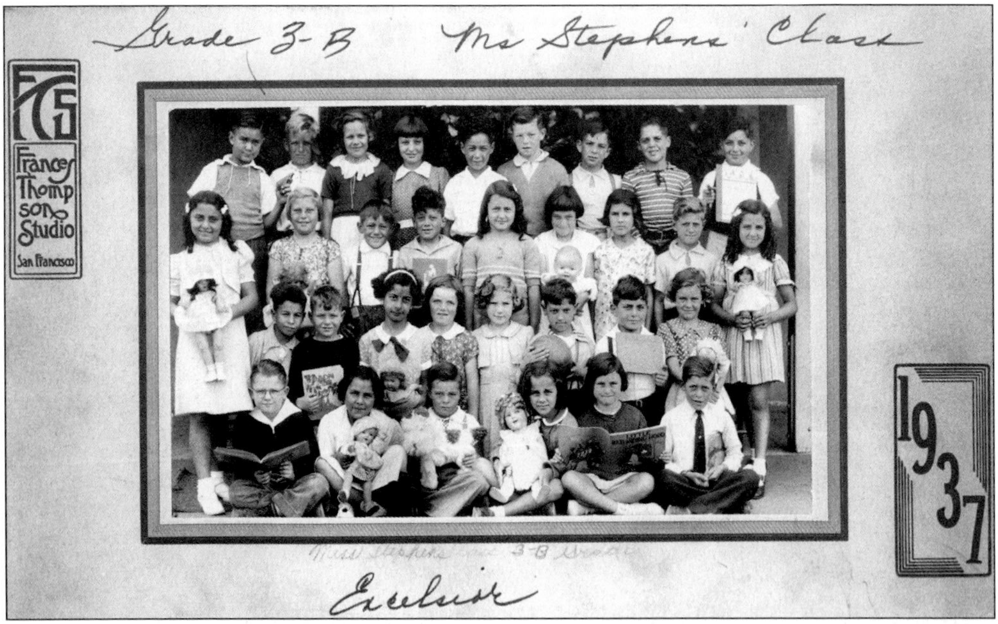

This 1937 photo of Miss Stephen's third-grade class at Excelsior Elementary School was taken by Frances Thompson, the school district photographer. These Depression-era kids somehow got 50¢ to buy these photos. The schoolchildren, from left to right, are (first row) Robert Feldman, Betty ?, Donald Mallen, Violet Joo, Virginia Gandolfi, and Curt Koch; (second row) Joseph D'Amico, Steven ?, Francis Chessari, Jacqueline Redmond, Laverne Garibaldi, James Blaine, Joe Farrah, and Frances Dunshee; (third row) Benvenuta Genna, Florence Hagenah, John Jurisich, Gus Xepoleas, Emily Powell, Carol Dunne, Vittoria Damante, Julio DePucci, and Diane Ceciello; (fourth row) Henry Sosso, Robert Larsen, Jacqueline Ostoja, June Campagna, Robert Raby, Don Van Trich, Michael Boswich, Rudy Bertolozzi, and Carl Fortina.

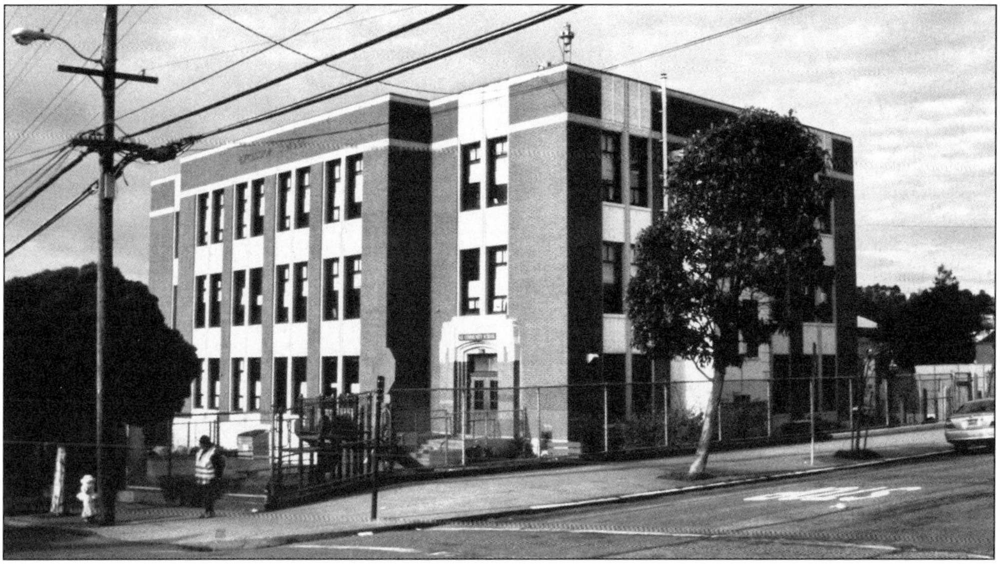

The new Monroe Grammar School was built on the same location as the old school at Excelsior Avenue between Lisbon and Madrid Streets. The original building was a huge, comprehensive grammar school made of red brick with a large auditorium, a full industrial arts and homemaking section, a dental office, and at one time a gymnasium. Unfortunately the beautiful red brick building was demolished in the 1970s because it was deemed unsafe in the event of an earthquake. After attending Monroe, students up until 1939 graduated into Balboa High School. In 1940 James Denman Junior High School opened; henceforth, students went to Denman for the seventh, eighth, and half of the ninth grade, and then to Balboa.

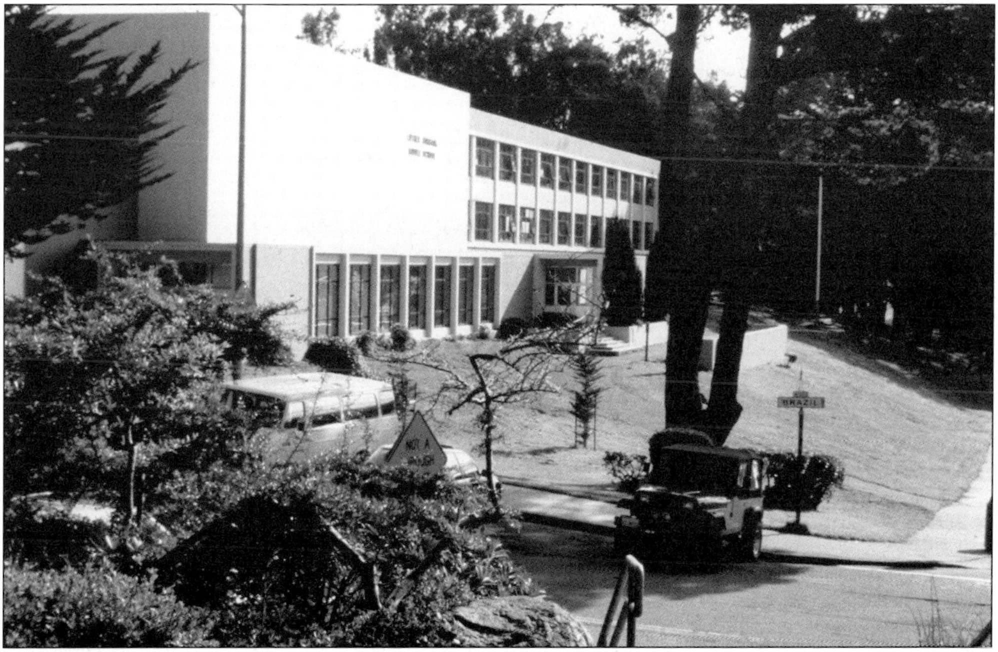

The Luther Burbank Middle School has a great location in McLaren Park facing Dublin Street between Persia Avenue and Brazil. This was also the location where the Excelsior Merchants Association held its Easter egg hunts.

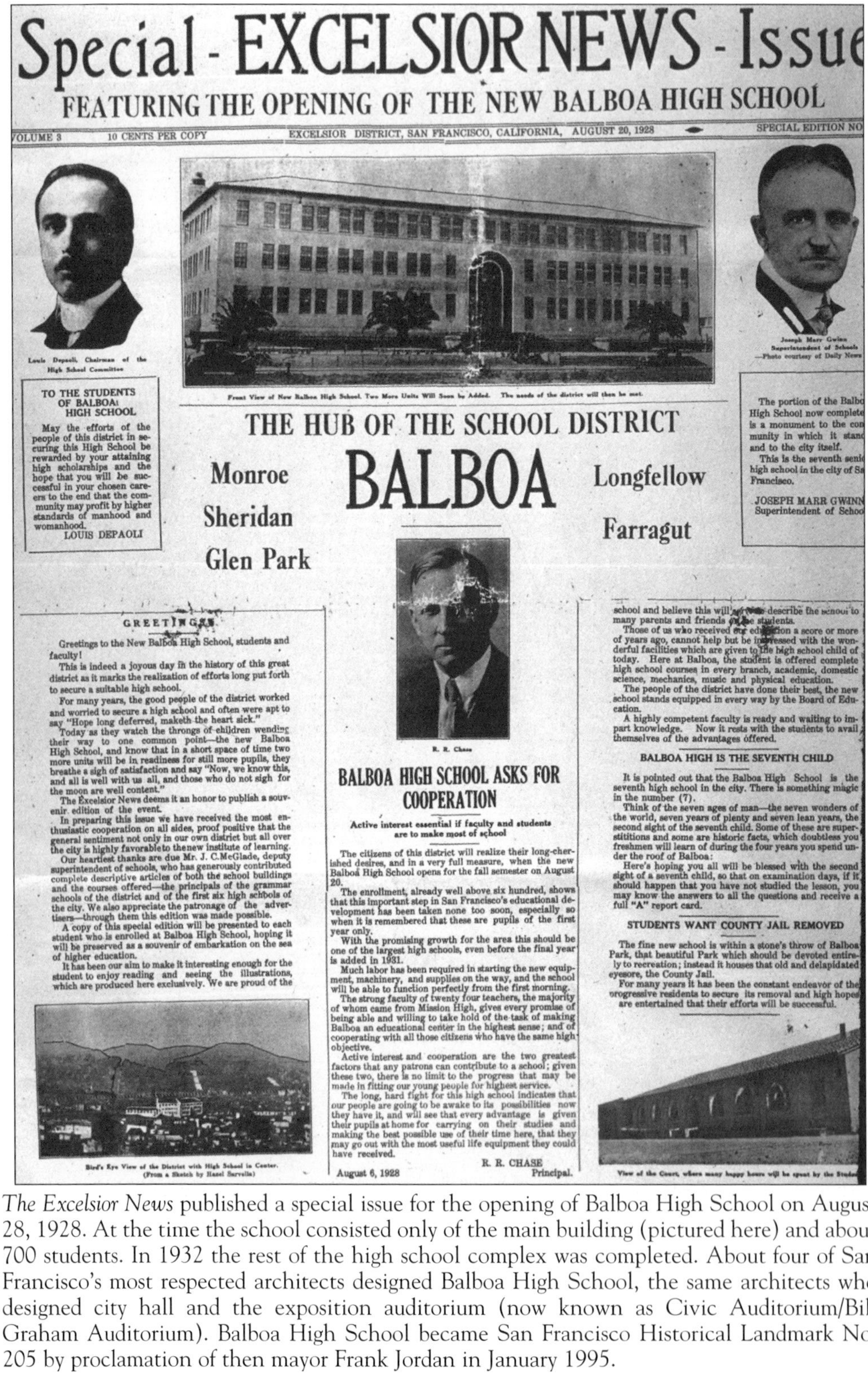

Special - EXCELSIOR NEWS - Issue

FEATURING THE OPENING OF THE NEW BALBOA HIGH SCHOOL

VOLUME 3 | 10 CENTS PER COPY | EXCELSIOR DISTRICT, SAN FRANCISCO, CALIFORNIA, AUGUST 20, 1928 | SPECIAL EDITION NO

Louis Depaoli, Chairman of the High School Committee

Front View of New Balboa High School. Two More Units Will Soon be Added. The needs of the district will then be met.

Joseph Marr Gwinn Superintendent of Schools —Photo courtesy of Daily News

TO THE STUDENTS OF BALBOA HIGH SCHOOL

May the efforts of the people of this district in securing this High School be rewarded by your attaining high scholarships and the hope that you will be successful in your chosen careers to the end that the community may profit by higher standards of manhood and womanhood.

LOUIS DEPAOLI

THE HUB OF THE SCHOOL DISTRICT

BALBOA

Monroe

Sheridan

Glen Park

Longfellow

Farragut

The portion of the Balboa High School now complete is a monument to the community in which it stands and to the city itself.

This is the seventh senior high school in the city of San Francisco.

JOSEPH MARR GWINN
Superintendent of Schools

GREETINGS

Greetings to the New Balboa High School, students and faculty!

This is indeed a joyous day in the history of this great district as it marks the realization of efforts long put forth to secure a suitable high school.

For many years, the good people of the district worked and worried to secure a high school and often were apt to say "Hope long deferred, maketh the heart sick."

Today as they watch the throngs of children wending their way to one common point—the new Balboa High School, and know that in a short space of time two more units will be in readiness for still more pupils, they breathe a sigh of satisfaction and say "Now, we know this, and all is well with us all, and those who do not sigh for the moon are well content."

The Excelsior News deems it an honor to publish a souvenir edition of the event.

In preparing this issue we have received the most enthusiastic cooperation on all sides, proof positive that the general sentiment not only in our own district but all over the city is highly favorable to the new institute of learning.

Our heartiest thanks are due Mr. J. C. McGlade, deputy superintendent of schools, who has generously contributed complete descriptive articles of both the school buildings and the courses offered—the principals of the grammar schools of the district and of the first six high schools of the city. We also appreciate the patronage of the advertisers—through them this edition was made possible.

A copy of this special edition will be presented to each student who is enrolled at Balboa High School, hoping it will be preserved as a souvenir of embarkation on the sea of higher education.

It has been our aim to make it interesting enough for the student to enjoy reading and seeing the illustrations, which are produced here exclusively. We are proud of the school and believe this will [illegible] describe the school to many parents and friends of the students.

Those of us who received our education a score or more of years ago, cannot help but be impressed with the wonderful facilities which are given to the high school child of today. Here at Balboa, the student is offered complete high school courses in every branch, academic, domestic science, mechanics, music and physical education.

The people of the district have done their best, the new school stands equipped in every way by the Board of Education.

A highly competent faculty is ready and waiting to impart knowledge. Now it rests with the students to avail themselves of the advantages offered.

R. R. Chase

BALBOA HIGH SCHOOL ASKS FOR COOPERATION

Active interest essential if faculty and students are to make most of school

The citizens of this district will realize their long-cherished desires, and in a very full measure, when the new Balboa High School opens for the fall semester on August 20.

The enrollment, already well above six hundred, shows that this important step in San Francisco's educational development has been taken none too soon, especially so when it is remembered that these are pupils of the first year only.

With the promising growth for the area this should be one of the largest high schools, even before the final year is added in 1931.

Much labor has been required in starting the new equipment, machinery, and supplies on the way, and the school will be able to function perfectly from the first morning.

The strong faculty of twenty four teachers, the majority of whom came from Mission High, gives every promise of being able and willing to take hold of the task of making Balboa an educational center in the highest sense; and of cooperating with all those citizens who have the same high objective.

Active interest and cooperation are the two greatest factors that any patrons can contribute to a school; given these two, there is no limit to the progress that may be made in fitting our young people for highest service.

The long, hard fight for this high school indicates that our people are going to be awake to its possibilities now they have it, and will see that every advantage is given their pupils at home for carrying on their studies and making the best possible use of their time here, that they may go out with the most useful life equipment they could have received.

R. R. CHASE
Principal.

August 6, 1928

BALBOA HIGH IS THE SEVENTH CHILD

It is pointed out that the Balboa High School is the seventh high school in the city. There is something magic in the number (7).

Think of the seven ages of man—the seven wonders of the world, seven years of plenty and seven lean years, the second sight of the seventh child. Some of these are superstititions and some are historic facts, which doubtless you freshmen will learn of during the four years you spend under the roof of Balboa:

Here's hoping you all will be blessed with the second sight of a seventh child, so that on examination days, if it should happen that you have not studied the lesson, you may know the answers to all the questions and receive a full "A" report card.

STUDENTS WANT COUNTY JAIL REMOVED

The fine new school is within a stone's throw of Balboa Park, that beautiful Park which should be devoted entirely to recreation; instead it houses that old and delapidated eyesore, the County Jail.

For many years it has been the constant endeavor of the progressive residents to secure its removal and high hopes are entertained that their efforts will be successful.

The Excelsior News published a special issue for the opening of Balboa High School on August 28, 1928. At the time the school consisted only of the main building (pictured here) and about 700 students. In 1932 the rest of the high school complex was completed. About four of San Francisco's most respected architects designed Balboa High School, the same architects who designed city hall and the exposition auditorium (now known as Civic Auditorium/Bill Graham Auditorium). Balboa High School became San Francisco Historical Landmark No. 205 by proclamation of then mayor Frank Jordan in January 1995.

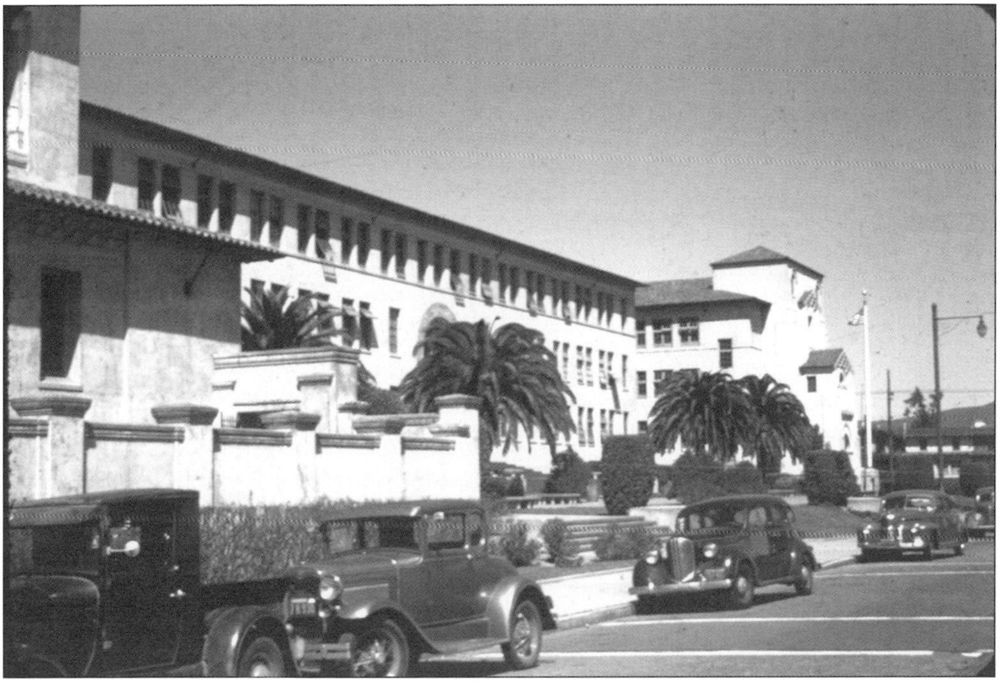

This photo was taken after 1932 when all of Balboa High School's buildings were completed and ready to accept the 3,200 Excelsior-area students. Today, bronze numerals embedded in concrete on its main stairway entrance represent 114 graduating classes. Balboa's 8,000-member alumni association is dedicated to preserving school traditions and honoring those who have contributed to the betterment of the school; it names facilities after them and affixes impressive plaques throughout the school. The main building is called Robert R. Chase Hall after the first and longest term principal (1928–1951). "Big Bob," the six-foot-tall-plus Yale graduate and former principal of Bernal Grammar School in Bernal Heights, is remembered by many students for the whistle he carried with him at all times and blew when he saw something he didn't approve of. The Nick Kafkas Quad is named after a 37-year civics faculty member, while the Emily Powell Library Building is named after Lew Powell's daughter for her outstanding volunteer service to Balboa since 1970. The Leta Wheeler Library is named for the longest serving librarian at the school (over 40 years). Sections of the Emily Powell Library building are named in honor of respected science teacher Allan Hummel and English department head Don Hofvendahl. Balboa's auditorium is named after 1958 graduate Calvin Simmons, the first African American to be named conductor of a major U.S. symphony orchestra and who died in a tragic canoeing accident at Lake Placid at age 32. The Orron Qualls Boys Gym is named after a basketball coach, the girl's gym after Rena Case, who often sponsored the Girls Athletic Association. The athletic field is named after Carl Mitchel, varsity football coach from 1935 to the late 1950s who, in the fall of 1957, led the football team to Balboa's first city championship over San Francisco Polytechnic. The stadium is named after Archie Chagonjian, a varsity football coach. The "Little Theater" is named after Salvatore Billeci, music director and composer of the *Songs of the Buccaneers*, including the beloved "Balboa Hymn."

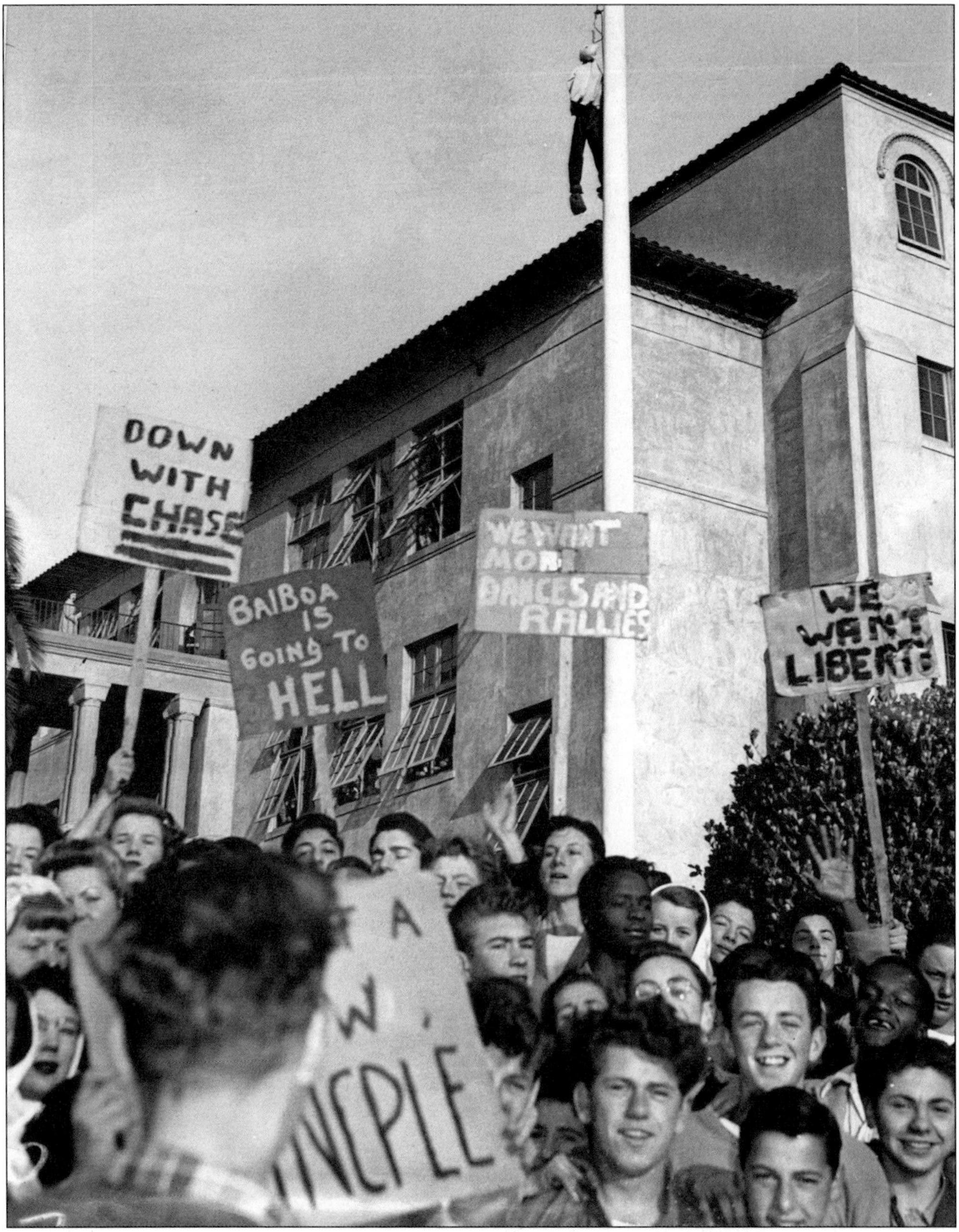

An interesting bit of forgotten history occurred on Friday, February 1, 1946, when the front page of most San Francisco newspapers carried a story and a photograph of a huge student strike in front of Balboa High School where Principal Robert Chase was hung in effigy on the school's flagpole for banning dances (he didn't like jitterbugging) and rallies and suspending Jack Caruso, varsity football star, and five other popular students for playing hooky. The students were to be reassigned to Continuation High School near Sixth and Mission Streets, considered a serious punishment. Later that day, after negotiating with strike leader Paul De Angelo and other students, all known as Balboa Buccaneers, Chase reversed most of his decisions and school resumed for the day. (International News Photo.)

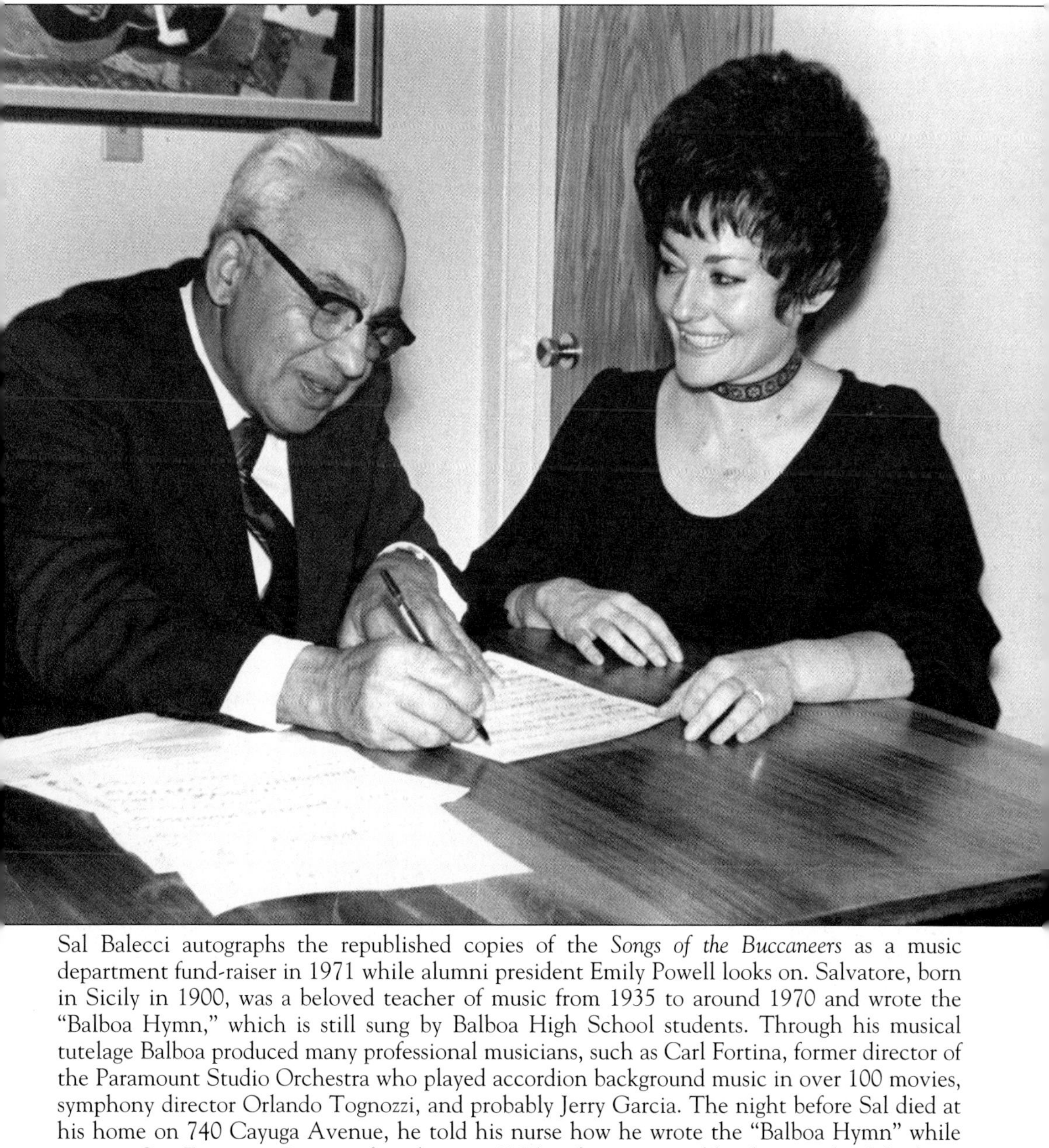

Sal Balecci autographs the republished copies of the *Songs of the Buccaneers* as a music department fund-raiser in 1971 while alumni president Emily Powell looks on. Salvatore, born in Sicily in 1900, was a beloved teacher of music from 1935 to around 1970 and wrote the "Balboa Hymn," which is still sung by Balboa High School students. Through his musical tutelage Balboa produced many professional musicians, such as Carl Fortina, former director of the Paramount Studio Orchestra who played accordion background music in over 100 movies, symphony director Orlando Tognozzi, and probably Jerry Garcia. The night before Sal died at his home on 740 Cayuga Avenue, he told his nurse how he wrote the "Balboa Hymn" while crossing San Francisco Bay in a ferry boat in 1935 and was inspired by the sounds of the bay's bells and whistles. Although very weak, he got out of bed, went over to his organ, and played and sang the hymn for his nurse, then went back to bed and died the next day. The Balboa section of this book is dedicated to Sal Balecci.

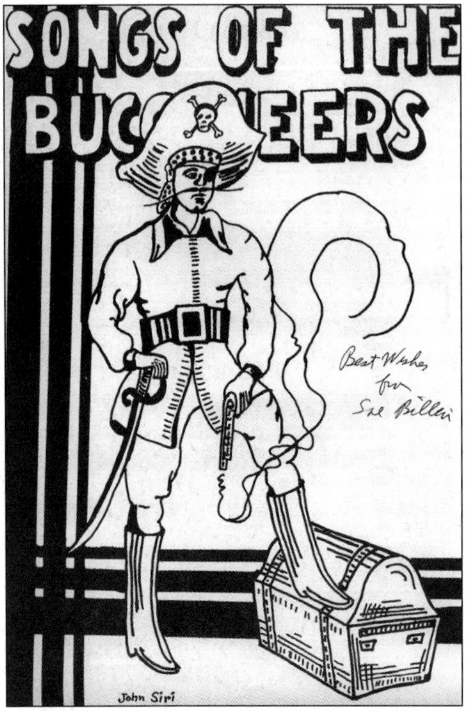

The artwork of the Balboa sheet music was done by John Siri, Balboa High School's "official" artist, who graduated in 1940. The Siri family—Paul, John, and Julius—worked at the popular Excelsior butcher shop Armanino's on Mission between Amazon and Geneva Streets. John Siri later opened several supermarkets called Siri's in San Francisco. The spirit of Sal Balecci's lyrics live on within these pages through his numerous compositions, such as "Smash 'Em, Bust 'em," "All Hail Balboa, Hail," "Always First on the Pacific," and the beloved "Balboa Hymn" the words of which are memorized by all Balboa graduates:

We're Loyal all and ever true
A Pledge of faith we give to you,
We follow where our colors lead
Our orange and our blue.

Balboa, loved by everyone
Where echoes ring of deeds well done.
Deep loyalty fore'er prevail
All hail Balboa, hail!

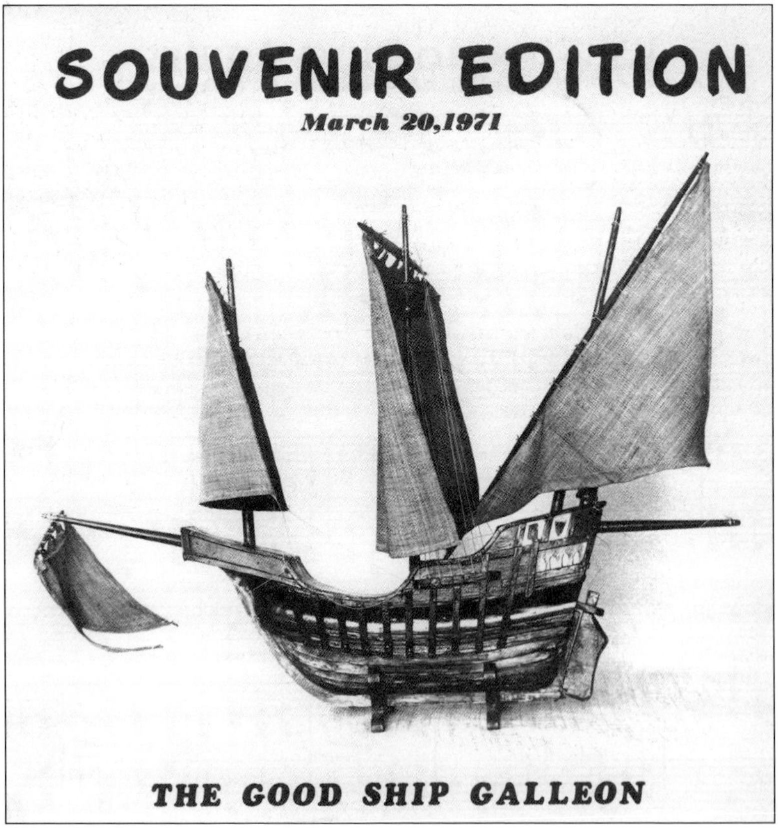

On the back page of the *Songs of the Buccaneers* is a photograph of the Good Ship Galleon, one of Balboa's symbols presented to the high school in 1928 by the students. On graduation day the Galleon is physically presented by the graduating senior officers to the incoming senior officers.

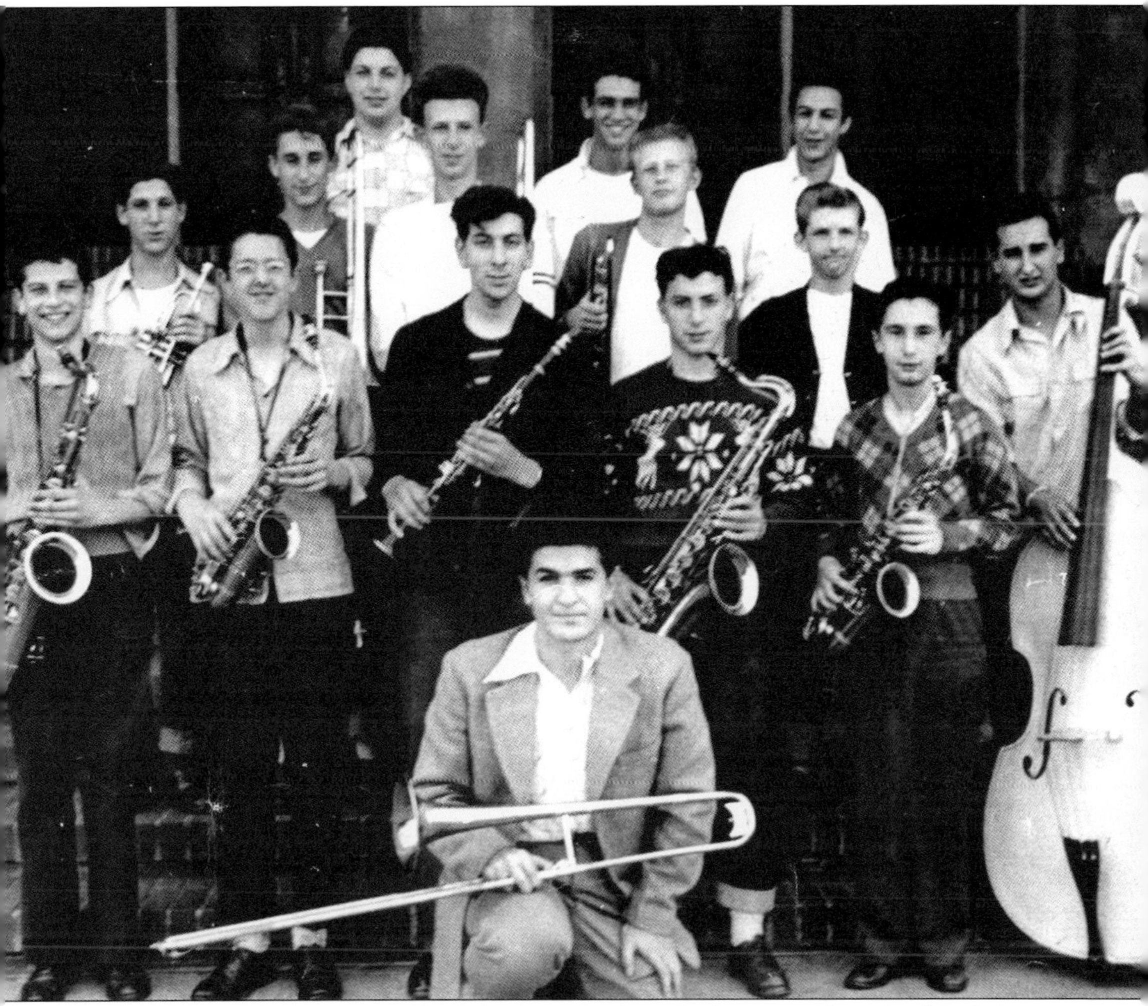

Balboa's music department was created in 1928. Through the years, the school had dance and jazz bands from different eras that were always called the Blue Boys. This photo of the 1945 Blue Boys, who all went on to become professional musicians, shows band leader Don "Rocky" Garofalo in the foreground. Band members, from left to right, included (front row) Mario DiRenzi, Rudy Paladini, Olando Tognozzi, Al Scaccalosi, and Cliff Partridge; (middle row) Al Sunseri, Rusty Young, Glenn Roland, Carl Hauser, Richie Mills, and Hector Ramos; (back row) Carl Fortina, Vic Casassa, and Robert Raby. These Excelsior boys still meet at annual gatherings.

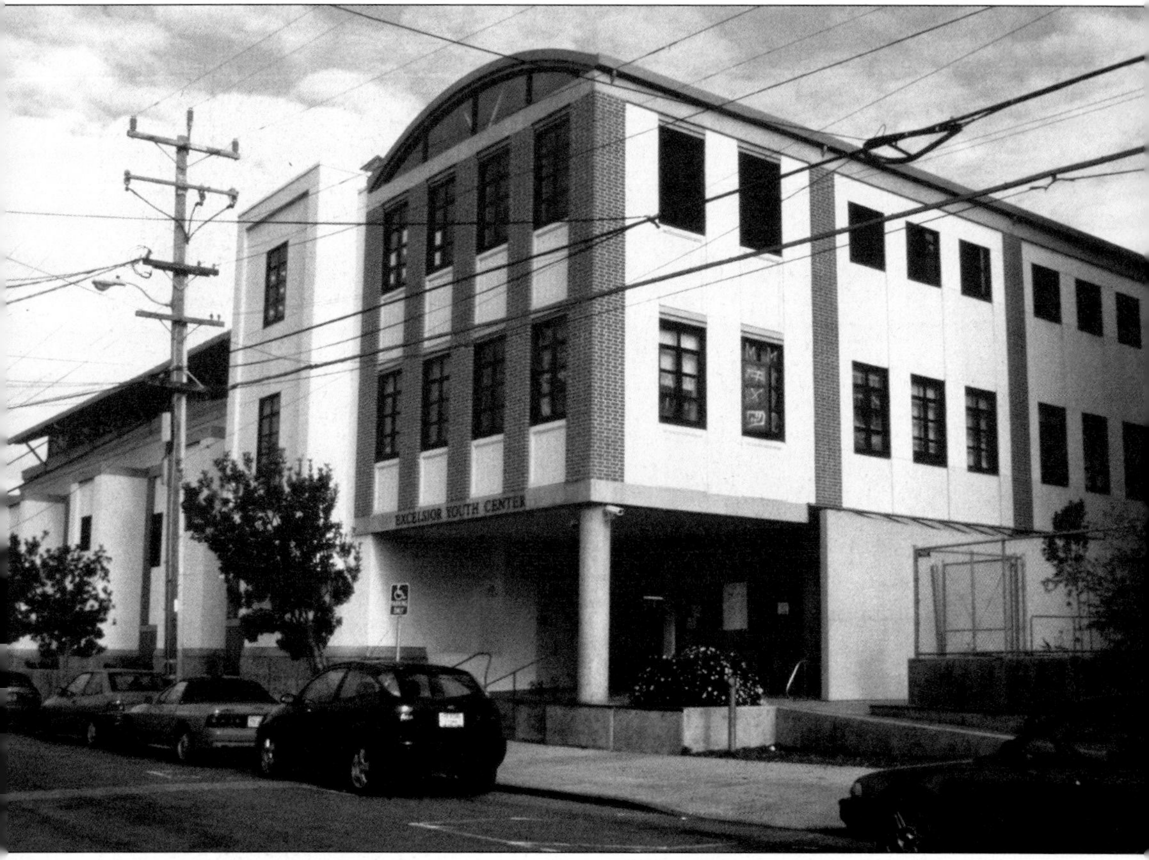

This view of London Street between Avalon and Excelsior shows the Excelsior Elementary School, housing the Excelsior Youth Center. A little anecdote: Excelsior activists had been lobbying city hall for over 40 years for a youth center with no luck. However, in the 1990s while the author and others were escorting mayoral candidate Willie Brown through the business area, he commented, "If you guys can deliver me the Excelsior I will see that you get the youth center you've been requesting." Willie Brown did win the Excelsior and the election, and within about 12 months after taking office there was a ground-breaking ceremony for the $10 million youth center, which provides all kinds of activities as well as a pool table, basketball court, rooms for cooking classes, and more.

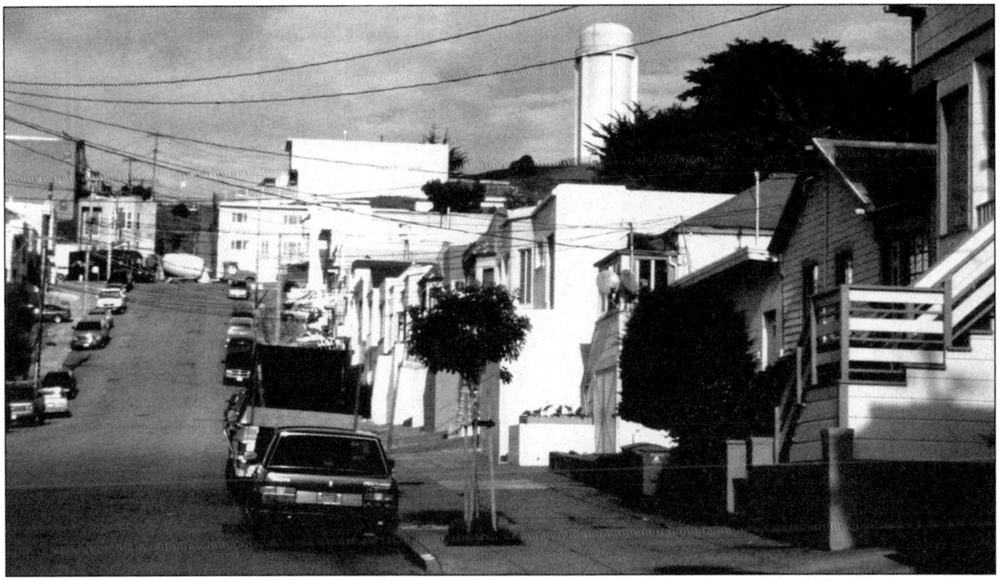

Excelsior's blue water tower in McLaren Park can be seen from most parts of the city. Water is pumped up to the tower and stored to provide water pressure. Since the city is built on a hill and water does not flow uphill on its own, it needs a little help.

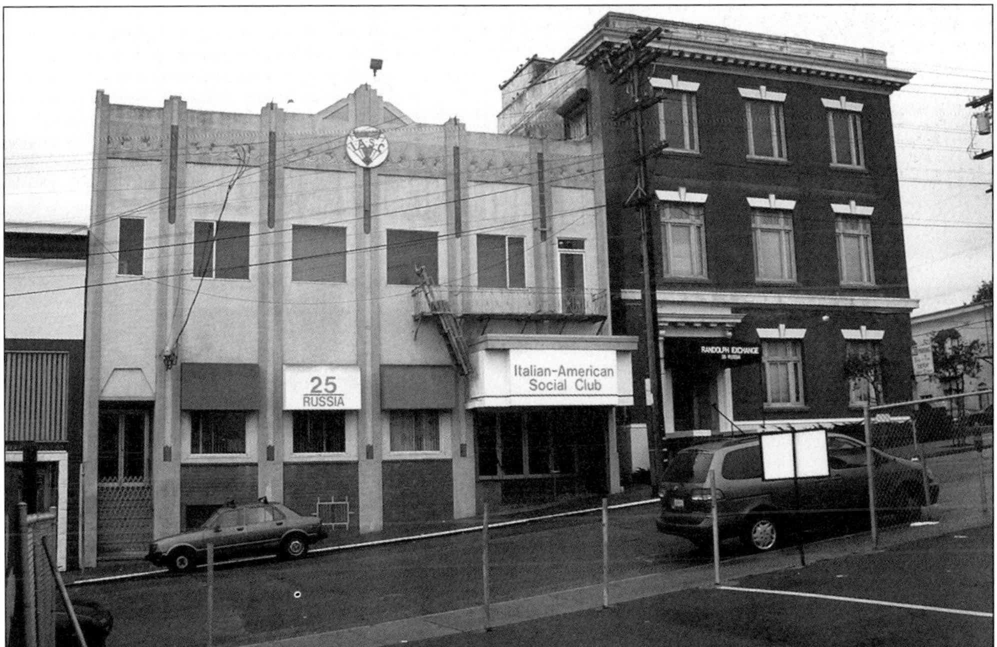

A very well-known address is 25 Russian Avenue, location of the exclusive Italian-American Social Club. Potential members must have Italian blood before they can even be considered for membership, although the club does open its restaurant to the public for lunch and dinner several days a week. This building was constructed around 1933 and is the site for all kinds of private parties, weddings, banquets, and funerals. The building to the right was the Outer Mission's main telephone exchange until around 1938. It has been converted to apartments and is now called the Randolph Exchange.

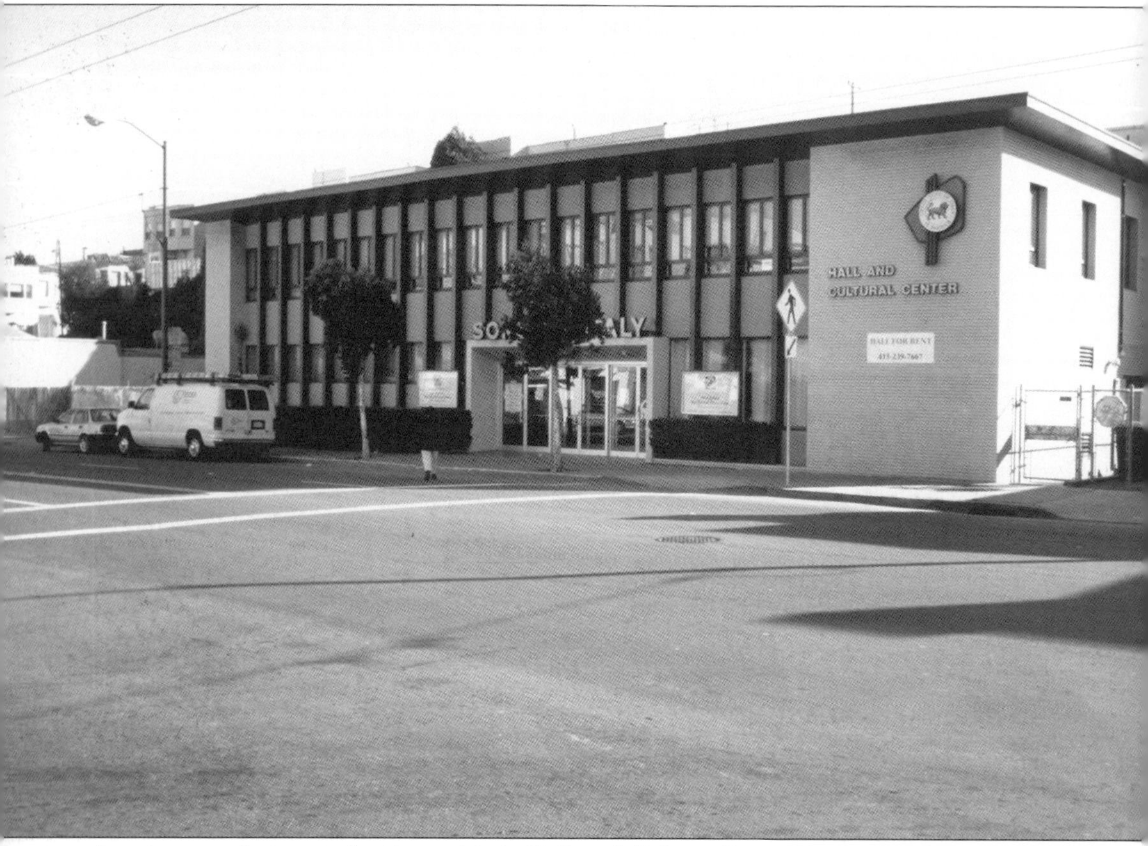

Another social giant is the Sons of Italy Hall and Culture Center, located on Mission Street between Italy and France. This club is also a great venue for parties and any kind of social event.

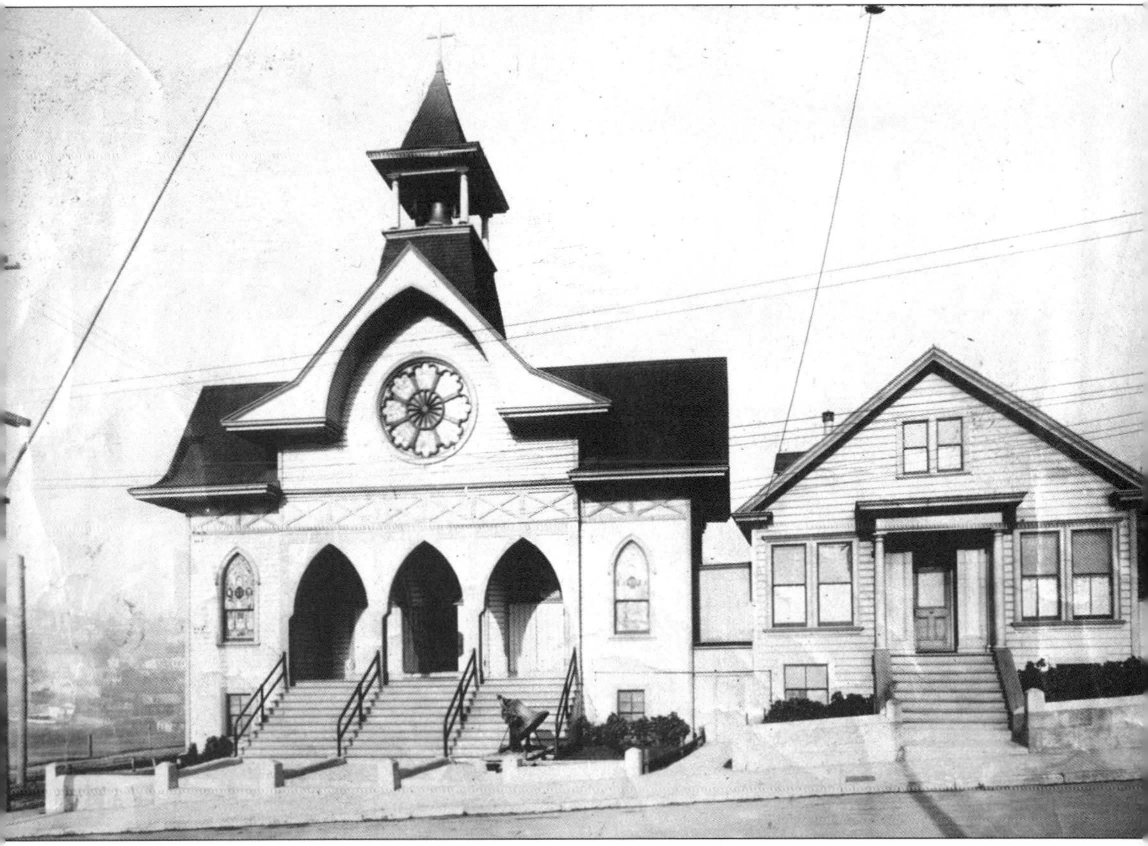

Corpus Christi Church was constructed in 1898 at a cost of $7,000. Before the church was built, those who wished to attend a mass in Italian had to harness up the wagon, pack up the family, and travel to Saint Peter and Paul's Church in North Beach, at the very other end of San Francisco. That trip, according to John Consiglieri, who was born across from the church in 1917, was three-and-a-half hours in one direction. Alternatively, someone from the community would go to North Beach to bring back a priest to the Excelsior Homestead and he would stay at the home of one of the parishioners overnight. The next day the priest would say a mass in one of the barns or homes, and then one of the farmers would take him back to North Beach.

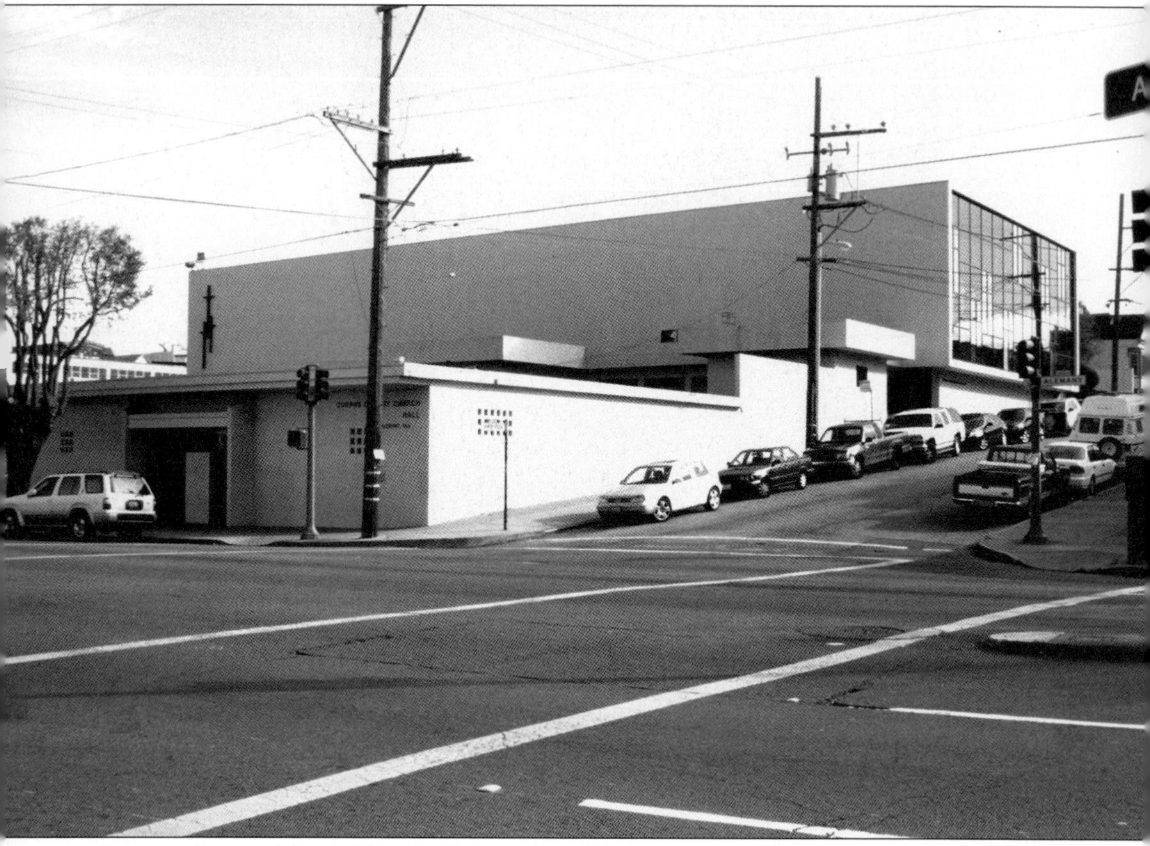

The new Corpus Christi Church, designed by San Francisco architect Mario Campi, was built in 1952. The front wall in this photo was a radical new design. Some of the locals went to a different Catholic church until they got used to the new design. Each pane of glass was a different color, which produced different visual effects in the church entrance and was very beautiful. One particular pastor did not like the colored panels and had them removed and replaced with a light amber-colored glass.

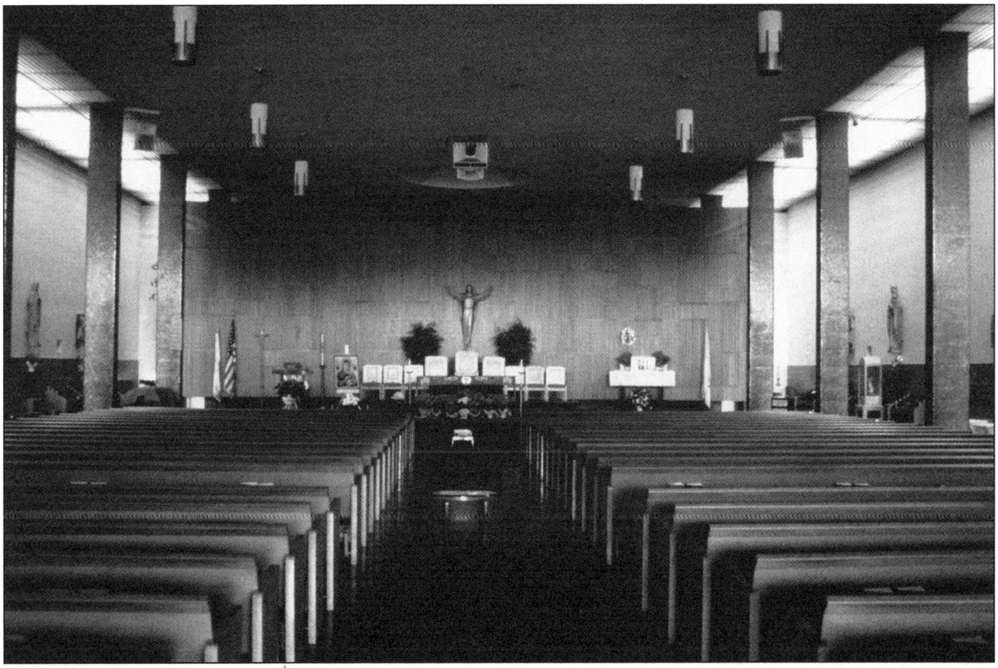

The interior of Corpus Christi is far more impressive than the outside. The author and his wife were married here in what was only the second wedding in the new church. Due to the newness of the church, no one was familiar with its rear-facing entrance, and the groom and the best man almost missed the wedding.

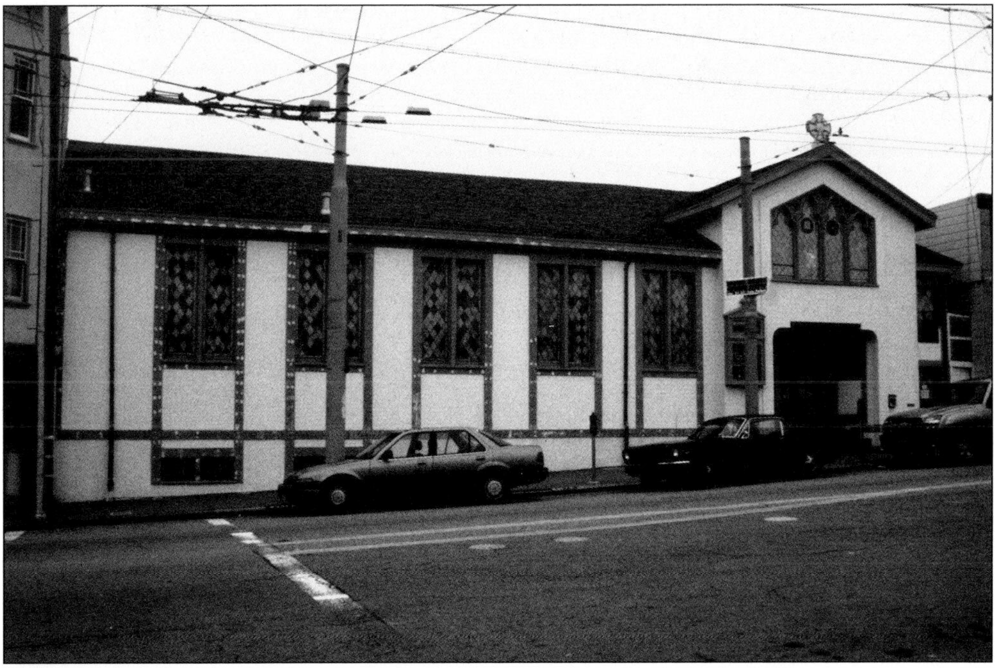

The Ocean Avenue Presbyterian Church was designed by the famous architect Julia Morgan, who also designed many other beautiful buildings in the Bay Area, including Hearst Castle, which is located about 150 feet down Ocean Avenue from Mission Street.

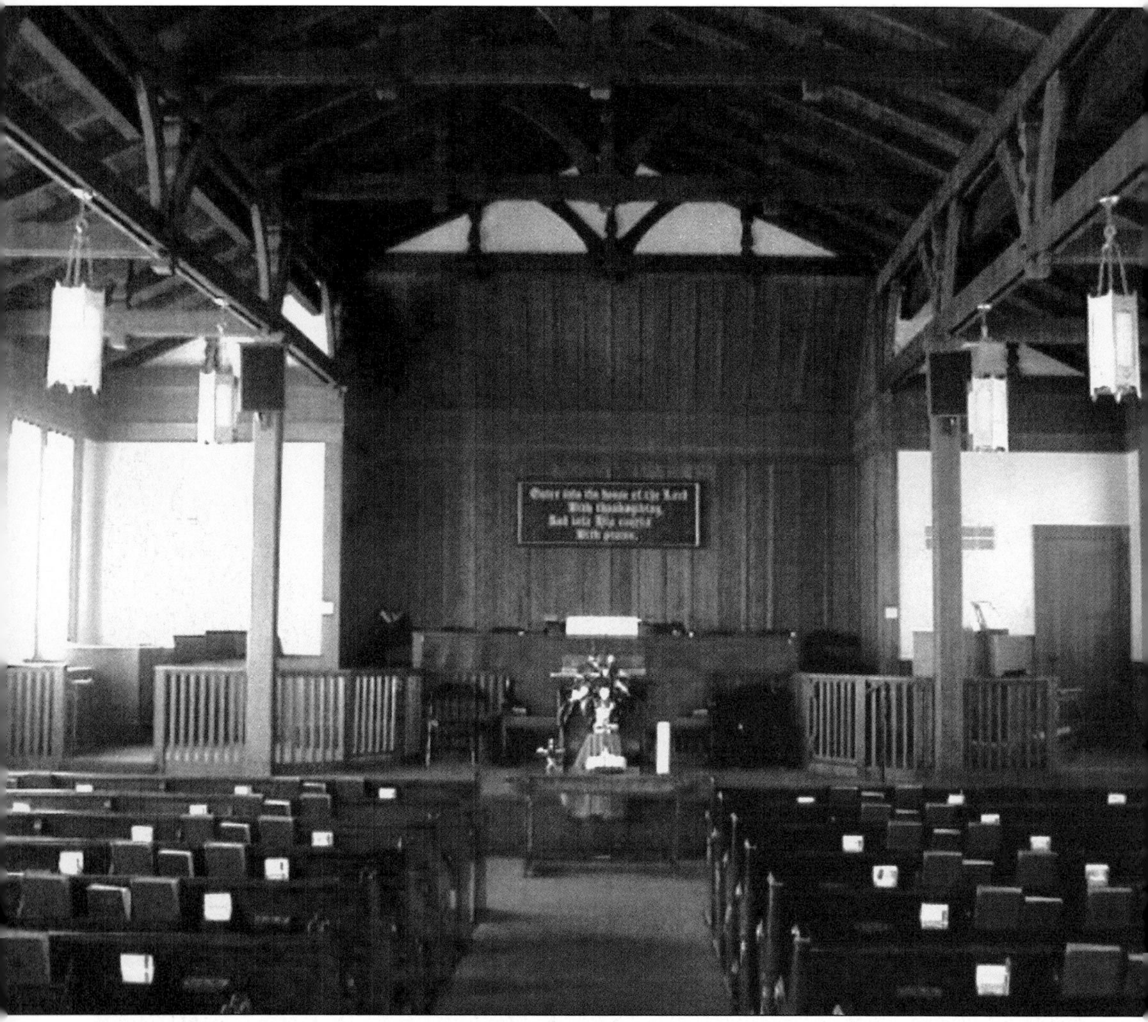

The interior of the Ocean Avenue Presbyterian Church shows the marvelous simplicity and the use of fine woods characteristic of the work of well-known architect Julia Morgan. This building was founded in 1920 and dedicated in 1922 and is now the oldest original church in the Excelsior. The original Presbyterian church, which existed from 1909 through 1920, was the Bethany at Madrid and Excelsior, and while the Ocean Avenue church was being completed services were held for about three months at the Bell Theater at Mission and Leo Streets.

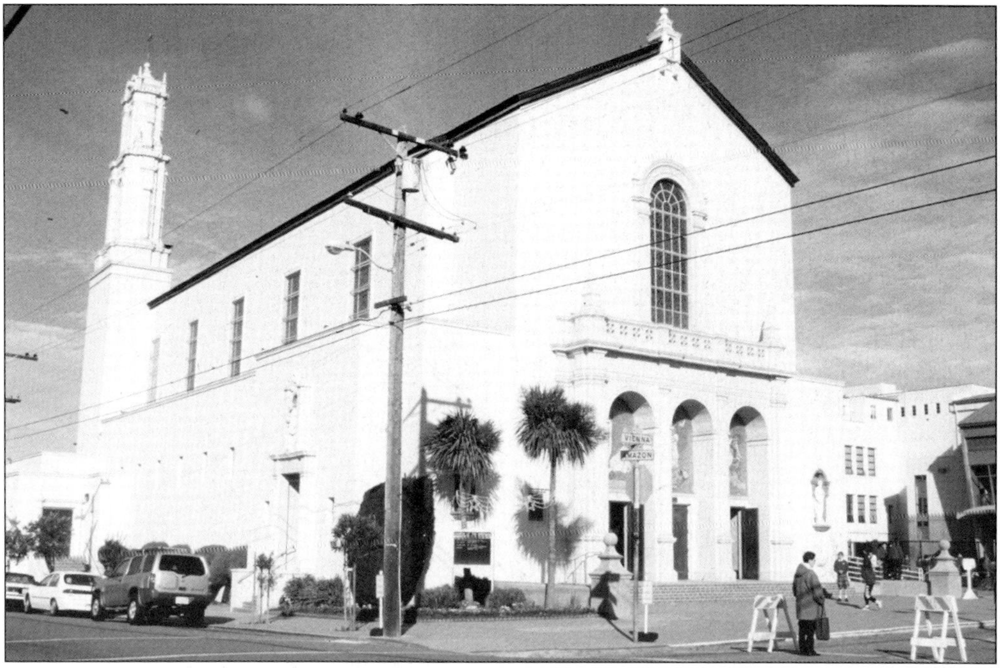

Built in 1950 on Vienna and Amazon Streets, the Epiphany Catholic Church was constructed with funds raised under the direction of the Right Reverent Monsignor Maurice J. O'Keefe. Adjacent to the church is a school for grades one through eight. The school has a large cafeteria used by the students as well as for social events. The Epiphany Parish was founded in 1914.

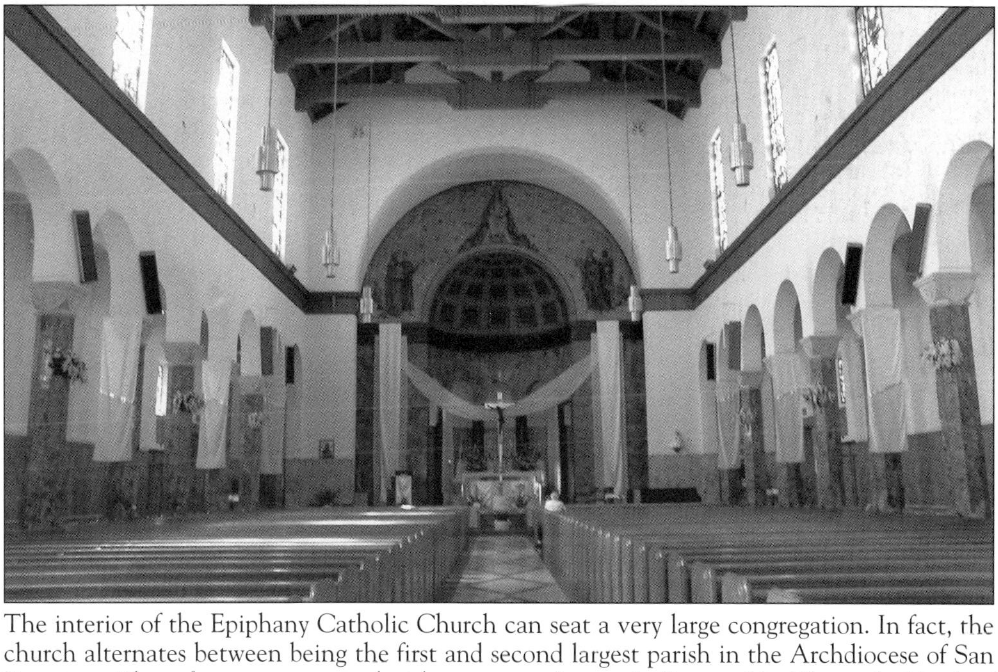

The interior of the Epiphany Catholic Church can seat a very large congregation. In fact, the church alternates between being the first and second largest parish in the Archdiocese of San Francisco. The columns are covered with a veneer of green Italian marble. The arched back of the altar is Italian tile in a mosaic of the Epiphany. All windows are stained glass depicting other religious scenes.

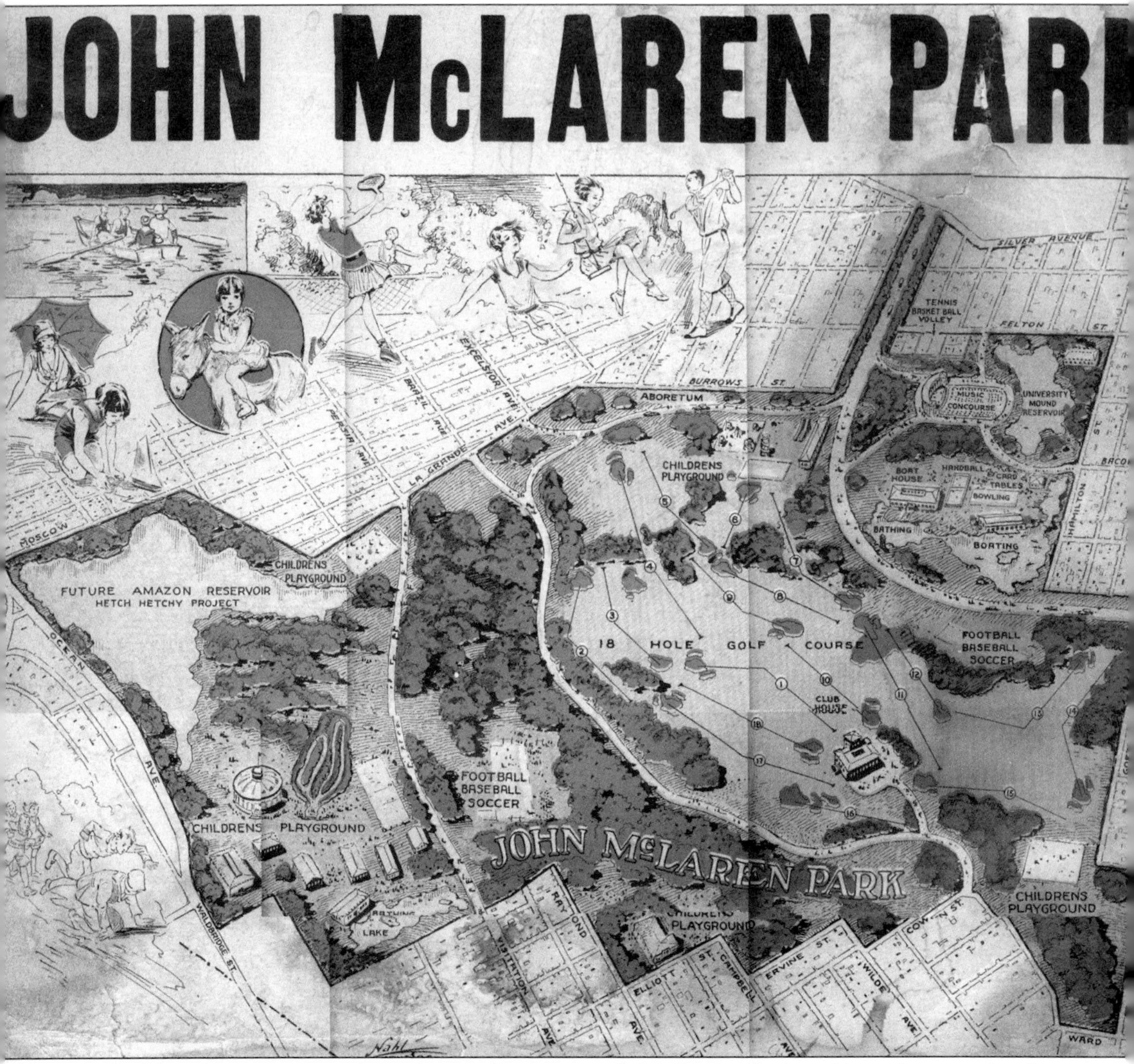

This bond campaign poster shows the proposed McLaren Park—although it is hard to distinguish what they really had in their minds. There are no instructions; once you read and study it, you are still not sure as to its mission. It is possible that this poster for the bond issue may have been prepared so that the vote at the time it was presented would fail. But later on the park and its boundaries were established. It clearly shows a golf course, a carousel, a reservoir, football field, and many other proposals. This map is very difficult to decipher, and it has no date. The streets that surround the park are very confusing; some are correct, many do not even exist, and some are in the wrong location. Despite all this, McLaren Park does somewhat resemble this poster.

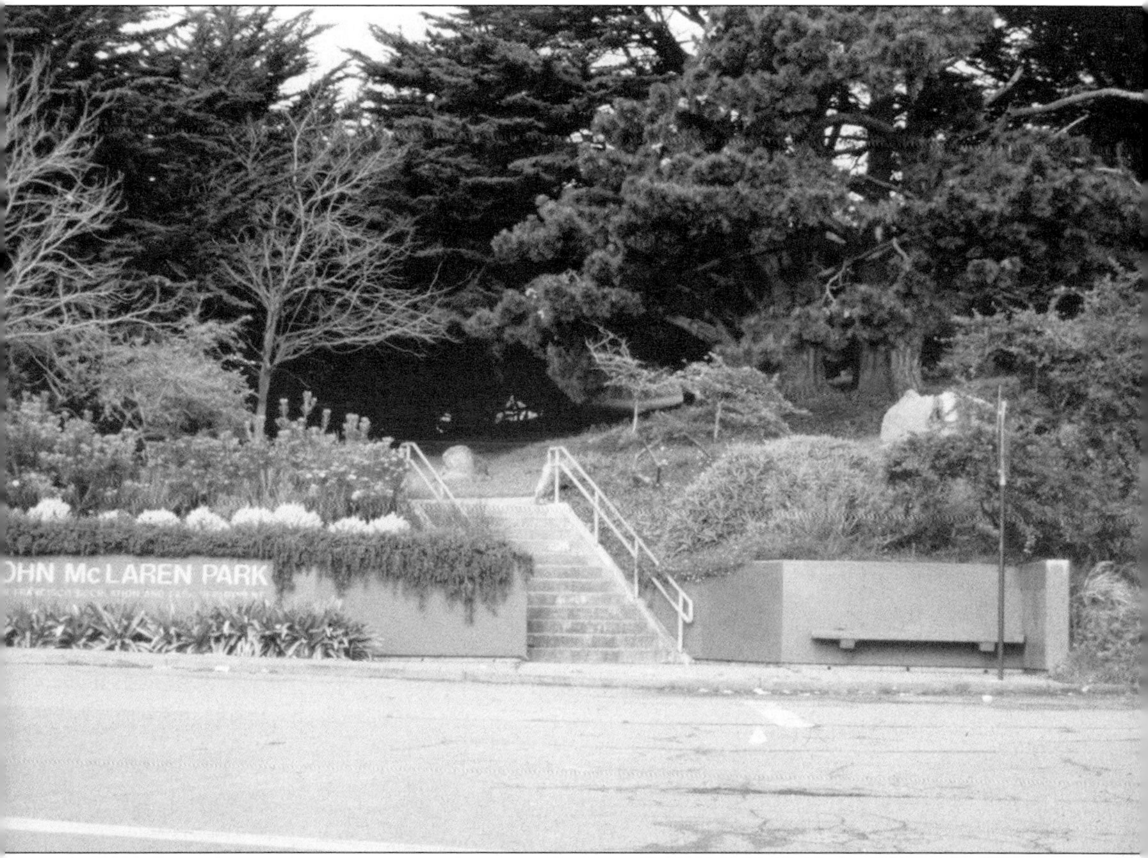

This is one of many entrances to McLaren Park and is located at the end of Brazil Street directly opposite the Luther Burbank Middle School on Dublin Street. The John McLaren Park is the second largest park in San Francisco. Many people complain that the park is not being maintained properly; however, because it is a wilderness park in a metropolitan area, it is only manicured along the perimeters and at a few other places, such as the amphitheater and barbecue pits in the center.

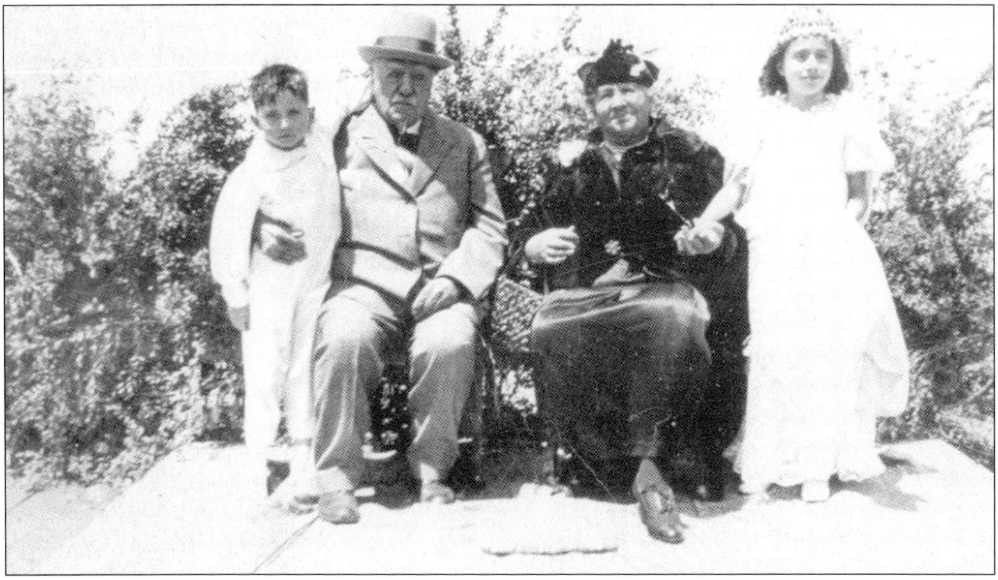

John McLaren himself attends a May Day festival somewhere in the Excelsior, although the location and year are unknown.

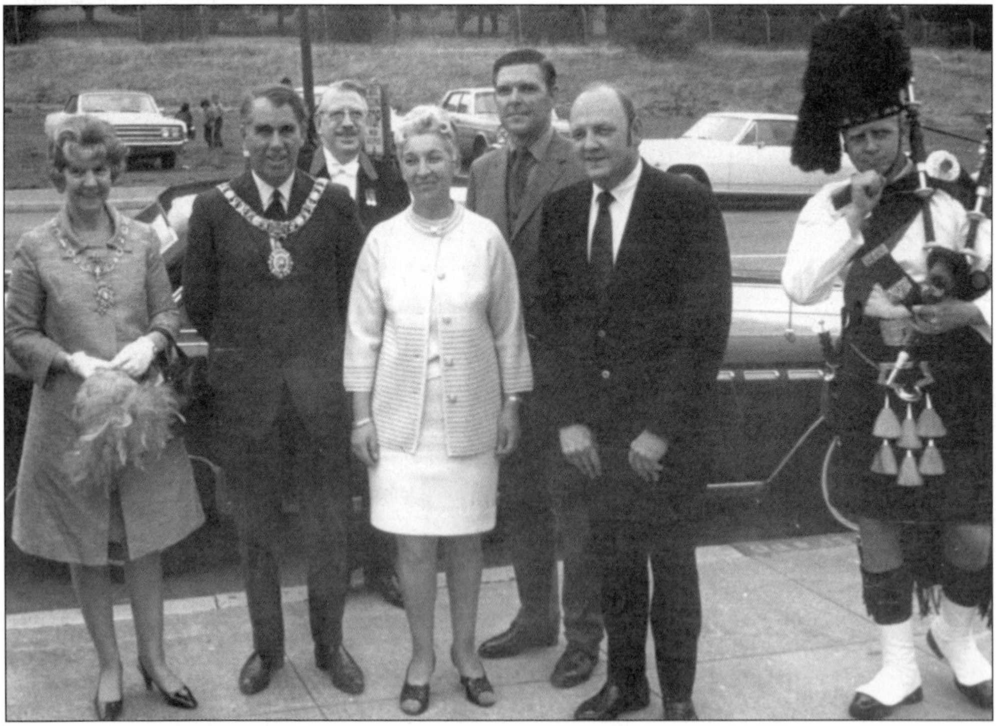

A tree-planting ceremony in McLaren Park with a reception at the John McLaren School was one of the many celebrations marking the 100th anniversary of Golden Gate Park. Attending the reception at the John McLaren School, from left to right, are the Lord and Lady Provost of Edinburgh, Scotland; the Lord Provost's aide; the school's principal (name unknown); unidentified; the author, Walter G. Jebe Sr.; and an unidentified bagpiper. The Lord and Lady Provost hosted this occasion.

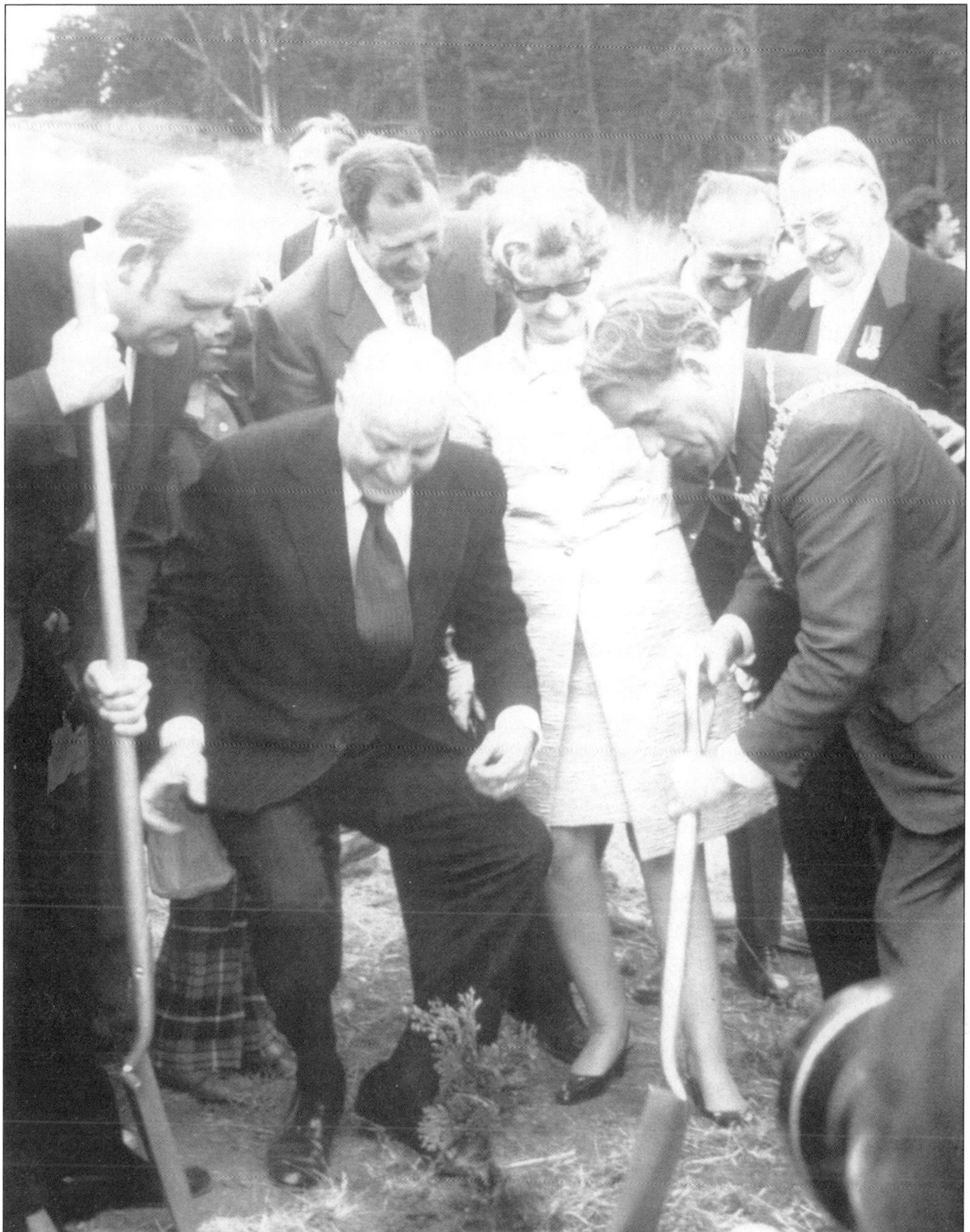

The tree-planting ceremony in McLaren Park commemorated the 100th anniversary of Golden Gate Park, which was developed by John McLaren. Shown here in front, from left to right, are Walter Jebe Sr., president of the John McLaren Society (with shovel); Mayor Joseph Alioto; the Lady Provost; and the Lord Provost of Edinburgh, Scotland. The man behind the Lord Provost is his aide. The Lord and Lady Provost were the guests of the John McLaren Society.

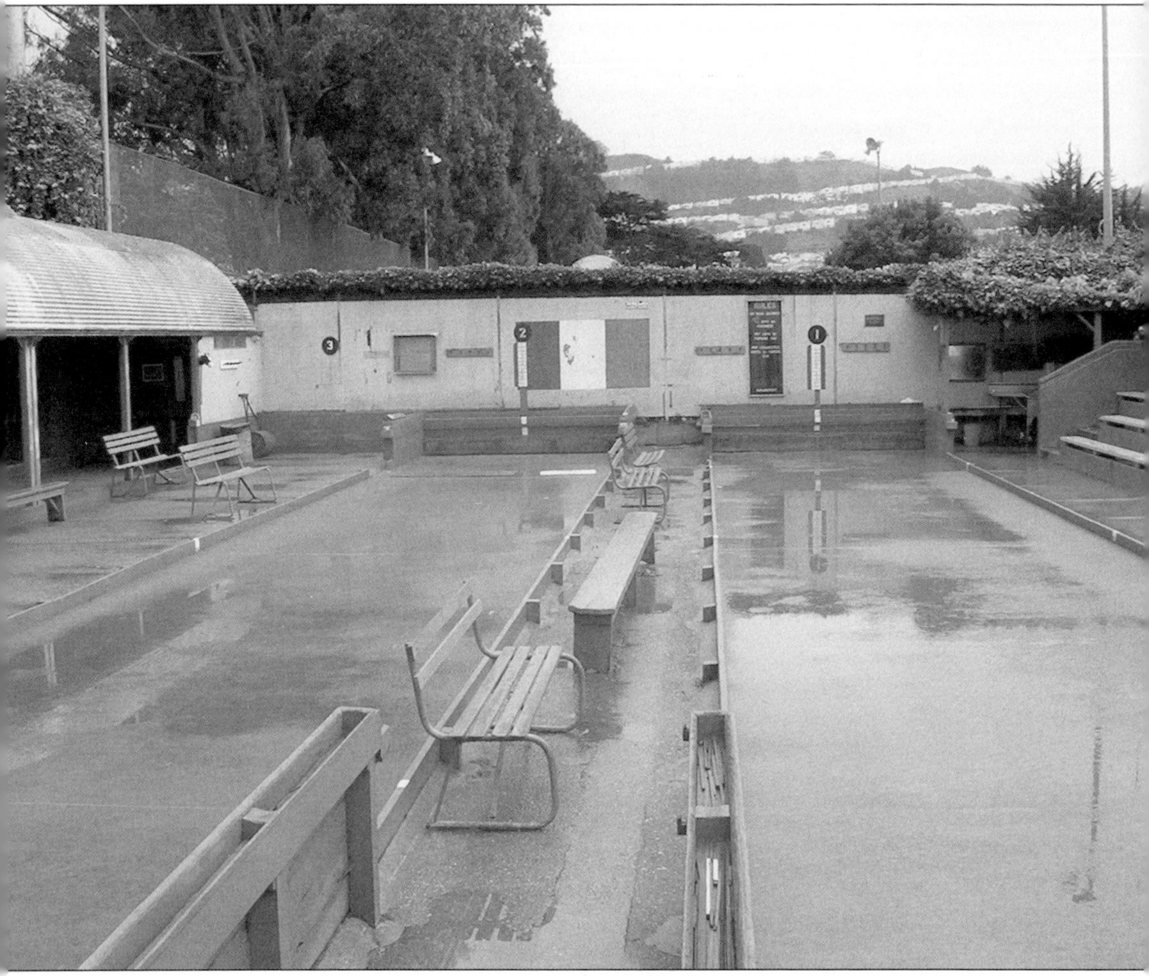

This is a picture of the only remaining bocce ball court in the Excelsior built by the city, located in Crocker Amazon Park at Moscow Street and Italy Avenue. Originally it was the location of the horseshoe pits. The Excelsior District for many years predominantly consisted of Italians, and neighbors with names such as Basso, Bottarini, Conti, Siri, Cosentino, Actis, Valenti, Facciano, Pardini, and Fortina participated in its construction. Many of them loved to play bocce, and in the 1920s and 1930s there were many "homemade" bocce ball courts in empty corner lots in the Excelsior. These were gathering places to play and to socialize and boast about the quality of their homemade wine, often late into the night. There was even a bocce court within the premises of the El Lido bar on the 4800 block of Mission Street. One of the other public bocce courts was next to the Kodak building by the bay, at the end of Van Ness Avenue, donated by the Eastman Kodak Company. Many residents made their own wine in their garages, and there was much excitement around harvest time as trucks laden with grapes arrived from places like Cloverdale, Sonoma, and Napa north of San Francisco. The trucks had grape presses with big cast iron wheels hitched behind them, which made a tremendous amount of noise as they rumbled down the streets of the Excelsior, bringing the children out yelling, "Fuji! Fuji!" as they chased the trucks and begged for grapes.

Four
NEIGHBORHOOD NOTABLES

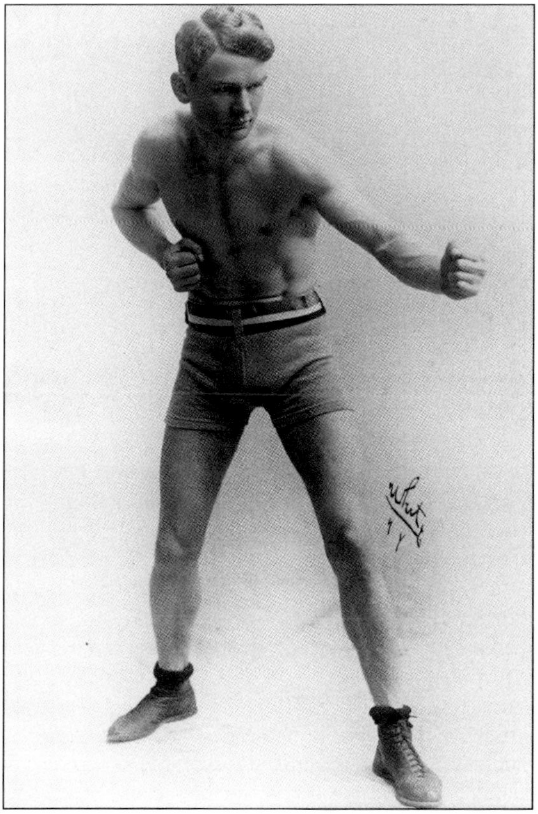

Excelsior boxing icon Llewellyn Arthur Powell was lightweight champion of California in 1906. Born in 1883 in Wellington, New Zealand, his family immigrated to Garden Street in the South of Market District of San Francisco in 1887. He was the main trainer for virtually all of the professional boxers who came out of the Excelsior District, which became a sort of incubator for prizefighting in the San Francisco Bay Area. Powell's energetic and inspiring personality made a lasting impact on the youth of his era.

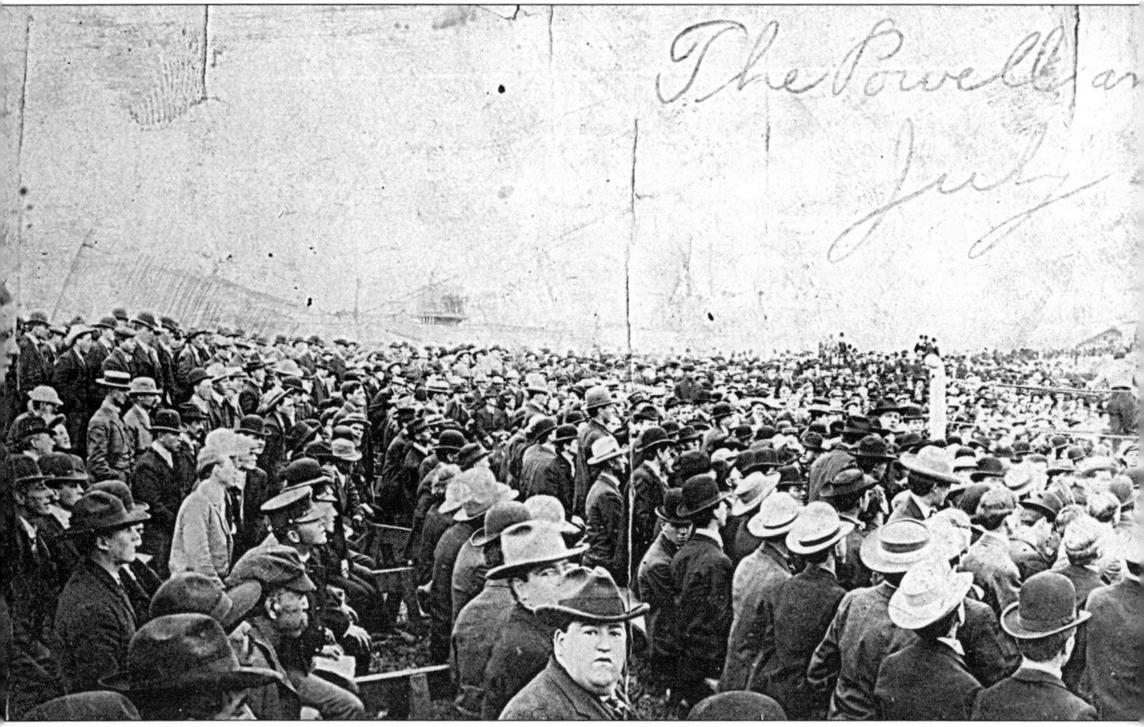

After the great earthquake of 1906 destroyed all of the pavilions, Lew Powell fought and won the first fight after the quake on July 4, 1906, at Ocean Beach beneath the Cliff House versus Willie Wolfe. Thousands of avid fans surrounded the fighters on the sands, and it proved a great

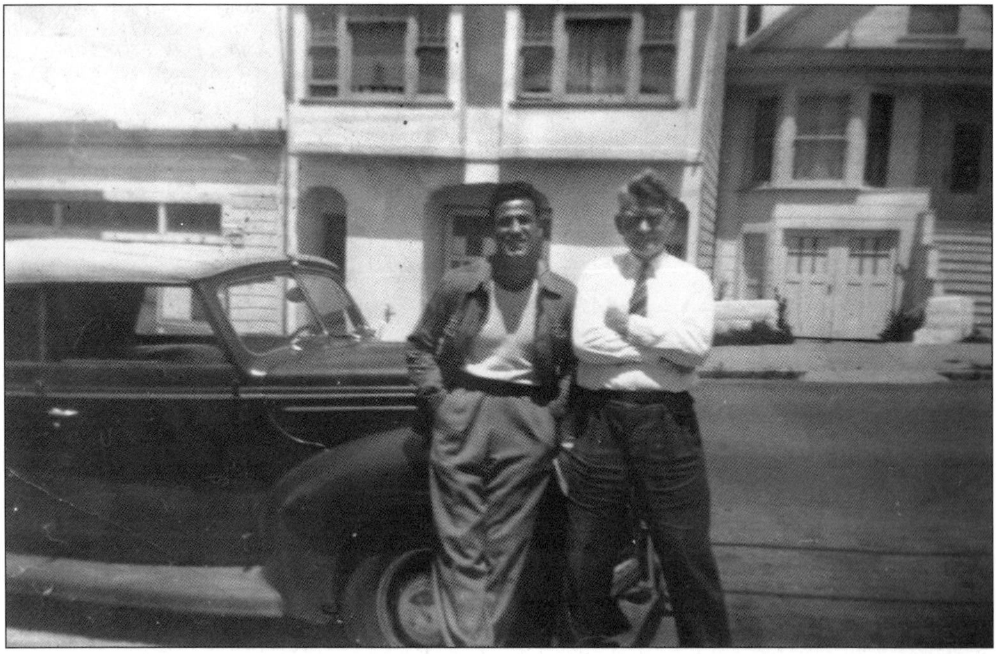

Many years later, in 1940, Powell (right) met with former middleweight champion Fred Apostoli to discuss Apostoli's comeback.

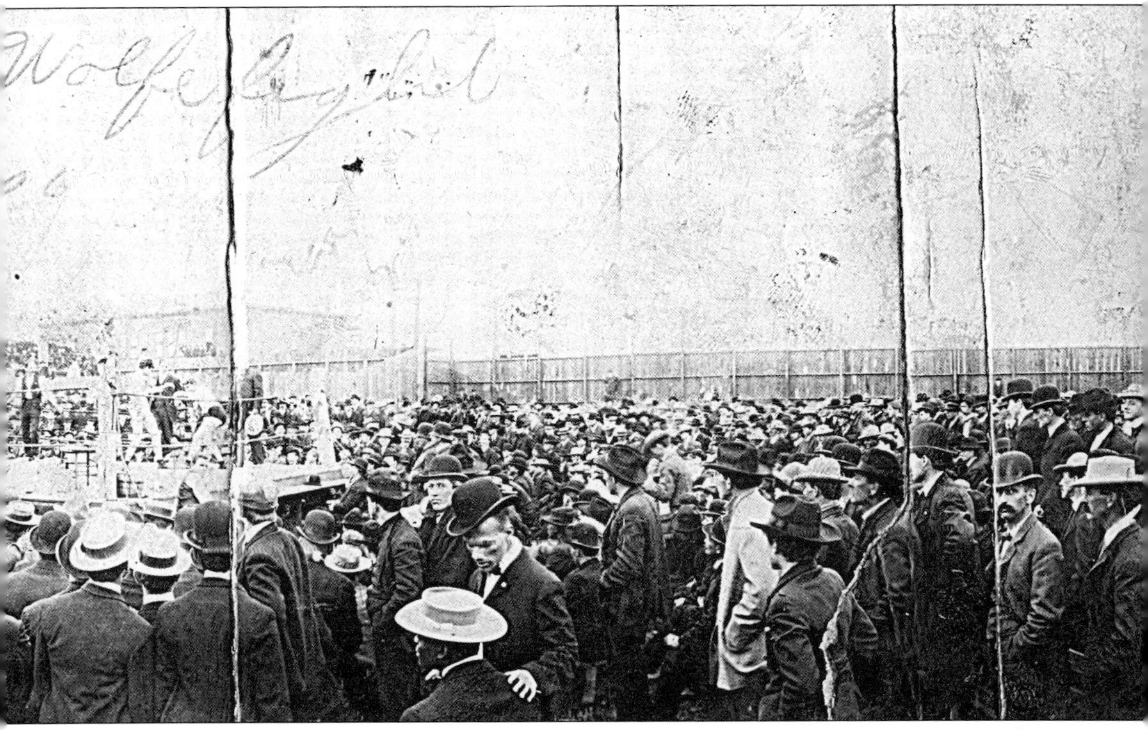

morale boost for a city recovering from the shock of the earthquake. Powell fought more than 100 fights from 1904 to 1913, losing only five.

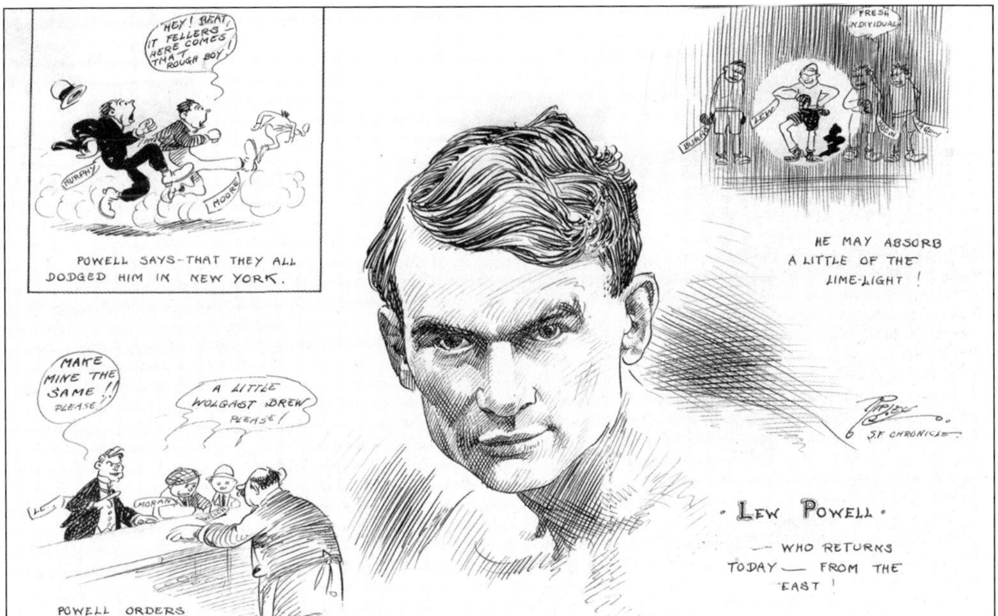

In 1910, *Chronicle* sports cartoonist Robert Ripley did this pen and ink sketch and cartoon of Lew Powell. Ripley later became famous for his "Believe It Or Not" series and exhibition at Fisherman's Wharf. During that era, sports cartoonists such as Ripley and George Herriman found Powell a favorite boxing subject.

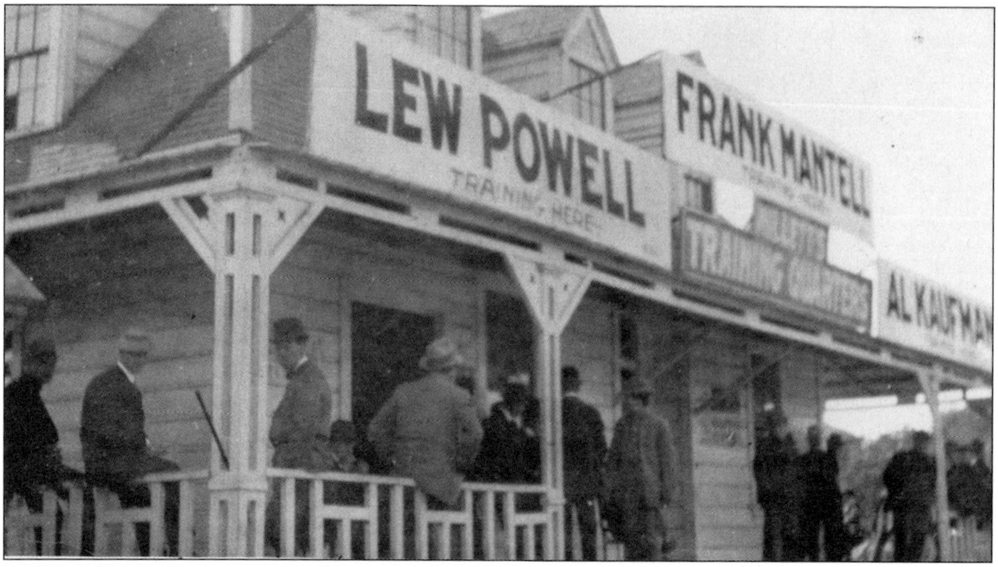

Millett's Training Camp in Colma was located behind Molloy's on Old Mission Road. Molloy's is still there, run by Lanty Molloy, who displays fight pictures and other San Francisco memorabilia on his tavern walls. The training camp ceased to exist many years ago. In its heyday, boxing was king and San Francisco/Daly City/Colma was the "golden mecca" for topnotch pugilists. Fighters such as Lew Powell trained here as well as the famous "swashbuckling playboy" Stanley Ketchell, a hero at 19 and dead at 24, the victim of a jealous suitor on a Missouri ranch. During this period of the early 1900s, boxing was banned in San Francisco, so fans from the Excelsior District would make the easy walk to San Mateo County to watch boxers train. The boxing matches were held at infamous kingpin promoter "Sunny" Jim Coffroth's open air arena on Sickles Avenue and Mission Street in Daly City, 50 feet from the San Francisco/San Mateo border, which conveniently makes an indentation just at that location. Over this border, boxing, wagering, gambling, and other vices were still legal.

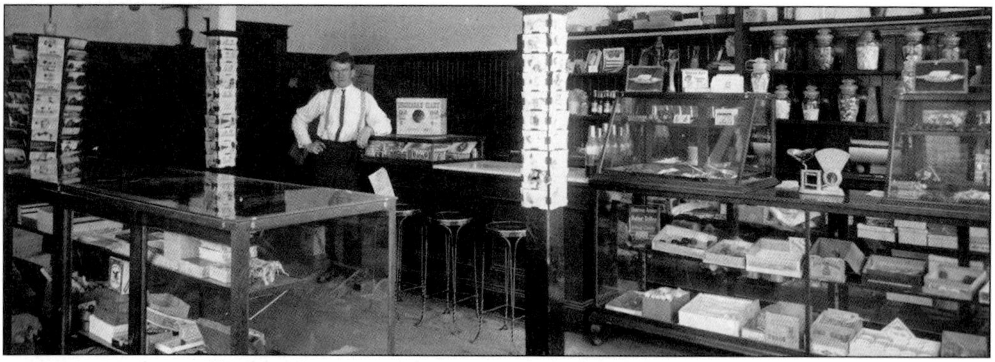
In 1913, Lew Powell opened a variety store, the Edinburgh, at the corner of Edinburgh and Brazil. Shown here on opening day December 1913, Powell's store was stocked with penny and nickel candy, cigars and cigarettes, toys, school supplies, and "notions"—small personal and sewing items. If a child had a penny he or she could select from the candies in the lower cabinet: licorice straps, penny suckers, candy cigarettes, pumpkin seeds, butterballs, tootsie roll, or bubblegum. If the kid was lucky enough to have a nickel, he or she could move up to the upper cabinet to choose between Babe Ruth, U-No Bar, Hershey Bar, Big Hunk, or Nestle's Crunch. Lew also sold milk, bread, cookies, and cakes. It was a true "convenience store" for the era. Lew is shown leaning on his cigar display case next to the soda fountain area.

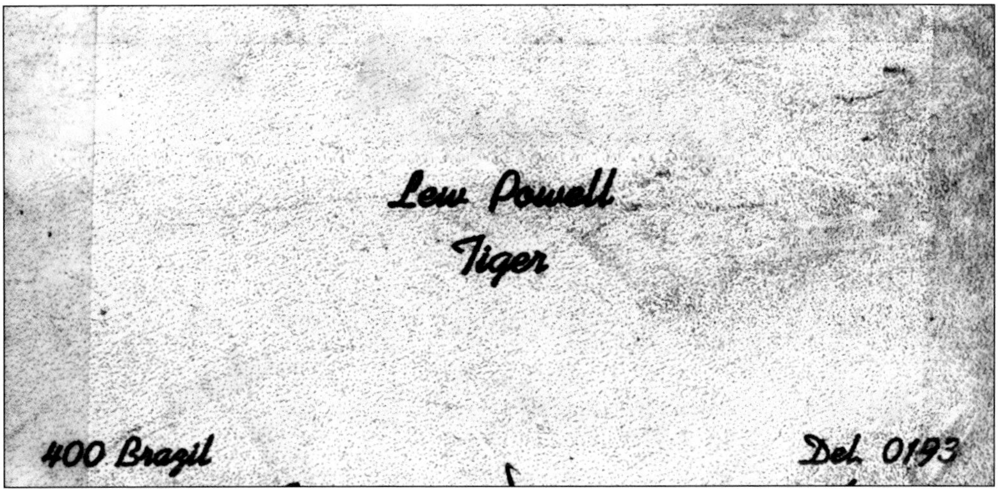

Because of Lew Powell's interest in sports and his exciting career as a champion boxer, many local boys came to his store to hang out even if they only had a penny or a nickel to buy a Coca Cola in its famous eight-ounce bottle. It was little stores like this that were the glue of the community, and ordinary citizens like Lew and others channeled the restless energy and potential of the neighborhood's youth to make something with their lives, if nothing more than just being good citizens. Lew called all the neighborhood boys who "hung out" in and around his store "Tigers." To this day, there are men in the Excelsior who refer to each other as Tigers, and some meet regularly at Excelsior District restaurants for lunch, such as the Balboa Geezers, the Balboa Legends, and the Excelsior Legends. Here's Lew's card, which would have been in the pocket of many people in the Excelsior. The current phone prefix for the area, 333, was based on "D-E-L" for Delaware Street, the area surrounding Balboa High School. Delaware Street was eventually renamed Delano Street, and the prefix was changed to "D-E-L-3," then the "L" was dropped, making it "D-E-3."

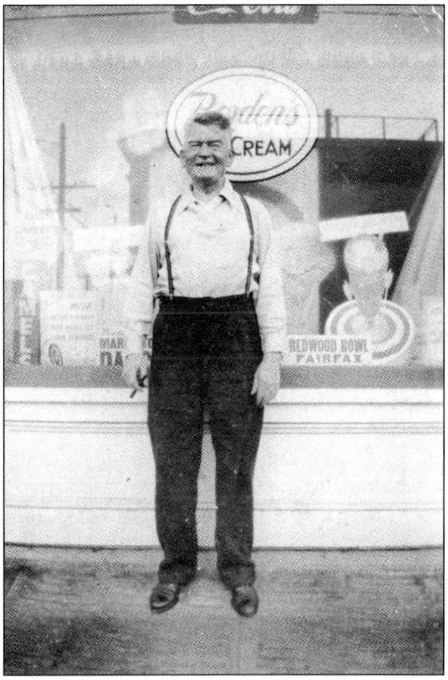

In 1929 Lew moved his store to the corner of Brazil and Madrid Streets and operated it there until 1952, when he retired to his ranch in Calaveras County. This photo shows Lew in front of his store at 400 Brazil Avenue in 1946, holding his signature Italian stogie, probably made by Toscanelli.

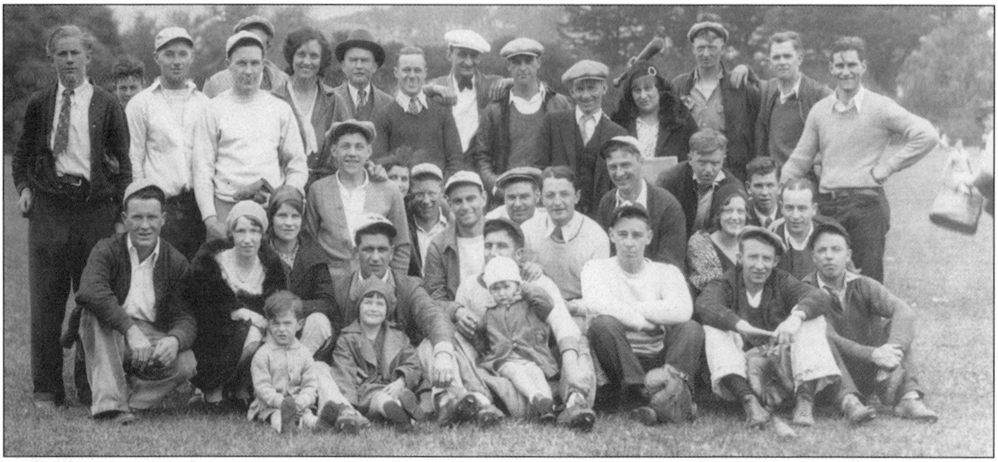

Lew Powell's original Tigers baseball team is shown here in 1931 in Balboa Park with Mount Davidson in the background. Lew formed his self-funded baseball team from the young men who hung out at his store, whom he had already nicknamed "Tigers." Coaching baseball was a natural transition for Lew, who had gone from champion boxer to neighborhood sports ring leader. Lew is in the back wearing his fedora while his wife, Clara, is on the right with a bat over her head. The Tigers played teams from other neighborhoods and practiced at Excelsior Park at the corner of Madrid and Russia Streets. The three young kids in the front are Tom Dillon, later to be inducted into the Balboa High School Athletic Hall of Fame, and Gwen and Emily Powell, the three mascots of the team.

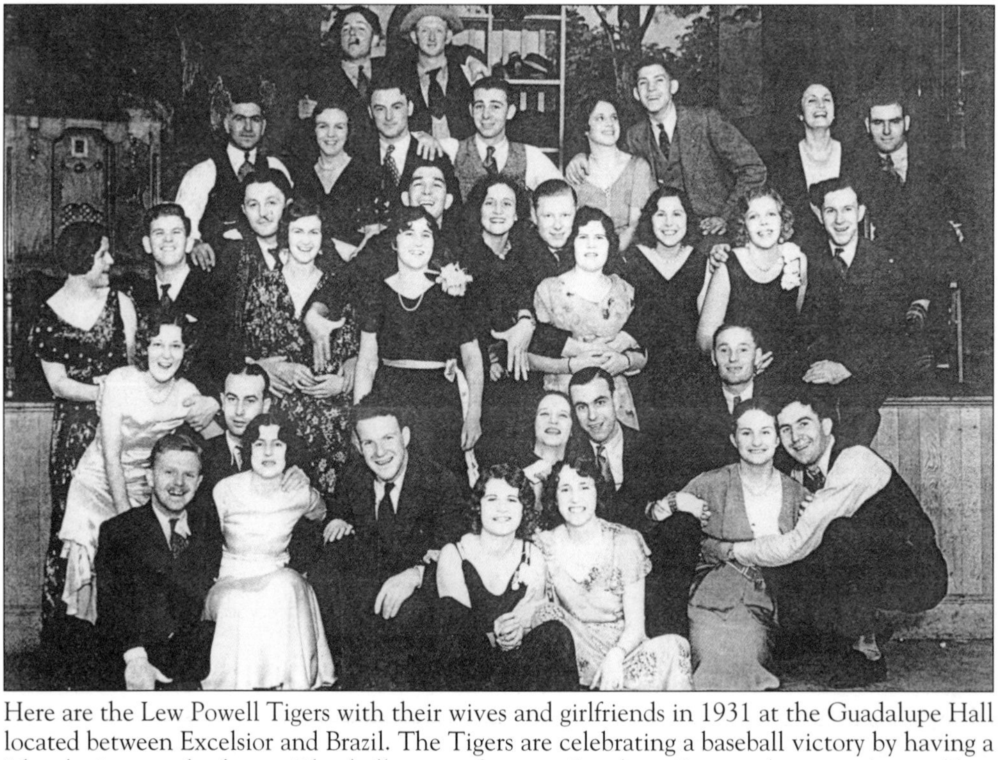

Here are the Lew Powell Tigers with their wives and girlfriends in 1931 at the Guadalupe Hall located between Excelsior and Brazil. The Tigers are celebrating a baseball victory by having a "shindig," a rowdy dance. The hall was a favorite Excelsior District location for wedding receptions and parties.

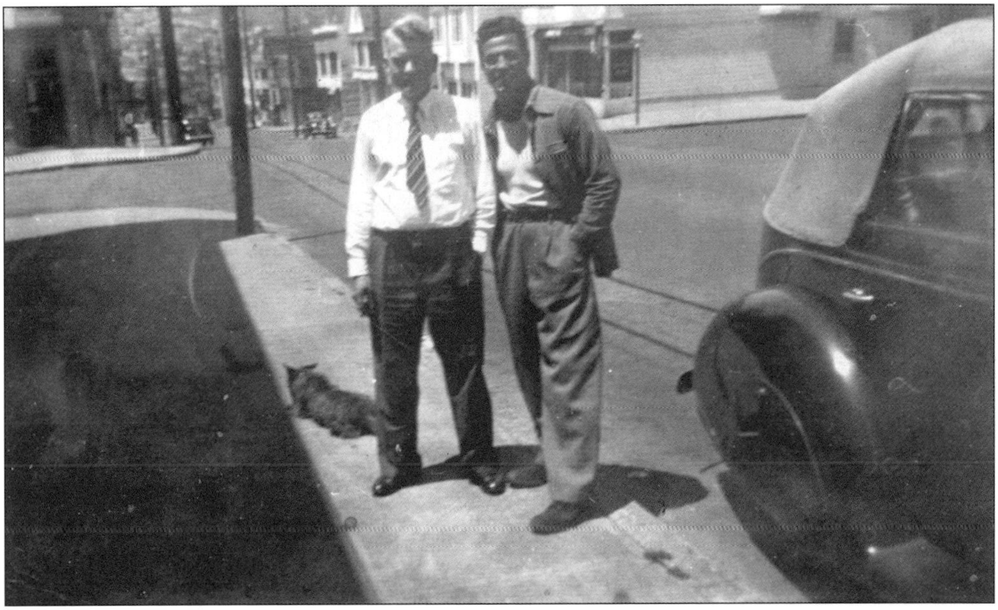

In 1940 Lew Powell met with former middleweight champion Fred Apostoli to discuss Apostoli's comeback plans. Though born in North Beach, Apostoli spent most of his time in the Excelsior District where he had relatives. After his boxing retirement, he and his wife, Yolanda, a championship female golfer, opened a restaurant called Apostoli's on Mission between Excelsior and Peru Streets. In this photo Augostino's grocery store is in the left background, Beccuti's Beauty Salon is on the right, while off to the far right and not visible is Kaufman's Dry Cleaners.

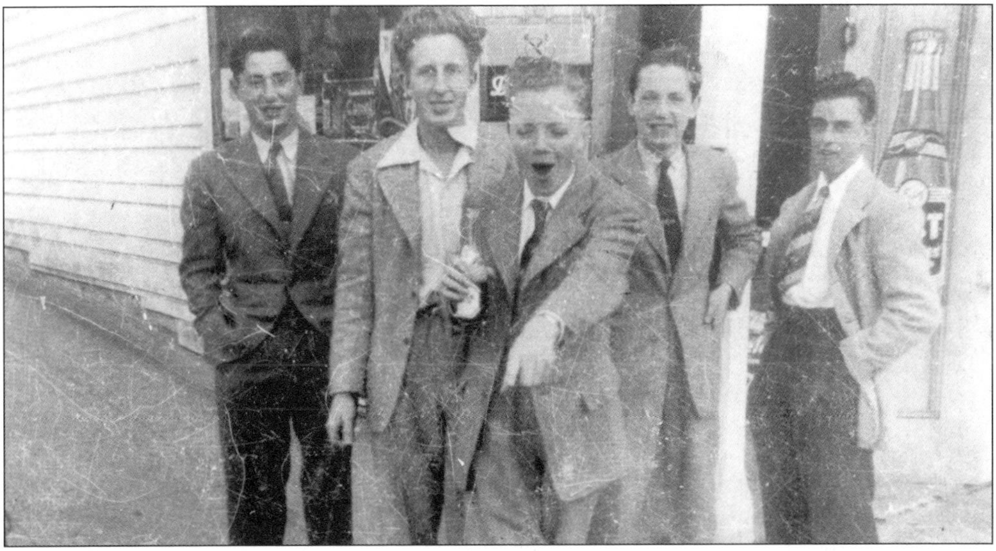

When the Japanese bombed Pearl Harbor on December 7, 1941, most of the Lew Powell Tigers gathered at Lew's store to discuss the shocking news. Within an hour after this picture was taken, loads of newspapers were dropped in front of the store and the Tigers went out selling these special issues door-to-door. This photo, taken by "Tiger" Jack Bermie, shows, from left to right, John Olson, Joe Bricker, Jim McCarthy, Ed Phillips, and Walt Woodall. Within two years, all of them were in uniform.

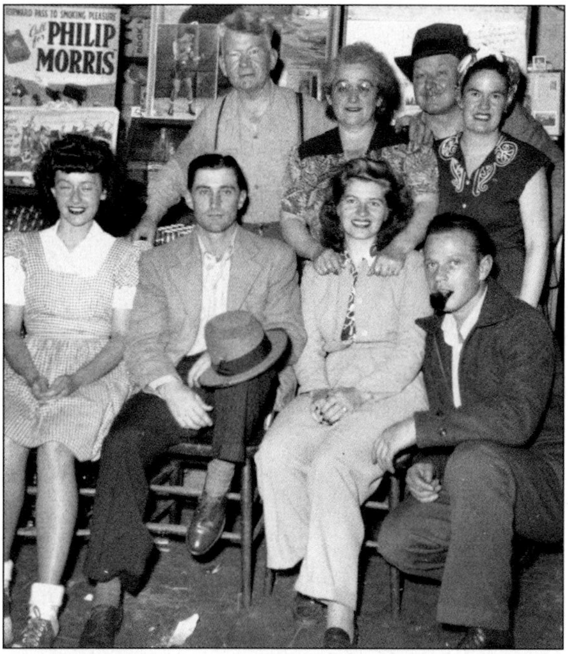

Although World War II was still raging, there were smiles in this summer 1945 gathering at Powell's store. Not visible is a large poster with over 100 blue stars and the names of Excelsior boys who went to war. In the front row far right is John Mikulin, boxer, fisherman, 1971 Officer of the Year, and in 1967 the founder of the Little People's Fishing Program, providing underprivileged kids the chance to learn to fish on San Francisco Bay. Mikulin was helped by Excelsior District friends boxer Ray Actis, Balboa Hall of Famer and Santa Clara football great Frank Zmak, and later by his famous son-in-law, meteorologist Pete Giddings. A plaque on the side of Castagnola's Restaurant at Fisherman's Wharf honors Mikulin's Little People's Fishing Program.

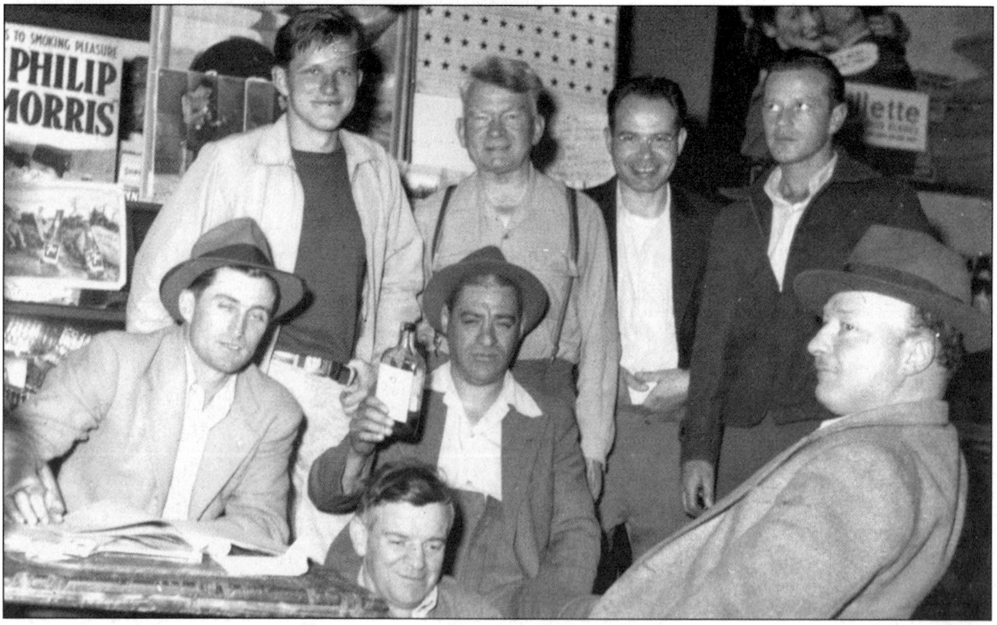

Gathered inside Lew Powell's store, *c.* 1945, from left to right, are (front row) Bebe Hughes; Tigers' coach and local barber Jake La Rosa; Harry Bell, father of local policeman and 1934 Balboa High School graduate Harry Bell Jr., Mary Bell, and well-known San Francisco attorney Stanley Bell; and (leaning back) Ernie Palany, a well-known opera singer and crack auto mechanic; (back row) Sam Mikulin, Lew Powell, Pete Re (Ray Actis's brother-in-law), and Johnny Mikulin. Johnny's brother Sam was a well-known ACME News Pictures photographer (later to become UPI), who accompanied Adlai Stevenson on his 1952 campaign tour for president. In the background is the World War II poster made by Emily Powell honoring Excelsior boys who had gone to war.

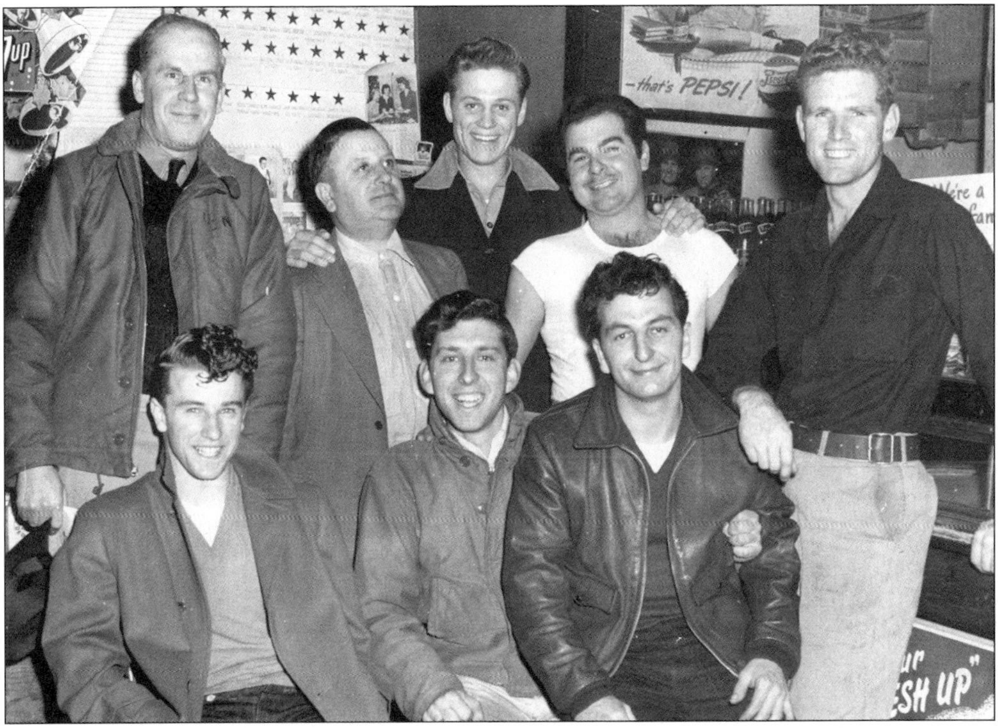

Another 1945 gathering of the Tigers, from left to right, included (front row) Ron Casassa, John Metropolis, Nini Chiesi, and Whitey Bernie; (middle row) Young Tigers football coach A. Gilfeather, George ?, and Benny CaMiddle; (back row) Charlie "Battlin'" Blagdon, boxer and retired UPI photographer who learned much of his skill and bought his equipment from Jebe's Camera Shop.

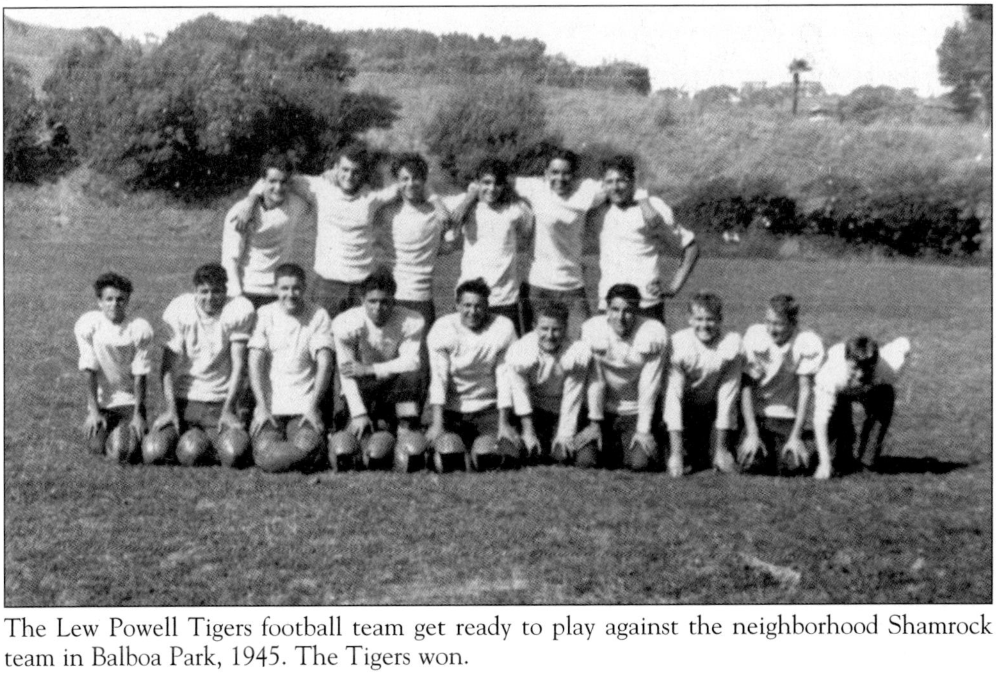

The Lew Powell Tigers football team get ready to play against the neighborhood Shamrock team in Balboa Park, 1945. The Tigers won.

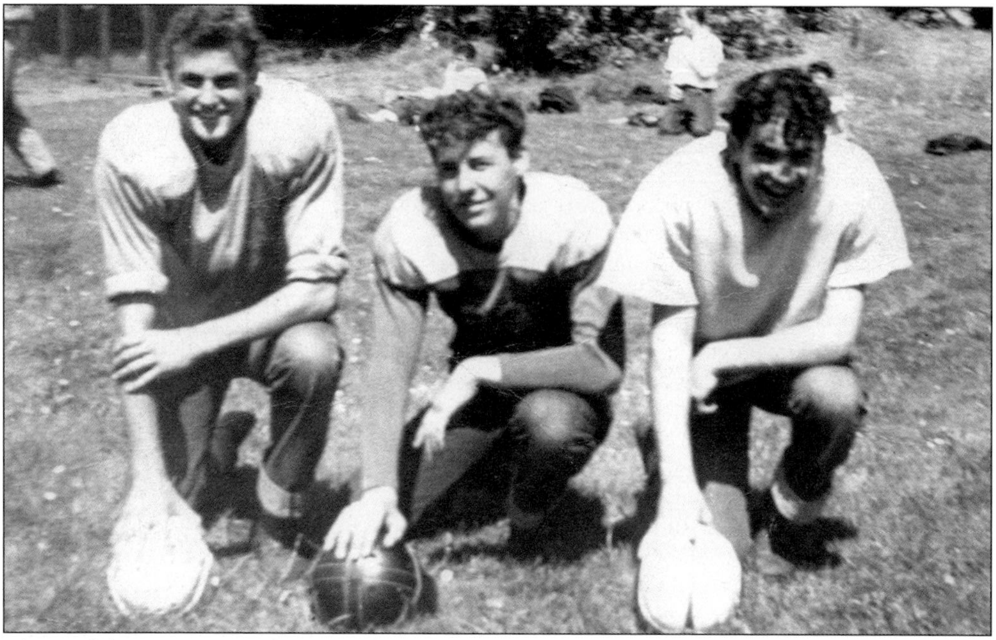

Three of the Tigers' top players smile for the camera. They are, from left to right, Frank Garre, who later became a professional baseball player and a member of the Balboa High School Athletic Hall of Fame; Joe "Gee Gee" Giordano, who became a Redwood City fireman; and Joe Dillon, who was also one of Balboa High School's top basketball players and became a lithographer after having gotten his start in the school's print shop.

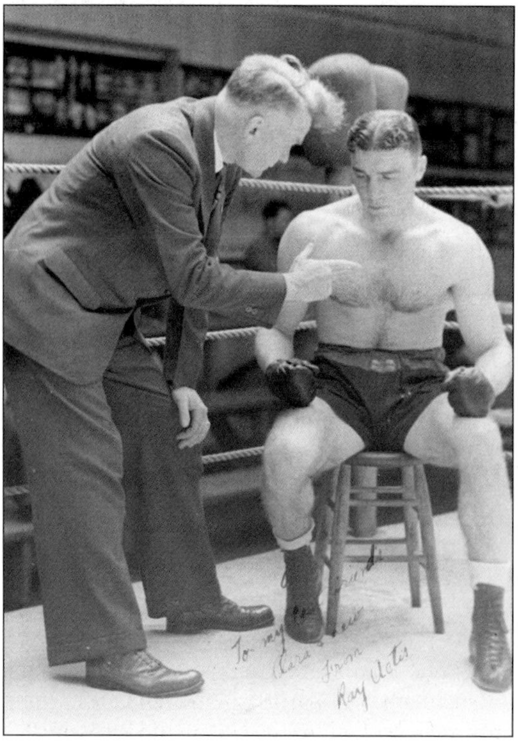

Lew Powell, while still a storekeeper, managed or trained a number of Excelsior neighborhood boxers who were known as the Prides of the Excelsior and had names such as Hoarace and Cliff Samuelson, Charlie "Battlin'" Blagdon, John Mikulin, Frank Caravaca, Otto Lopez, Willie Keane, Leif Magnusson, Willie Meeham, and Fred Apostoli. This photo was taken in 1936 at the Moose Taussig/Paddy Ryan Gym on Leavenworth Street, later known as the Newman/Herman Gym. Lew is seen here giving instructions to Ray Actis, known as the "Excelsior Assassin." During the Great Depression many young men like Ray became boxers, not because they liked hitting people, but because it was a way to make a good living for working-class men who used their strength in their daily jobs. Outside the ring they were gentlemen. Before his boxing career, Lew was a stonecutter and a box-maker, and Ray was a Works Project Administration construction worker and truck driver.

Ray Actis, "The Excelsior Assassin," "The Excelsior Exterminator," and "The Excelsior Extinguisher," was a light heavyweight managed by Lew Powell. Actis, who was of Italian heritage and whose family name was originally Actiscorporale, was called "The Italian Stanley Ketchell" because his vicious left hook was compared to that of Ketchel, a legendary early-1900s boxer. Actis scored 33 of his 39 professional wins by knockouts. Whenever Ray fought at Civic Auditorium or Dreamland Auditorium, the city's fight fans filled the facilities to watch the "Fistic Hope." Always to be remembered was Ray's fight against Billy Conn, "The Pittsburgh Kid," in 1938. Conn later went on to fight champion Joe Louis, who twice knocked him unconscious. Pete Ehrmann of *Ring* magazine wrote: "it was natural for most people to assume that . . . Billy Conn never got hit harder by anybody in his career. But every time the matter was brought up, 'The Pittsburgh Kid' would unhesitatingly set the record straight by mentioning what Ray Actis did to him. 'That Actis hit me harder that night out in San Francisco than Louis did when I fought him for the championship.' "

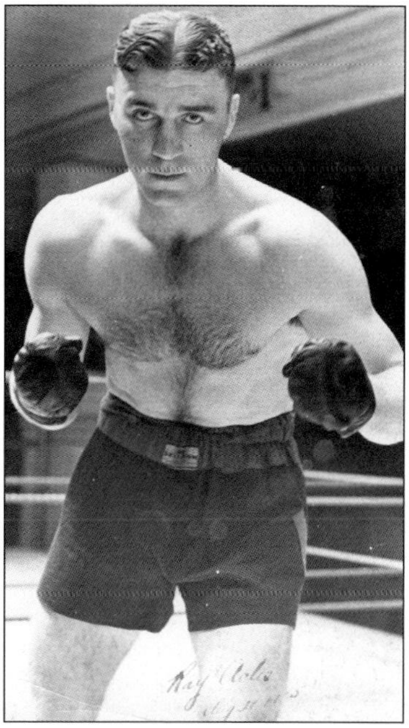

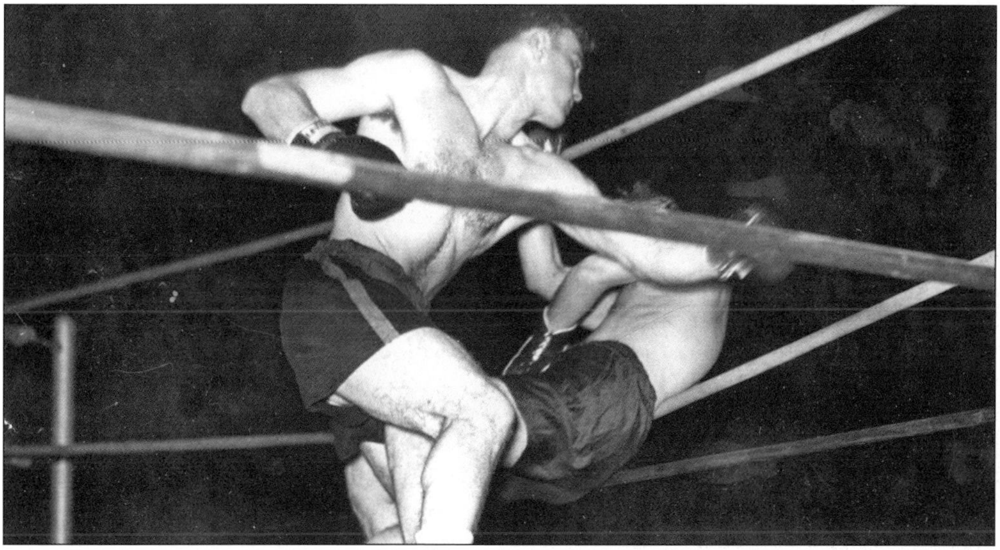

When Ray Actis stepped into the Civic Auditorium ring on May 13, 1935, to fight Jimmy Smith, local reporter Eddie Muller called Ray the "Excelsior Fistic Hope." Excelsior's Billy Burke, referee, counted a full 10 over Smith, and he was officially out after 2 minutes and 55 seconds of the first round. The photo shows Ray delivering his vicious left hook with his right cross ready to make the birdies sing for Smith. The headline above this photo in the *Chronicle* read humorously, "Mr. Smith 'Faw' Down . . . Go Boom." During the Depression, Actis was perhaps the biggest boxing name in San Francisco, the No. 5 light heavyweight contender in the world 1935–1937. Despite the publicity names of "Assassin," "Exterminator," and "Extinguisher," Ray was a legendary gentleman prizefighters. His good friend, the late lightweight Ray Lunny, remembered Actis's kindness when Lunny was a young aspiring fighter. Lunny wrote a poem about Ray in 1983; the last verse read: "Ray's cordial greeting to a little fighter / When they met at Taussig & Ryan's gym / Will always be remembered / With continued admiration for him."

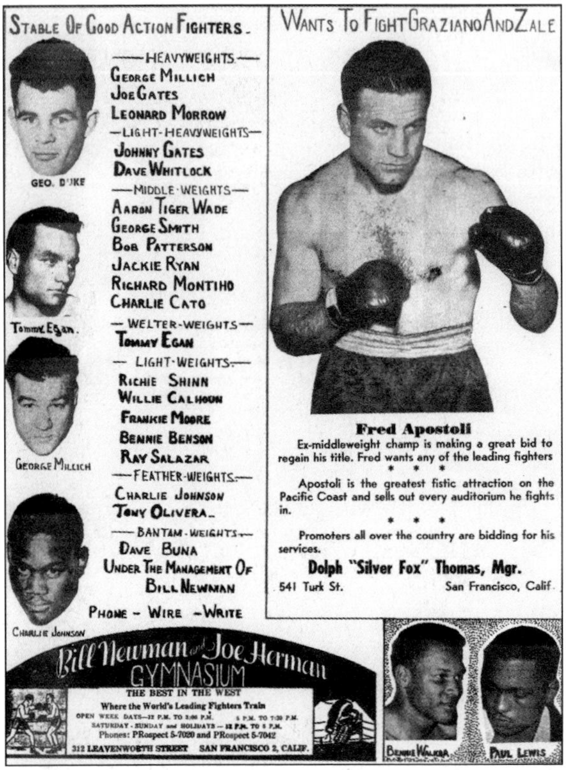

Fred Apostoli, a middleweight champion sometimes billed as the "Boxing Bellhop," started his boxing career in the mid-1930s, fighting dozens in the middle and light heavy ranks, including Billy Conn, Ceferino Garcia, Tony Zale, Ken Overlin, Freddie Steele, Young Corbett III, Melio Bettina, Marcel Thil, Lou Brouillard, and Babe Risko. During World War II, Apostoli served in the U.S. Navy and fought exhibition bouts onboard the USS *Colorado* in 1943. Although he was born in North Beach, when he desired to make a comeback in 1940, he came to the Excelsior, and as Tom Laird of the *San Francisco News* wrote, "If knowledge of boxing and training will bring back Freddie Apostoli, he is taking a big step in the right direction in making a deal with Lew Powell, the great lightweight of yesteryear. Lew knows all the answers."

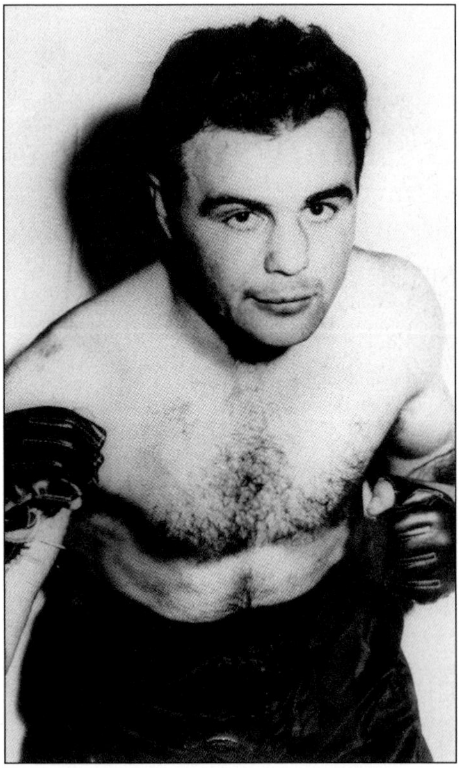

In September 1940 Balboa High varsity football coach Carl Mitchel and his team were disappointed when Tony Bosnich decided to become a boxer and give up football. Shown here in fighting pose, Bosnich got his start boxing at age 13 at the Corpus Christi Gym, and his boxing career included 50 professional fights from 1941 to 1950, including a 10-round decision he lost to Joey Maxim, world light heavyweight champ. Tony told a reporter once, "There weren't any jobs when I was fighting and boxing was a good way to earn a living." Part of Tony's boxing purse went to pay hospital bills for his younger brother, Frank, a star baseball athlete at Balboa who was pegged for stardom as a first baseman until his leg was amputated. Frank later died. Tony's three fights against neighborhood pal Pat Valentino were publicized as "grudge" fights, but Valentino said in a 1979 interview, "The neighborhood grudge fights were strictly for the fans' consumption. We were friendly then and still are now." In 1948 Tony Bosnich was fifth in the world heavyweight division. He was inducted into the Balboa Athletic Hall of Fame and received honors from the Northern California Veteran Boxing Association.

Pat Valentino was featured on the cover of this 1948 issue of Fight Parade with the caption "Pat Valentino, San Francisco Heavyweight, rated among first five best in the world." On the right side of the cover page and along the bottom are photos of the most well known referees at the time. Excelsior District's Billy Burke is second from left, at the bottom.

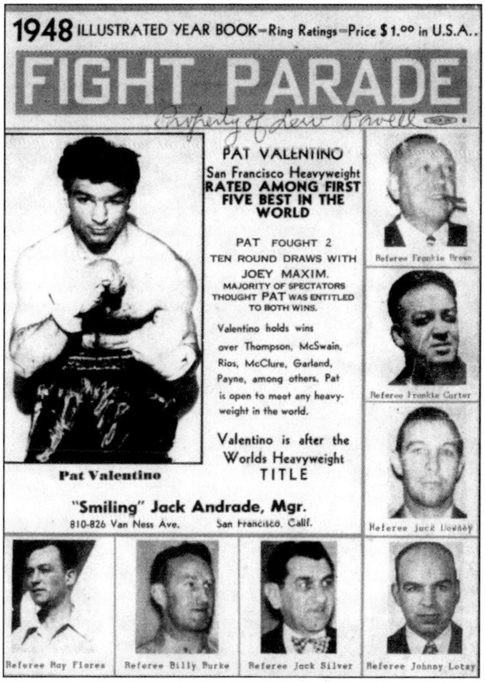

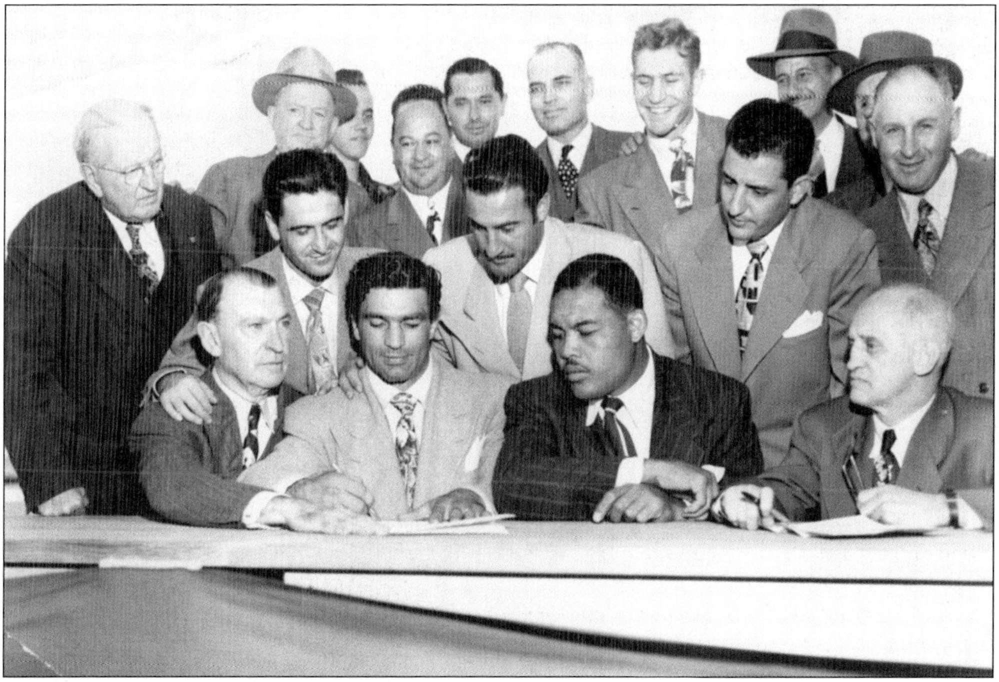

Shortly after Pat Valentino's loss to Ezzard Charles at the Cow Palace, Pat signed papers to fight an exhibition bout with retired undefeated heavyweight champion Joe Louis at Chicago Stadium on December 7, 1949. Pat and Joe Louis are pictured with Bay Area promoter Billy Kyne on Pat's right, and Pat's manager, Smiling Jack Andrade, between Pat and Joe. No one other than Pat knew at the time that he was blind in his right eye. Pat lost the fight in the eighth round.

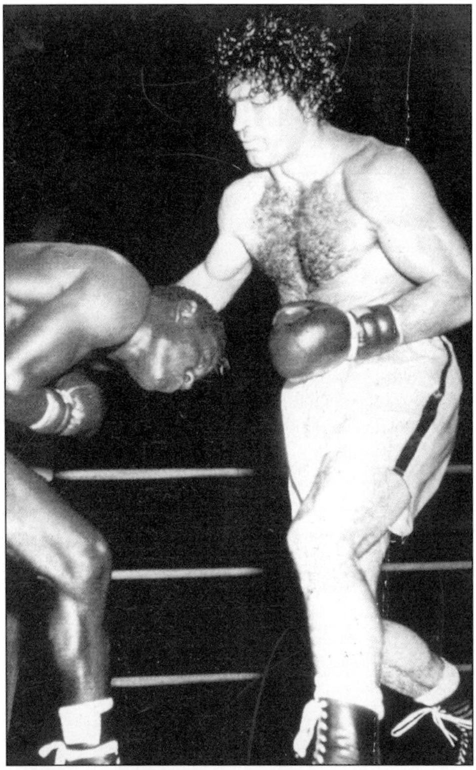

Pat Valentino was called "The California Grizzly Bear" and "The Pride of the Excelsior." Sports reporters and announcers found it difficult to pronounce Pat's real family name—Guglielmi. On October 14, 1949, fans turned out to witness Pat fight heavyweight champion Ezzard Charles. Here, Pat scores with a right to Charles's head in the seventh round. In the eighth, Charles hit Pat with a hook and a right cross and Pat went down. Referee Jack Downey stopped the fight and declared Charles the victor. On December 7, 1949, Pat lost to Joe Louis in an exhibition bout at Chicago Stadium. Pat was completely blind in his right eye from an injury caused by Tony Bosnich and exacerbated by Ezzard Charles. Pat's father would not allow him to go to high school. Pat and his seven siblings had to work in the family produce market at Persia Avenue and Mission. After the Louis bout, he retired and moved to Los Angeles, appeared in several movies, worked at Lockheed Aircraft, and owned and ran a bar. Pat's ring record was a respectable 48 fights with 25 knockouts. He was and still is "The Pride of The Excelsior."

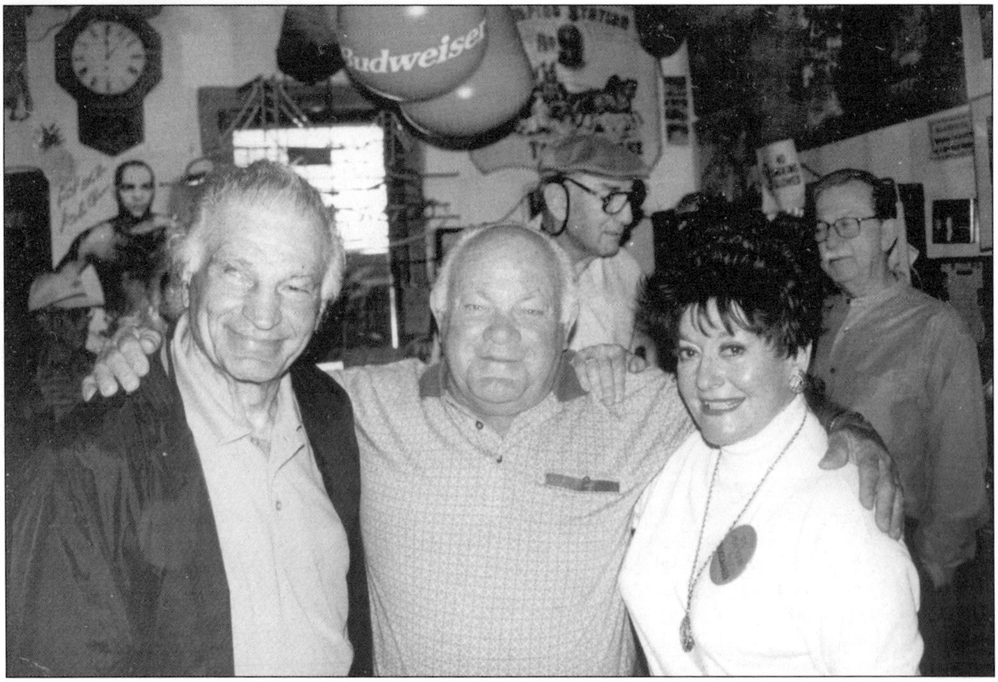

Pat Valentino, Sam Grado, and Emily Powell attend a lunch at the historic Silver Moon Saloon in Daly City given in Pat's honor. In the background is Jerry Flamm, noted San Francisco historian and author.

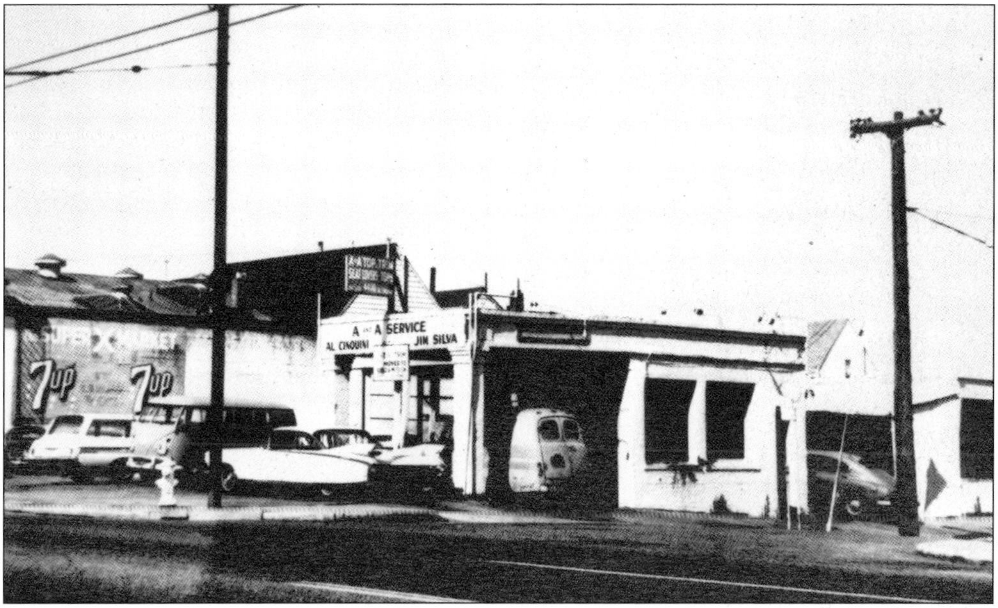

After the author discovered that the Excelsior and Outer Mission areas had the largest number of schoolchildren in the city and only a small, storefront library, he launched a drive for a new library for the Excelsior. It took 10 years and 20,000 signatures on a petition that was presented to Mayor Jack Shelley for consideration. Once it was decided that the Outer Mission badly needed a library, the city acquired this piece of property by eminent domain.

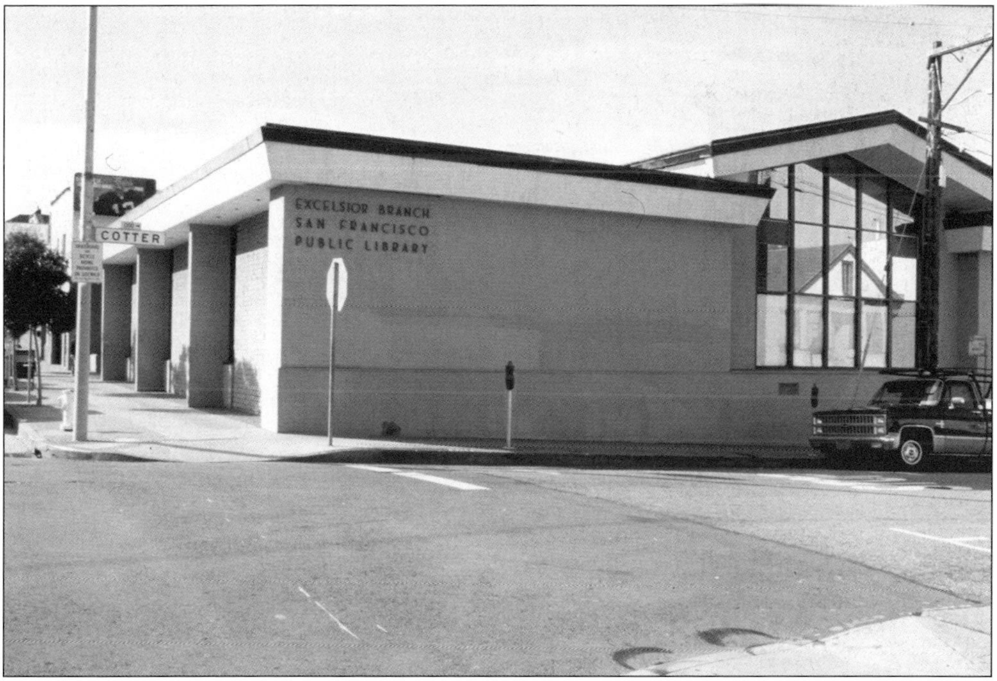

The Excelsior Regional Reference Branch Library was the second-largest library in San Francisco at the time and one of the first regional reference branches as well as the busiest in the branch system. At this writing, it is being remodeled and retrofitted.

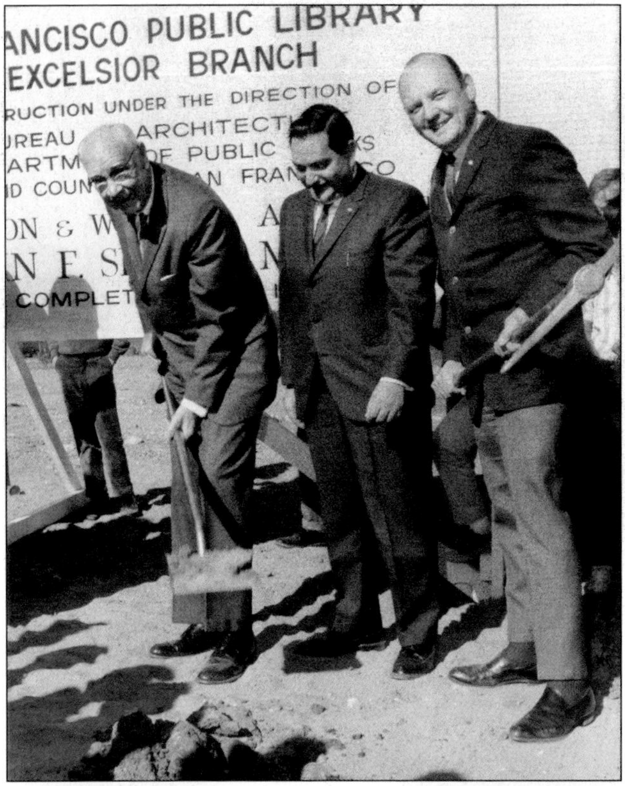

At last the ground-breaking for the new Excelsior Branch Library on Mission Street at the corner of Cotter Street is underway. Present at the ceremony are Mayor Jack Shelly, president of the Excelsior Business Association (left), and the author (right), who spearheaded the drive for a decent library for the area. In the 10-year period of gathering signatures for the library, Mayor Shelly was the only person in city hall who would listen to him, says the author.

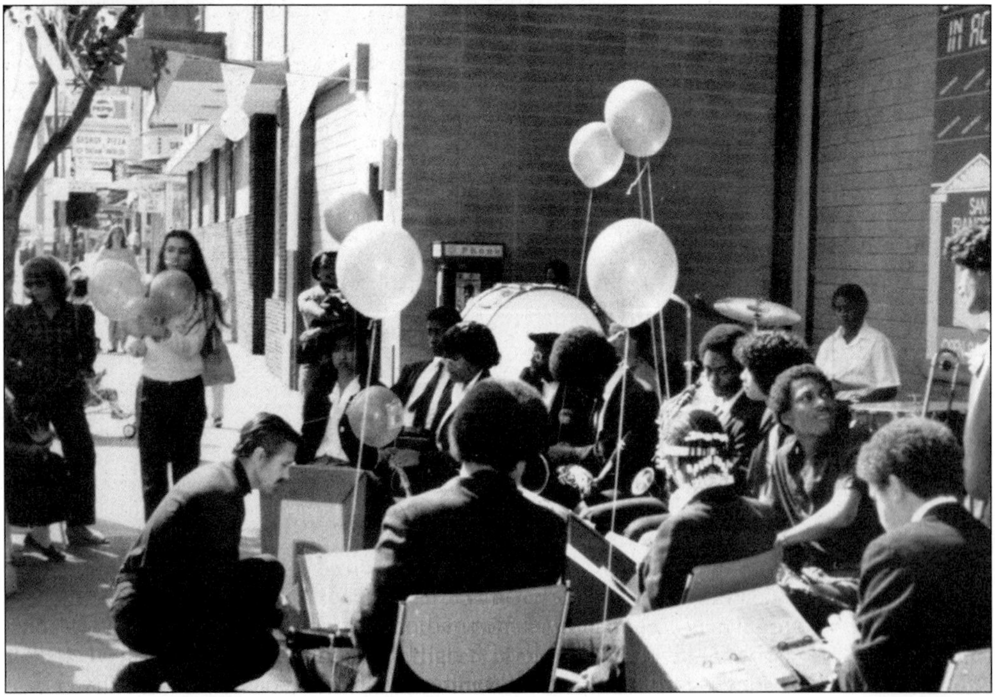

Opening day for the library was a festive occasion, with music provided by Balboa High School. Thank you, Buccaneers.

Geneva Excelsior Lions members present high quality AM /FM radios to Sister Emabelis, principal of the Epiphany School. Presenters were Lion Walter Jebe Sr., chair of the school symphony radio project, and Lion Chuck Bottarini, president of the Geneva Excelsior Lions Club (1968–1969). The radios were presented to the school after the author's daughter, Vivian, reported that no radios were available at the school for listening to the Standard Oil School Symphony broadcast. The author took the problem to the Lions Club board of directors, which approved the donation of one radio for each classroom.

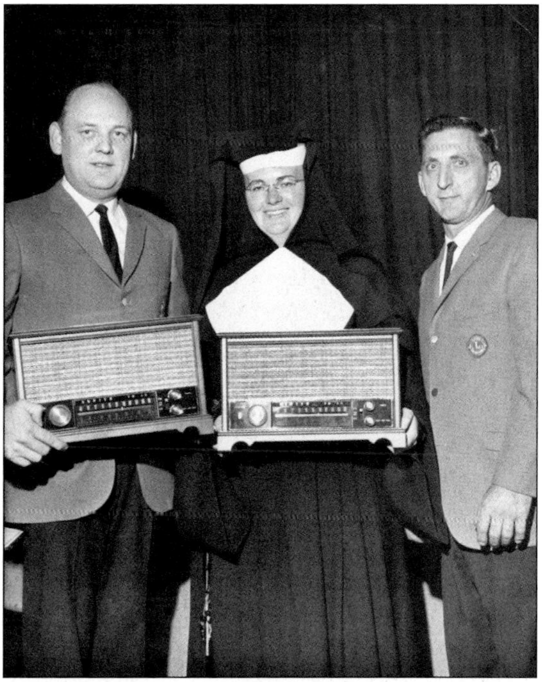

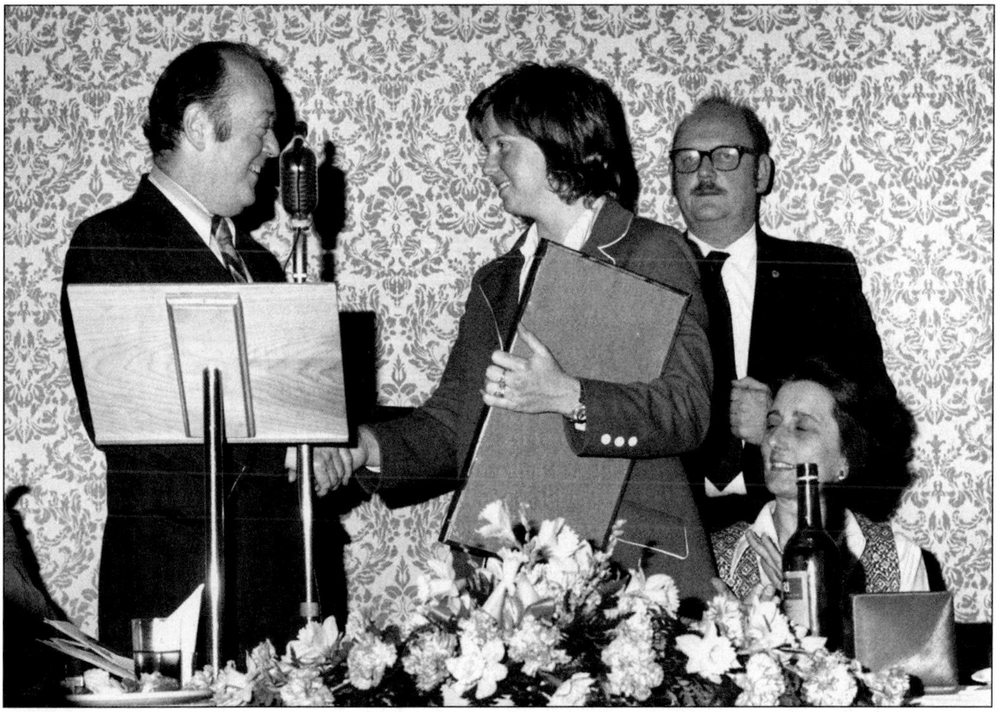

San Francisco native Lynn Vidali has won two medals in the Olympics for swimming: a silver medal in 1968 and a bronze in 1972. This special awards dinner at the San Francisco Athletic Club honoring Lynn was sponsored by the Geneva Excelsior Lions Club. Here, Sen. Milton Marks presents Lynn with a proclamation from the California State Senate. Lynn was a former student of the Epiphany School and Mercy High School.

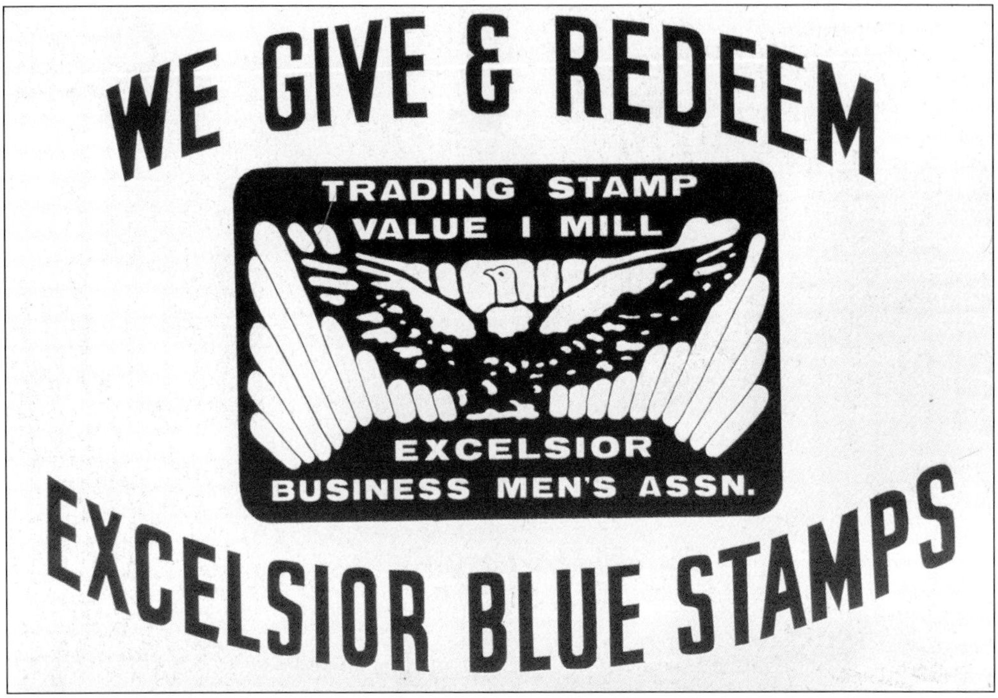

The Excelsior Business Association was fortunate to have some far-seeing members years ago who started their own trading stamp company in order to help local shoppers conserve. The benefits were two-fold: the saver of the stamp received redemption value while the merchant that gave the stamps got return customers because they collected the stamps. An added benefit over the years was that a small surplus developed that was used for promoting business in the area, such as planting trees on Mission Street, Easter egg hunts, free movies at the Granada, Christmas decorations, and so forth.

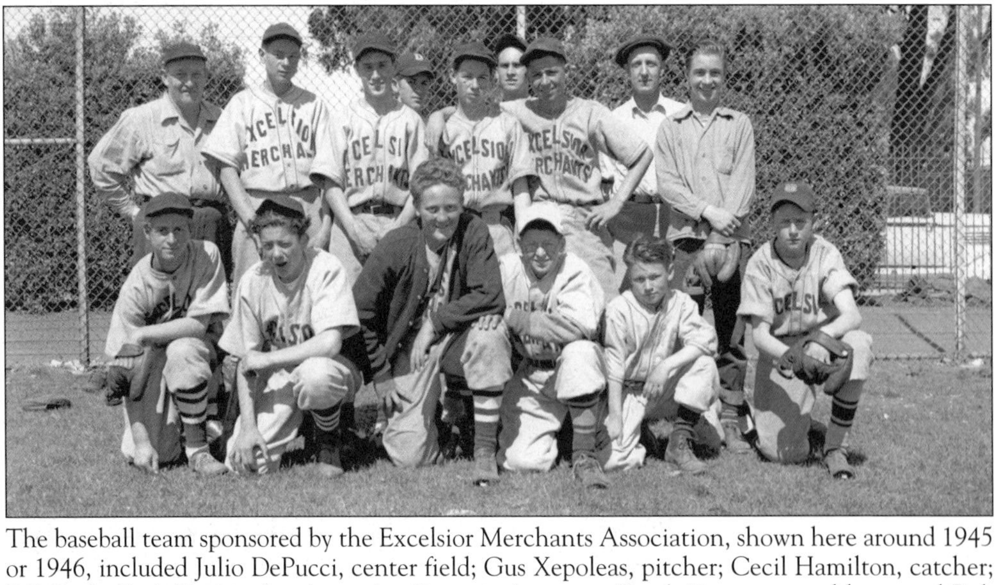

The baseball team sponsored by the Excelsior Merchants Association, shown here around 1945 or 1946, included Julio DePucci, center field; Gus Xepoleas, pitcher; Cecil Hamilton, catcher; Bill Rush; Dick Nesbit, first base; Art Demasi, shortstop; Frank Drago, second base; and Bob Crudo, left field.

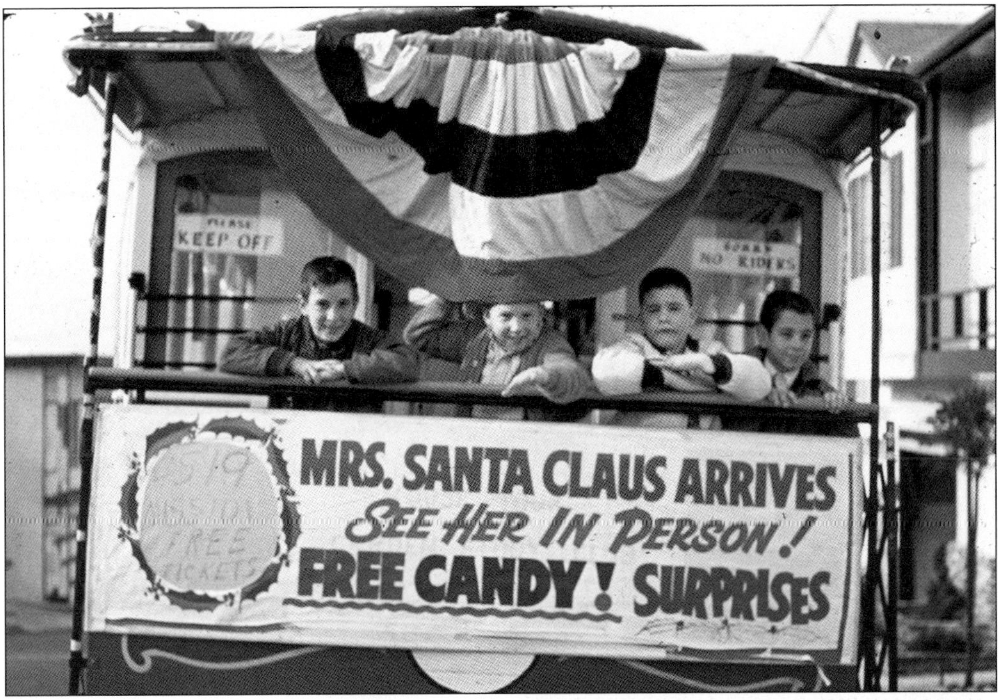

The cable car, Santa's village, and Mrs. Claus were among the many benefits Excelsior residents derived from using Excelsior Blue Stamps.

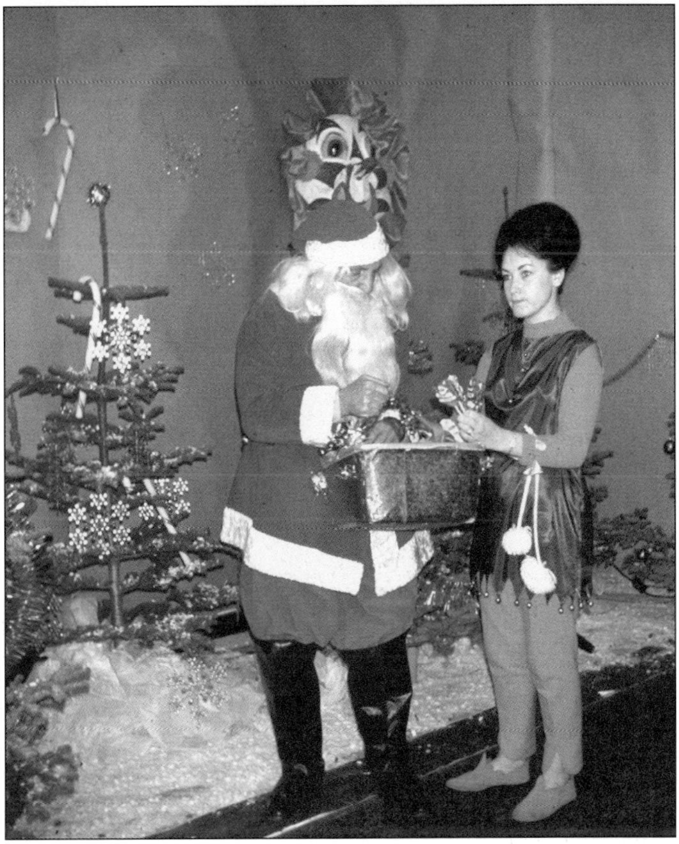

Another Blue Stamp benefit was this Santa's village, displayed in a vacant store at 4519 Mission Street.

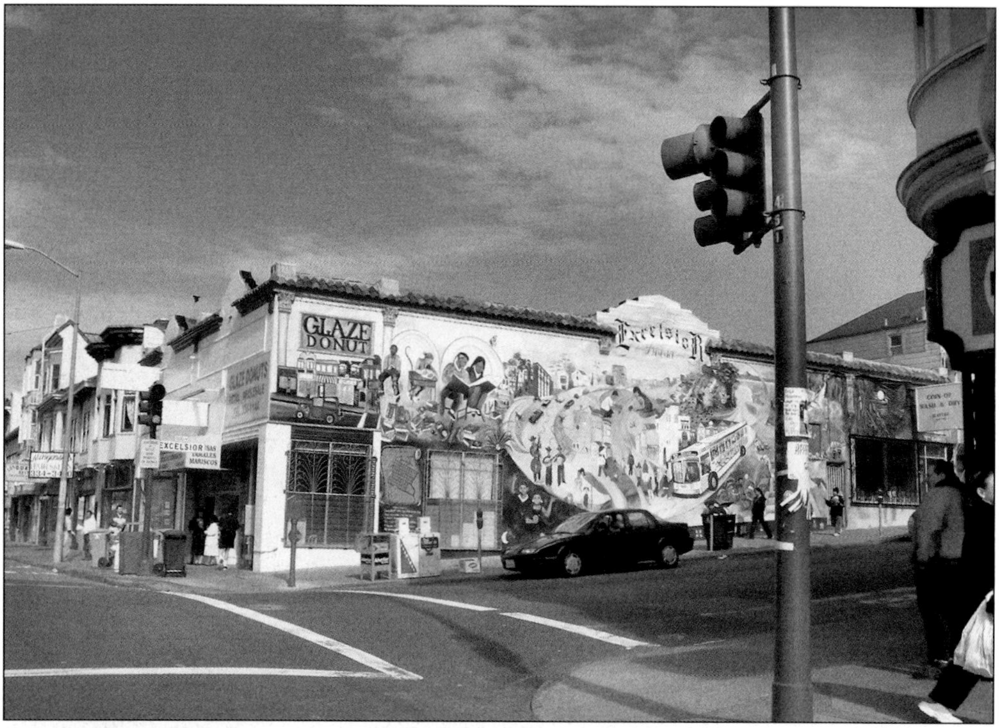

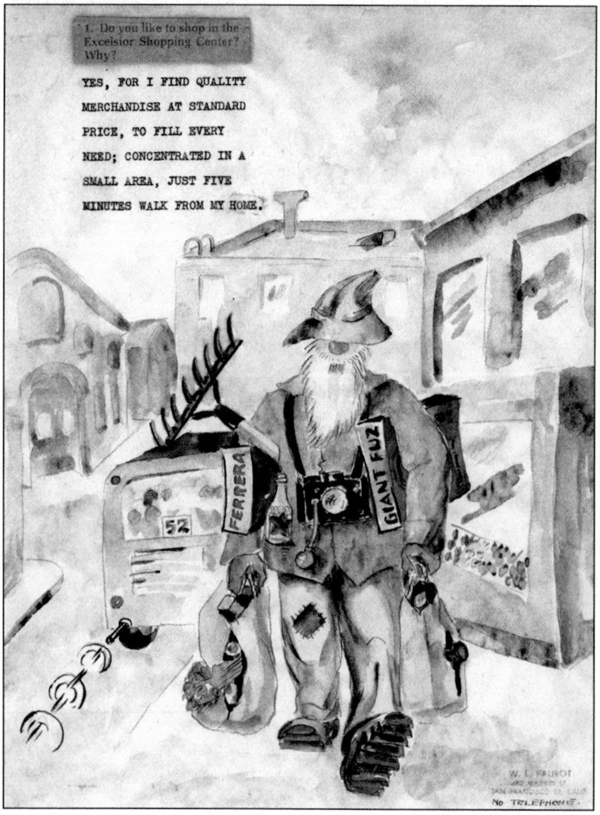

This mural, sponsored by the Excelsior Business Association and located at Excelsior and Mission Streets, was recently repaired and repainted. It was originally created as a way to get Excelsior youth involved in helping to stop graffiti.

This was the winner of a contest held by the Excelsior Merchants Association to stimulate business. Ads were placed in local newspapers informing residents of a contest for those who could best describe in writing or by drawing why it was convenient to shop in the Excelsior area. The caption included the following text: "Yes, for I find quality merchandise at standard price, to fill every need, concentrated in a small area, just five minutes walk from home."

The first trees planted on Mission Street in the Excelsior were a project of the merchants association in conjunction with its partner, the Blue Stamp Trading Company. The first tree to be planted, at Mission and Ocean Avenue, was an Australian bottle brush, chosen because they produce a beautiful red bloom, have roots that do not damage the sidewalk, and are semi-drought resistant. Here the first planting is being done by president of the San Francisco Board of Supervisors Harold Dobbs and Excelsior Merchants Association treasurer Angelo Bosso of Bosso's Pharmacy.

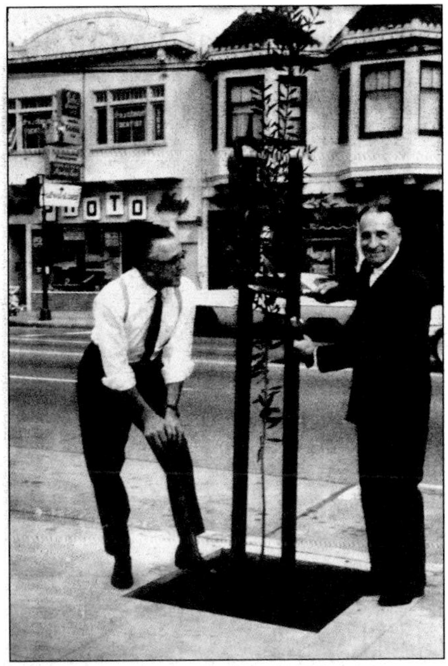

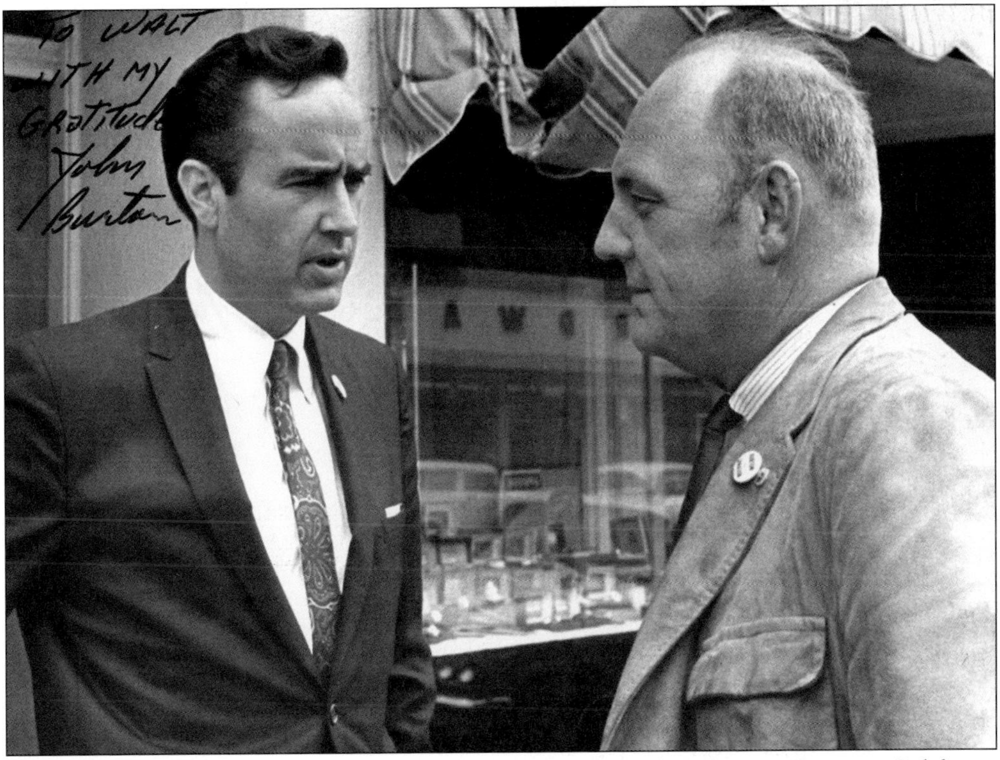

State Sen. Pro Tem John Burton (left), a man of numerous political positions, was a California assemblyman, congressman, state senator, and president pro tem of the California Senate. When this photo was taken, he and author Walter Jebe Sr. were having a very heavy conversation concerning ways that the state could help in improving the southeasterly part of the city.

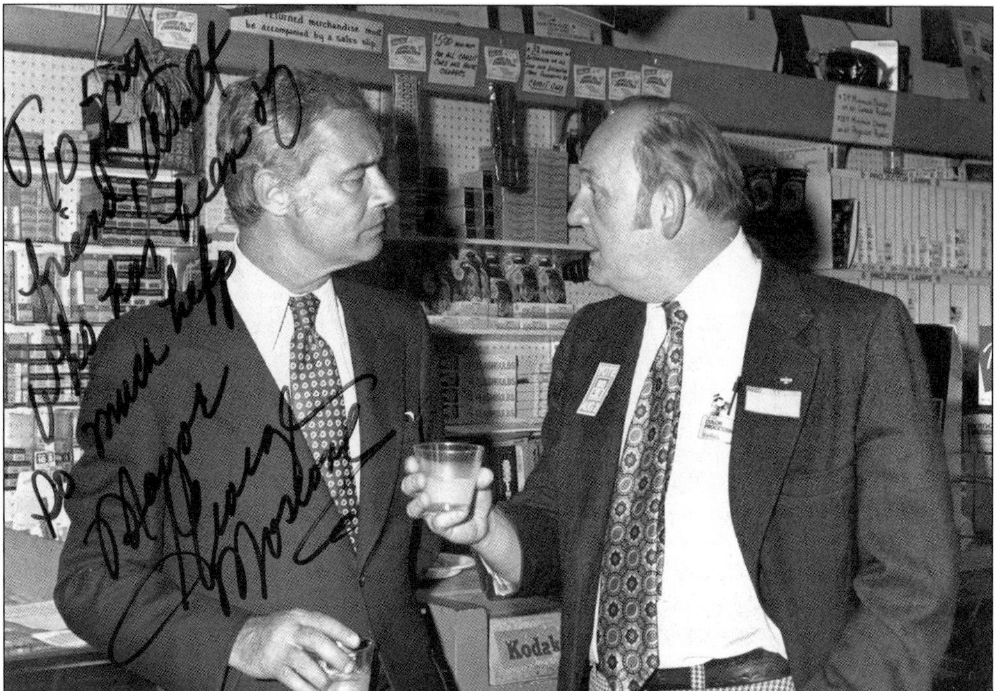

Mayor George Mosconi (left) and Walter Jebe Sr. attend one of the many political parties the author arranged as election time rolled around. The idea was to expose the candidates to a large group of people in a leisurely setting.

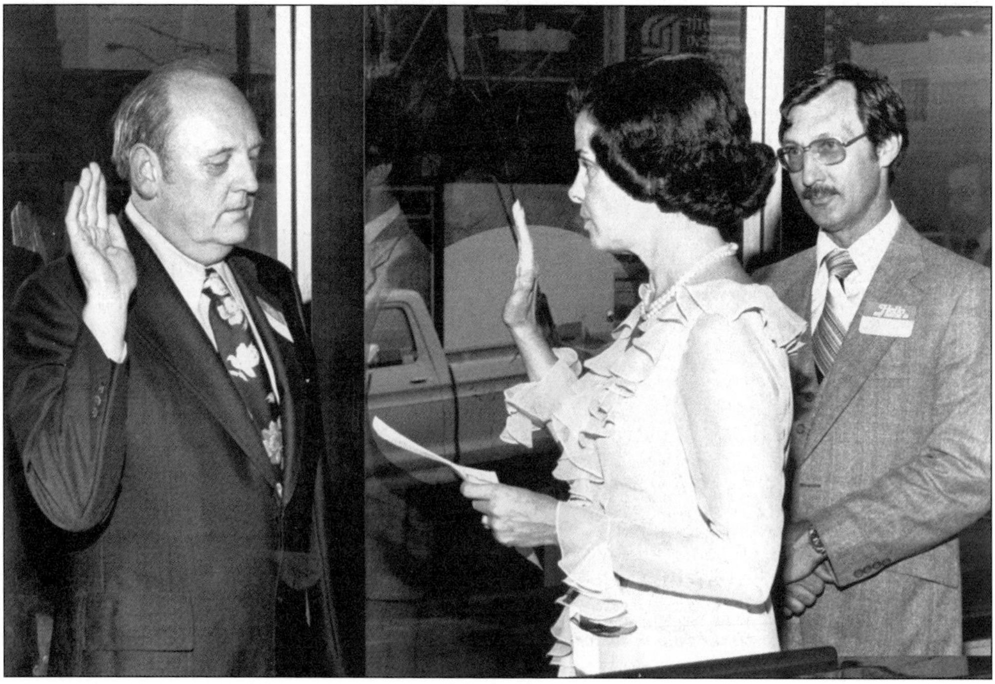

Mayor Diane Feinstein (center) swears in the author as a library commissioner at the Excelsior Library. To the mayor's right is Don Horenzi, a city supervisor from District 8 at that time.

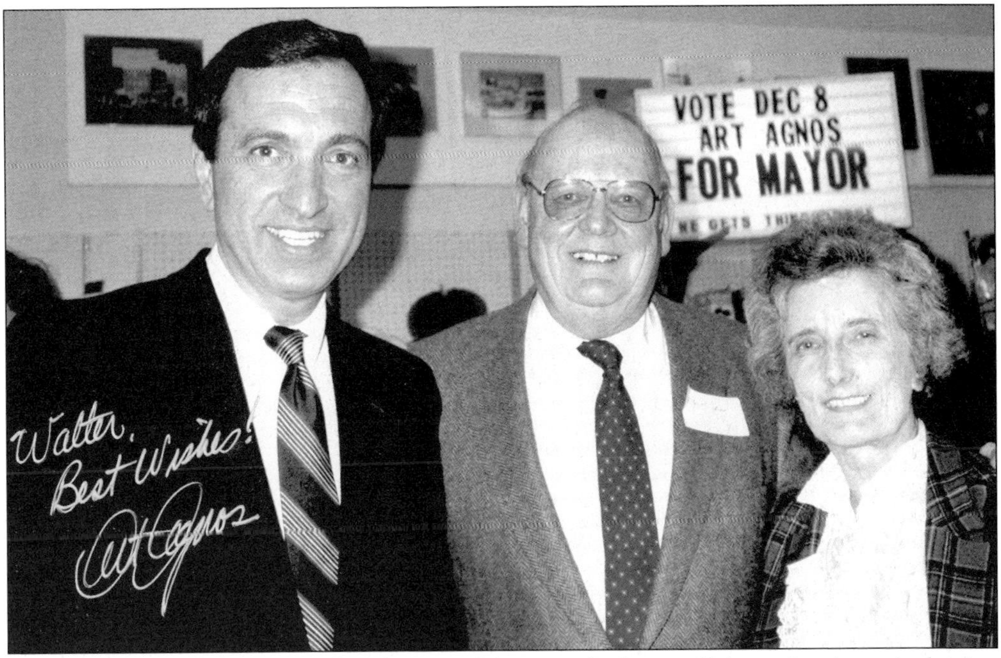

Author Walter Jebe Sr. (center) and Vivian Jebe were the hosts of Mayor Art Agnos's election party, given at Jebe's Camera Shop on Mission Street. Because there was no clear winner in the November election, a December runoff was held.

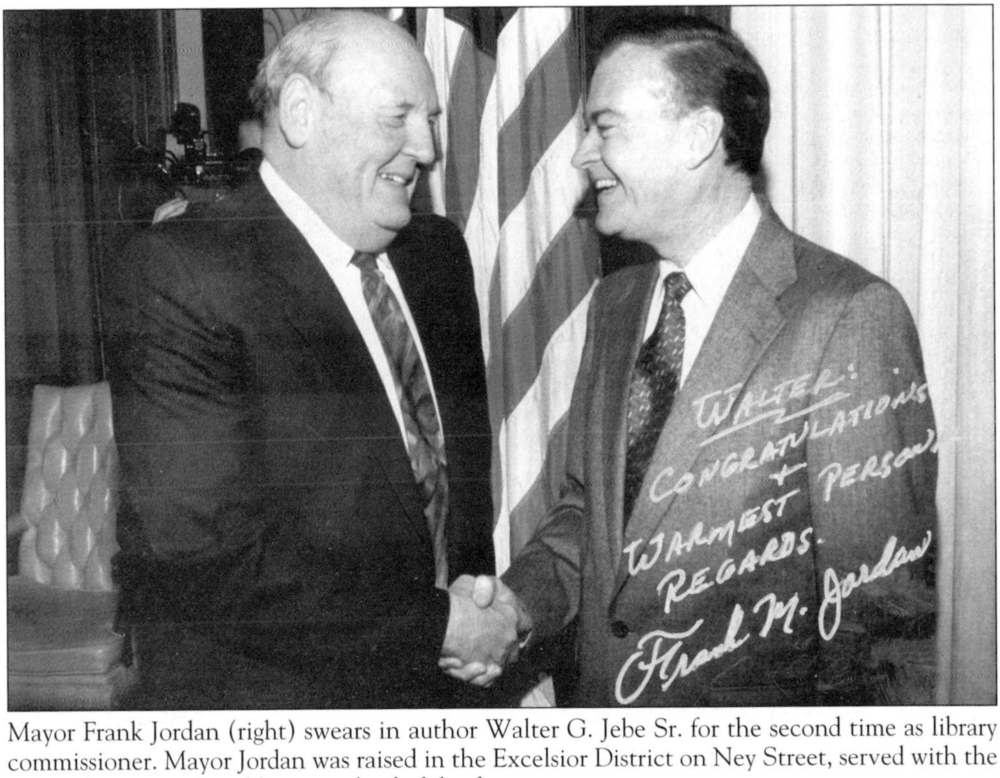

Mayor Frank Jordan (right) swears in author Walter G. Jebe Sr. for the second time as library commissioner. Mayor Jordan was raised in the Excelsior District on Ney Street, served with the police department, and became chief of the force.

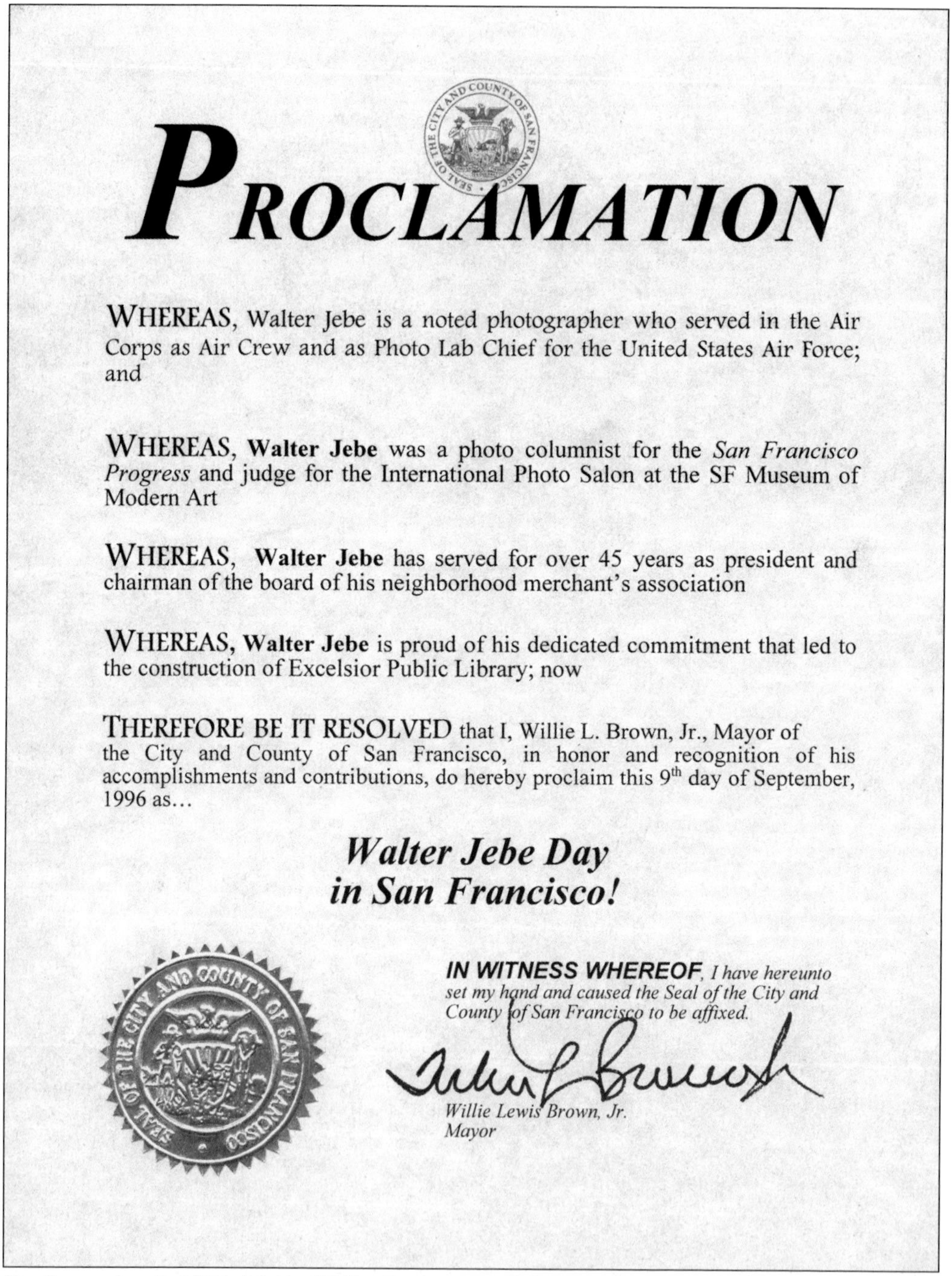
PROCLAMATION

WHEREAS, Walter Jebe is a noted photographer who served in the Air Corps as Air Crew and as Photo Lab Chief for the United States Air Force; and

WHEREAS, **Walter Jebe** was a photo columnist for the *San Francisco Progress* and judge for the International Photo Salon at the SF Museum of Modern Art

WHEREAS, **Walter Jebe** has served for over 45 years as president and chairman of the board of his neighborhood merchant's association

WHEREAS, **Walter Jebe** is proud of his dedicated commitment that led to the construction of Excelsior Public Library; now

THEREFORE BE IT RESOLVED that I, Willie L. Brown, Jr., Mayor of the City and County of San Francisco, in honor and recognition of his accomplishments and contributions, do hereby proclaim this 9th day of September, 1996 as...

Walter Jebe Day
in San Francisco!

IN WITNESS WHEREOF, *I have hereunto set my hand and caused the Seal of the City and County of San Francisco to be affixed.*

Willie Lewis Brown, Jr.
Mayor

On September 9, 1996, Mayor Willie Brown issued this proclamation declaring September 9, 1996, Walter Jebe Day in San Francisco. The author is a noted photographer who served in the Air Corps, was a photo columnist for the *San Francisco Progress*, and judged the International Photo Salon at the San Francisco Museum of Modern Art. He served over 45 years as president and chairman of the board of his neighborhood merchants association, and his commitment led to the construction of the Excelsior Public Library.

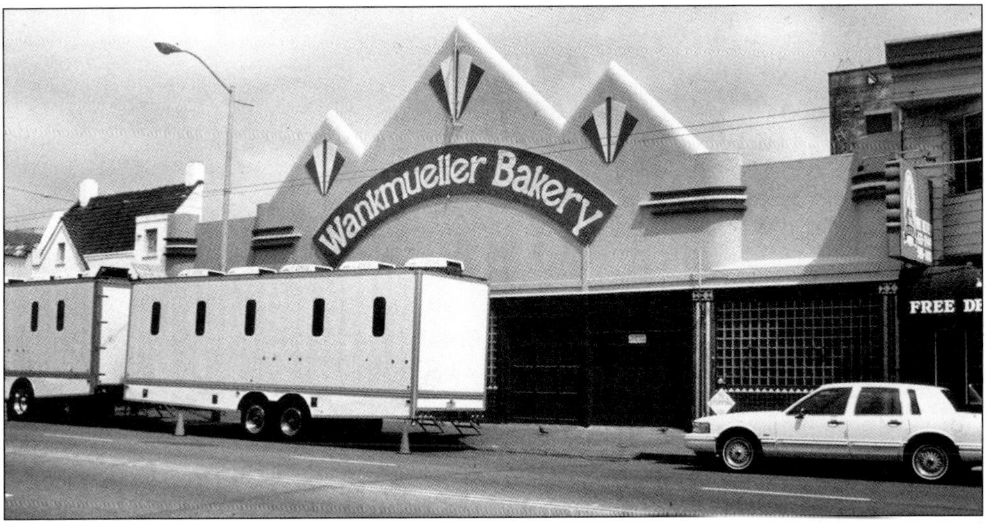

Getting Even with Dad, a MGM/UA production filmed in 1994, starred Ted Danson and Macaulay Culkin and is a comedy about a young boy who masterminds an outrageous plan to blackmail his dad into becoming the ideal father. A comic battle of wits and wills results as the boy gets his dad to do everything a kid could possibly want and teaches his dad the true meaning of the words "quality time." The "Wankmueller Bakery" sign is a prop for the movie; the real name of the bakery was the Royal Baking Company, once the largest French bread baking company in San Francisco. The van pictured here is a dressing room trailer for the actors. The Royal Bakery still exists and continues to bake great breads, rolls, and cookies.

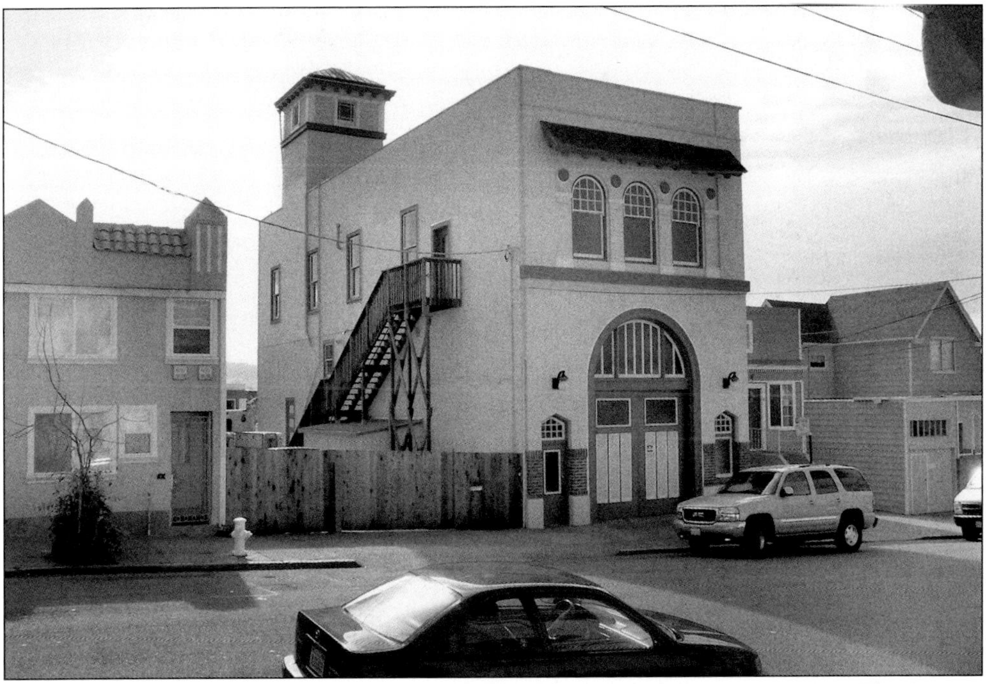

This photo shows the front of the firehouse featured in the 2001 Disney movie *The Princess Diaries*. This former fire station on Brazil Avenue was one of the many San Francisco settings used in the film, which starred Julie Andrews and Anne Hathaway.

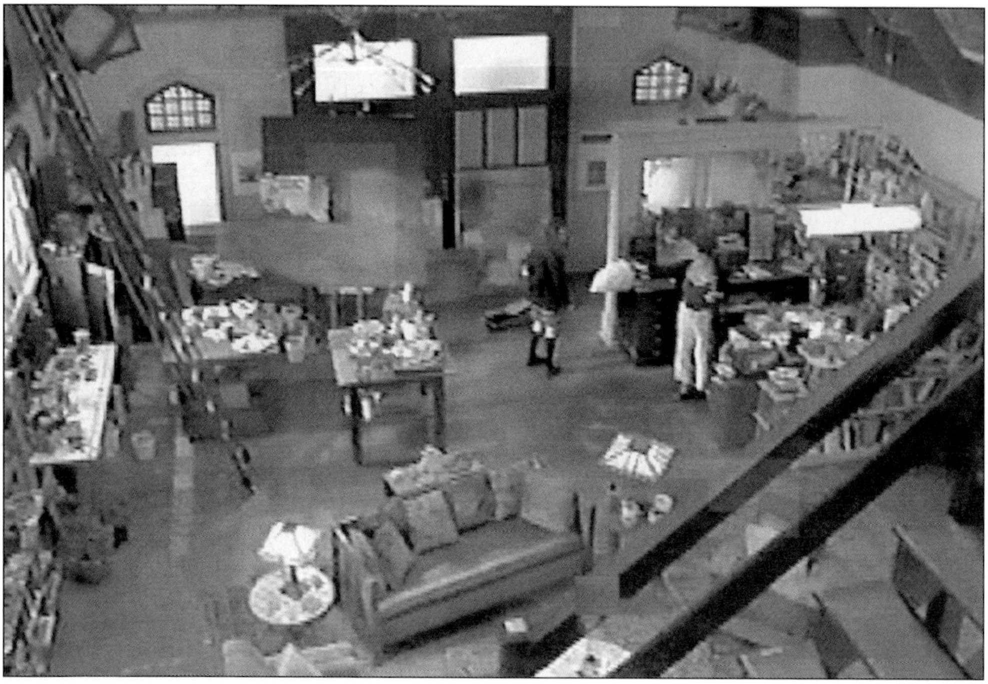

Another scene from *The Princess Diaries* shows the interior of the firehouse where the princess (Julie Andrews's granddaughter, played by Anne Hathaway) lives. In the film, Julie Andrews pays a visit to San Francisco to make contact with her granddaughter and have her returned to their homeland, only to find the princess living in this old firehouse on Brazil Avenue.

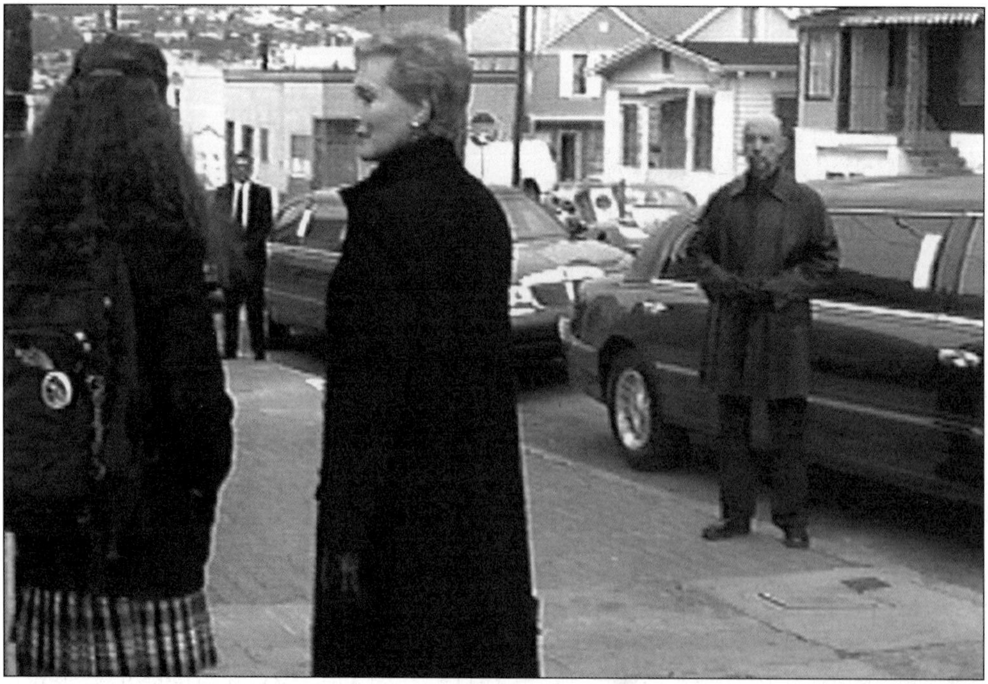

In this scene, Julie Andrews is speaking to her granddaughter while her driver and bodyguard wait to take them to their embassy in downtown San Francisco.

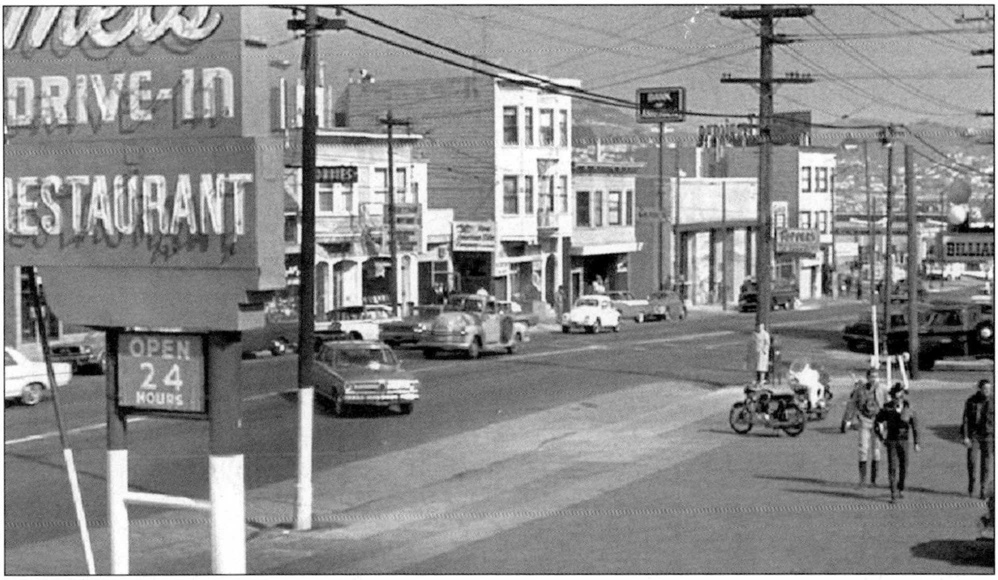

Spencer Tracy pulls into Mel's Drive-In at Pope and Mission Streets to order ice cream in this scene from *Guess Who's Coming To Dinner?* The 1967 Columbia Pictures film starred Spencer Tracy, Katharine Hepburn, Sidney Poitier, and Katharine Houghton.

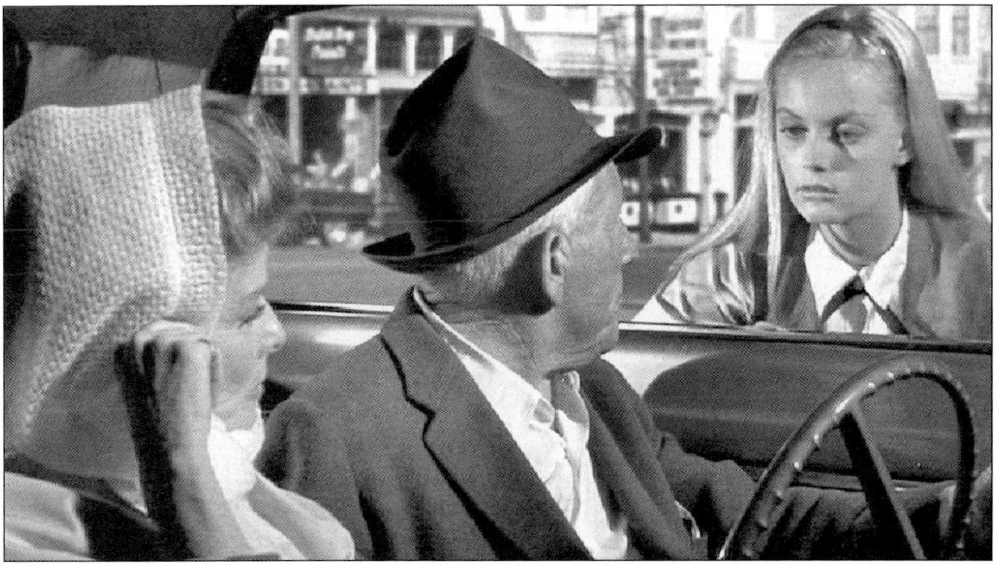
Pictured is another scene from *Guess Who's Coming to Dinner?*

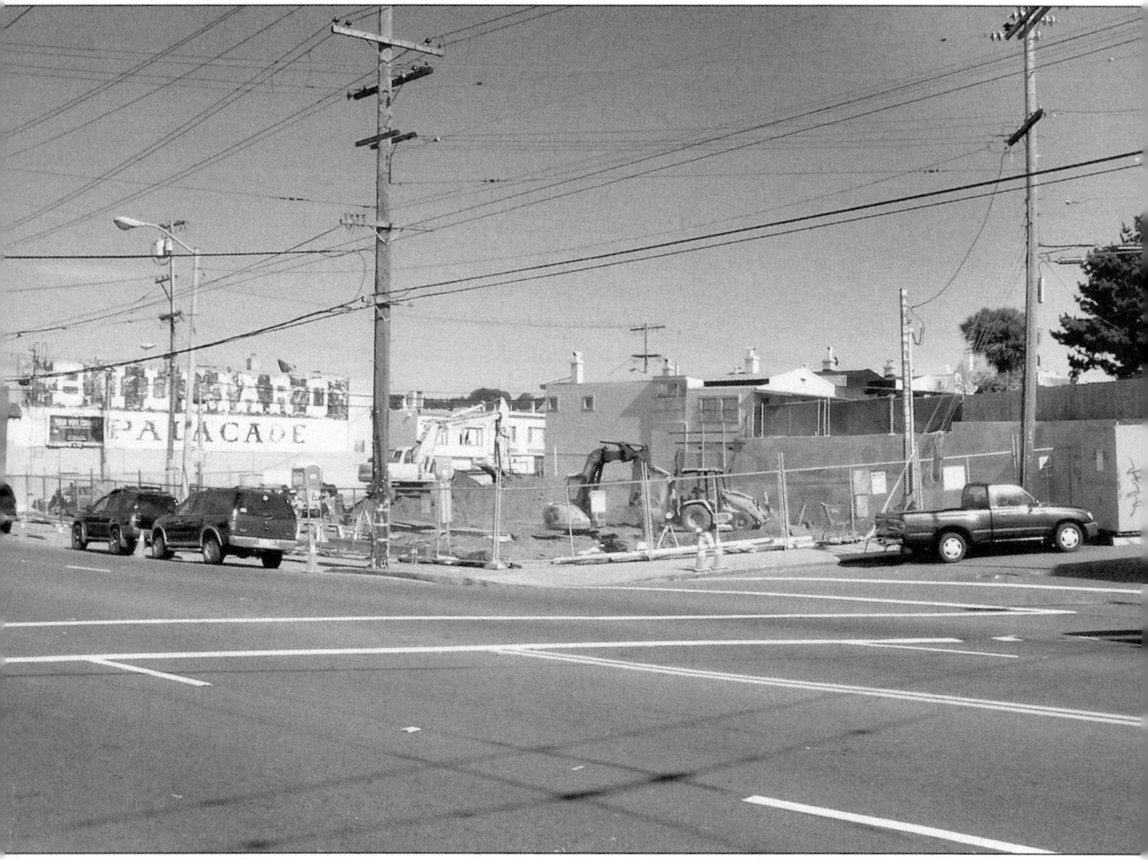

This is the former site of Mel's Drive-In at Mission and Pope Streets, the location used in *Guess Who's Coming to Dinner?* Mel's Drive-In has been demolished, and affordable housing for seniors is being constructed on the site.

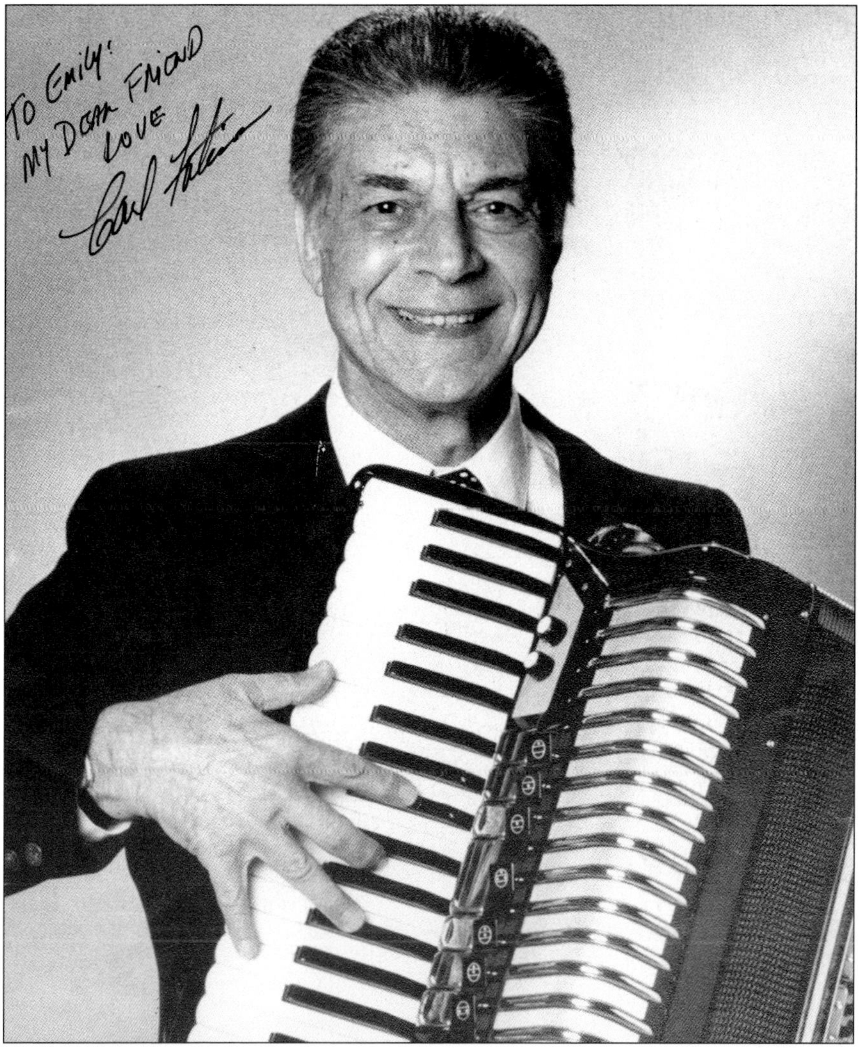

Carol Fortina, acknowledged as "The World's Most Famous Accordionist," was born in 1929 on France Avenue and attended Excelsior and Monroe Grammar Schools, James Denman Junior High, and Balboa High School. At age four his father bought him the smallest accordion that had ever been built (only eight inches long, with only 24 piano keys and 12 bass keys). At age six, Carl and his three-year-old sister, Chickie, formed a brother-sister act, Carl playing and Chickie dancing to English and Italian music. They performed at every major vaudeville theatre in San Francisco. At age 10, Carl won first prize at a three-day grueling accordion contest at the El Capitan Theatre. Since then he has played the accordion in over 550 motion pictures, including *The Godfather*, *Butch Cassidy and the Sundance Kid*, and *How the West Was Won*, and has played in more than 25,000 television episodes, including *Bonanza!*, *Gunsmoke*, and *Hill Street Blues*. He has worked with over 100 top recording artists, including Elton John, Elvis Presley, Cher, and Luciano Pavarotti. He has appeared on many live TV shows, including *The Dean Martin Show*, *The Carol Burnett Show*, and *The Lawrence Welk Show*, and has performed with every major film composer in the industry, such as Henry Mancini, Andre Previn, and Marvin Hamlisch. At Balboa High School, he also played the bass violin and was at times leader of the Balboa Blue Boys dance/jazz band. For many years Carl was conductor of the Paramount Studios orchestra in Hollywood.

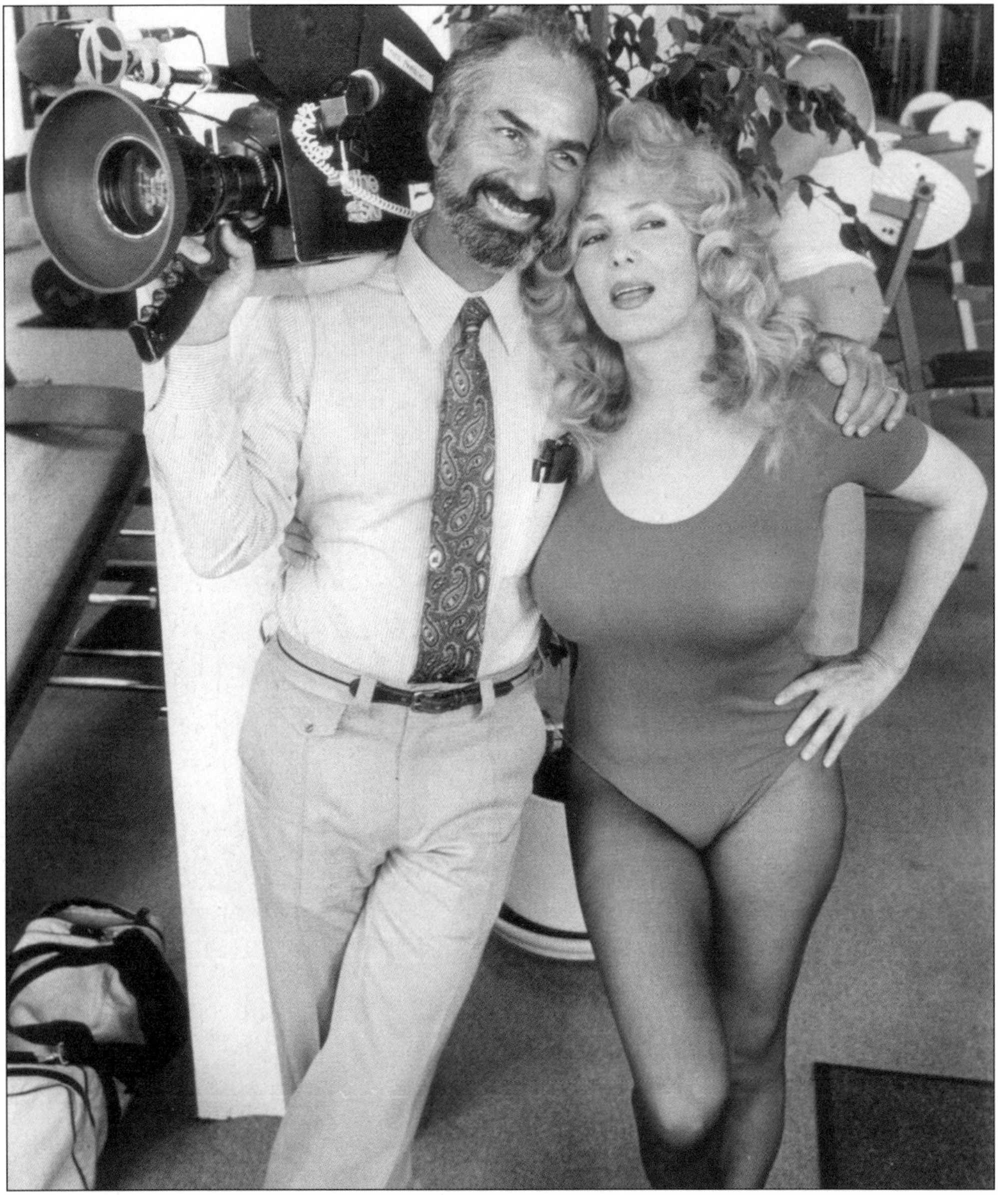

Fred Pardini attended Monroe Grammar School, James Denman Junior High, Balboa High School, and City College of San Francisco. He started his photojournalism career with the *San Francisco Call Bulletin* in 1955; then in 1960 he was a news photographer with the *Examiner* for 12 years. In 1966 he joined KGO-TV News as a cameraman and for 32 years shot millions of feet of film. He is the only photojournalist to have received the Press Club Award for a still photograph and an Emmy for a film news story. He has met and photographed many celebrities, including Eleanor Roosevelt, Marilyn Monroe, Elizabeth Taylor, and San Francisco entertainer Carol Doda, pictured here. He has won innumerable awards and was inducted into the Silver Circle and the Broadcast Legends Hall of Fame, as well as the Balboa High School Hall of Merit.

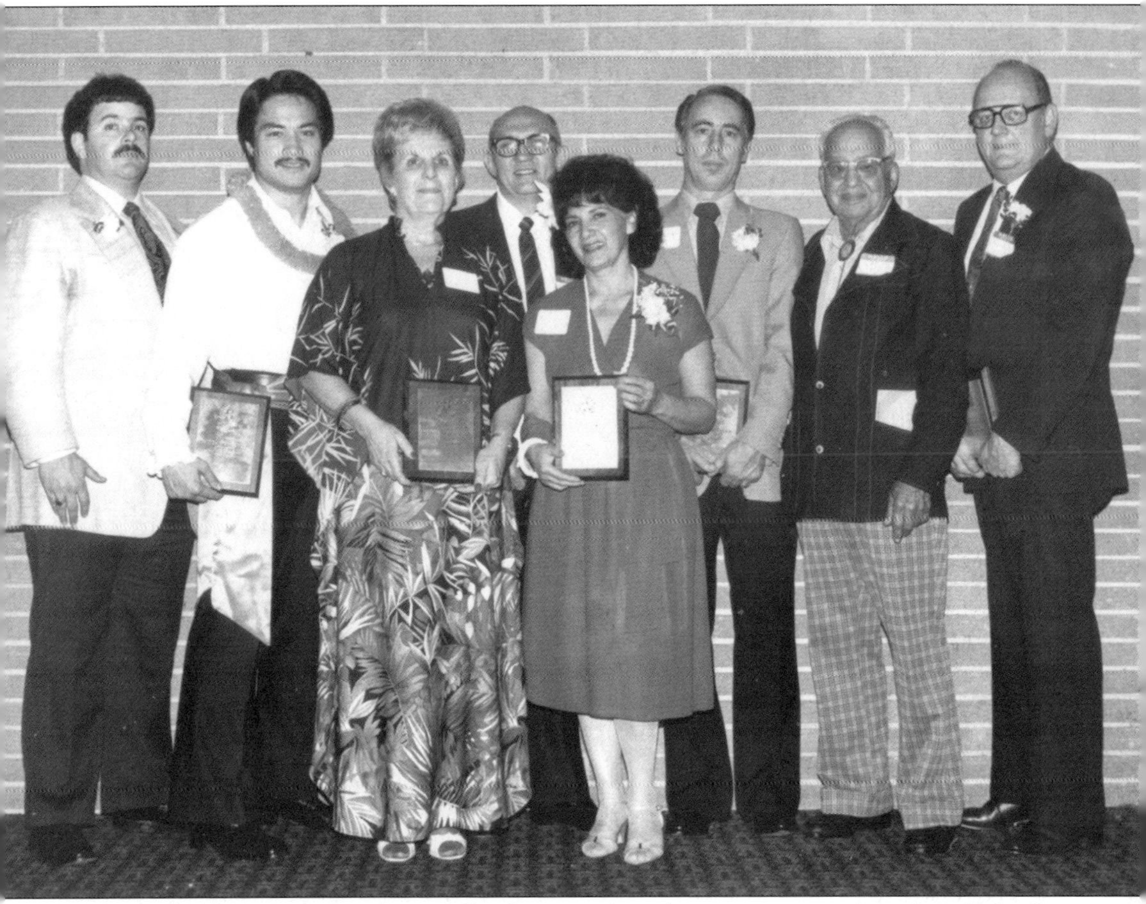

Balboa High School's 1983 first Hall of Merit Awards were presented to Jim Toland (journalism), Dan Hampton (heroism in the line of duty with the San Francisco Police Department), Alan Bushnell (educator, mathematician, and businessman), David Dal Porto (educator), Salvatore Billeci (music director at Balboa High School and composer of Balboa's and other schools' songs, as well as founder of the Northern California Micological Society and a world authority on fungi, especially mushrooms), and Walter G. Jebe Sr. (outstanding civic leader, developer of the new Excelsior Branch Library, delinquency prevention, art, and library commissions, and leader of the Excelsior Business Association). Shown in the first row are Ruth Fritzell, accepting an award on behalf of her brother, the late Jim Fritzell, a movie comedy writer and actor as well as one of the writers of the *M.A.S.H.* TV series; and Carmen Osuna, accepting an award for heroism on behalf of her husband, Herb Osuna, who was killed in the line of duty with the San Francisco Fire Department.

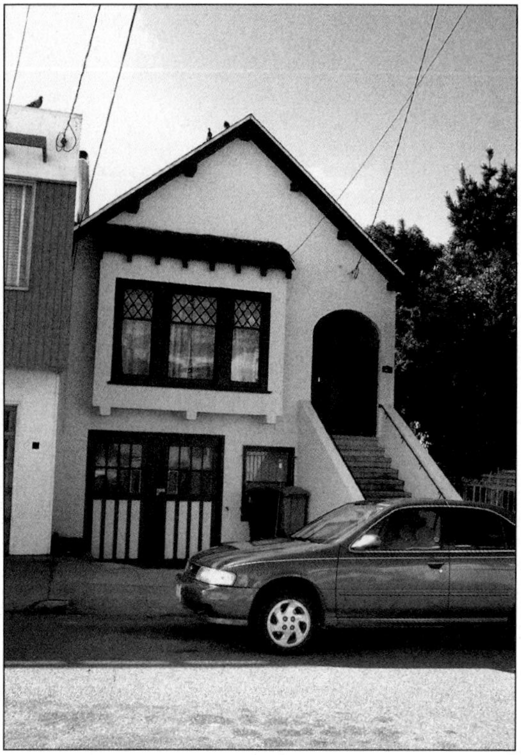

The Grateful Dead's Jerome "Jerry" Garcia was born August 1, 1942, at 121 Amazon Street in the Excelsior. After their father's death, Jerry and his brother, "Tiff," moved to 87 Harrington Street, pictured here. Jerry spent most of his childhood in this house with his maternal grandparents and a parrot named Loretta. Jerry attended Monroe Grammar School like his mother, Ruth, a San Francisco native. After graduating from James Denman Junior High School, he attended Balboa High School. Prior to his death on August 9, 1995, he had almost completed a book he had simply entitled *Harrington Street*, which featured his drawing of the house on the cover. The book was completed posthumously by his publisher.

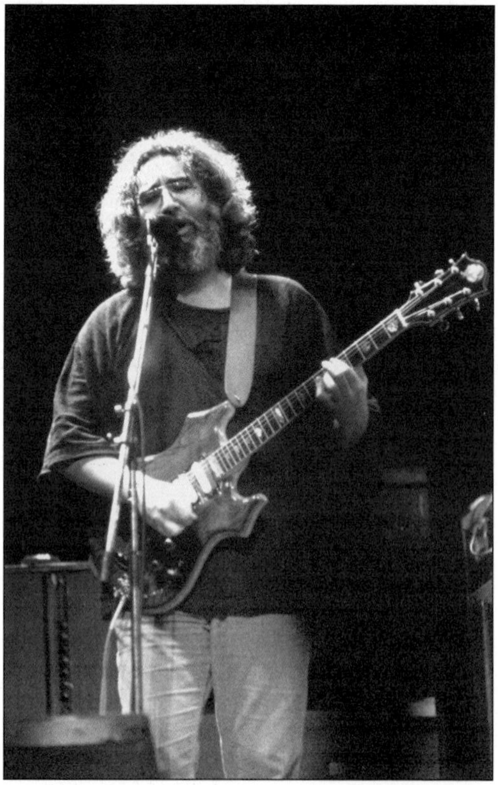

This Walter Jebe II photo of Jerry was taken at the Fillmore Auditorium in San Francisco. Jerry's father, Joe, was a jazz musician and bartender who came to the United States from Spain around 1920. His mother, Ruth, was a nurse of Swedish/Irish descent. Jerry's first musical memory and the best memory of his father (who drowned when Jerry was only five) was the sound of his dad's clarinet when they lived on Amazon Street. The Excelsior District has not forgotten Jerry. In 2003, Jerry Garcia T-shirts with reproductions of Jerry's stick figure drawings on the front and the words "Crocker Amazon Playground" on the back were sold to raise money for a new playground. Now the sale of the Jerry shirts helps Balboa High School's music department.

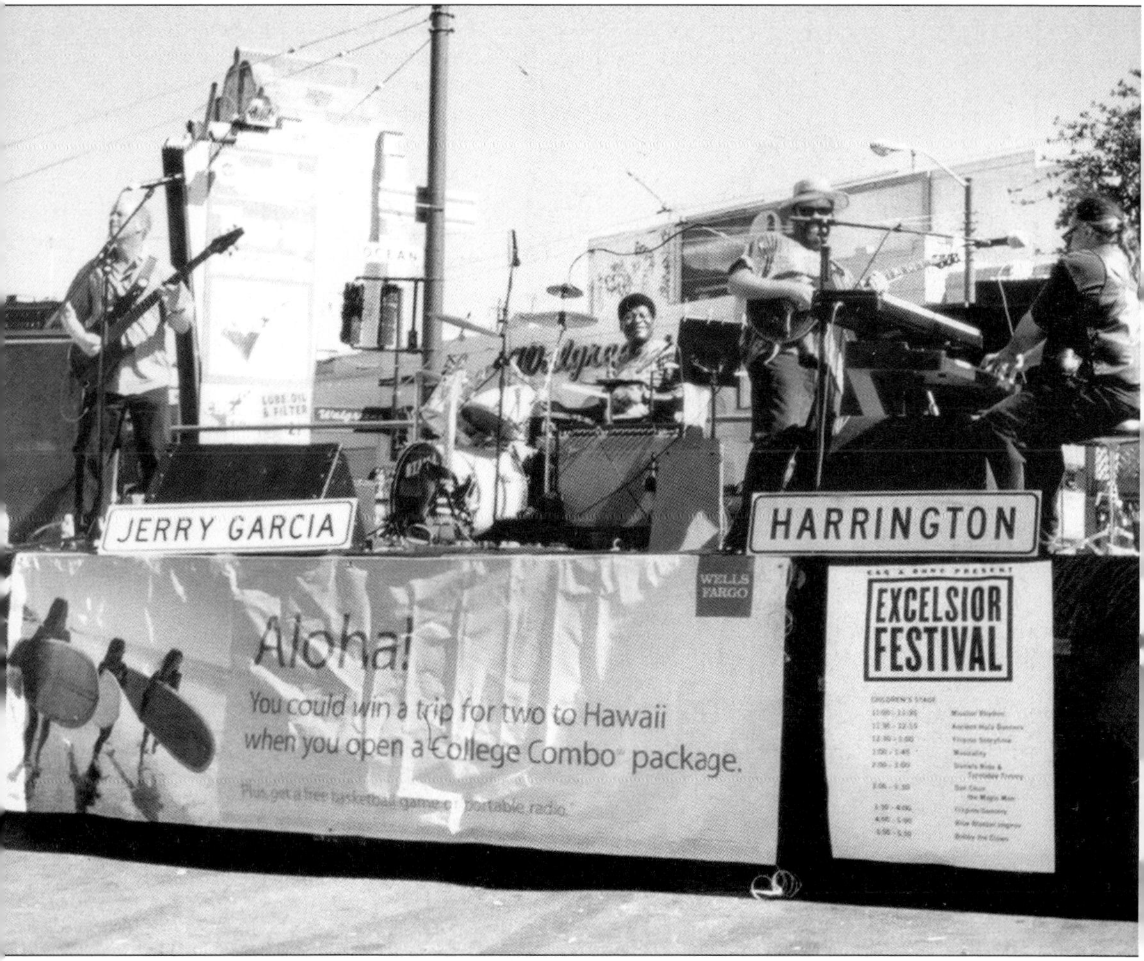

The first Excelsior District Annual Street Fair took place on October 12, 2003, with an estimated 4,000 in attendance. The event featured live local artists/musicians and performers plus a children's activity area and stage. There were ethnic food booths and other booths to promote neighborhood unity, sponsored by such organizations as the Geneva/Excelsior Lions Club, the Balboa Alumni Association, the Outer Mission Residence Association, the Excelsior Improvement Association. Handmade clothing and accessories were also for sale, while many local politicians set up booths of their own. The event was sponsored by the Excelsior Action Group.

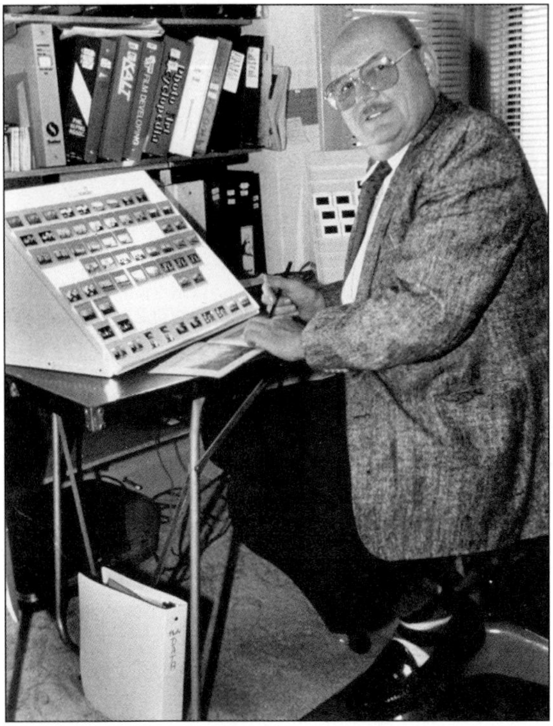

The author, Walter Jebe Sr., is shown organizing the pictures for this book. Through decades of business, political, and photographic experience in the Excelsior District, Jebe has a unique perspective on the area's history and relationship to San Francisco as a whole. He hopes readers of this volume will endeavor to preserve their own history for future generations.

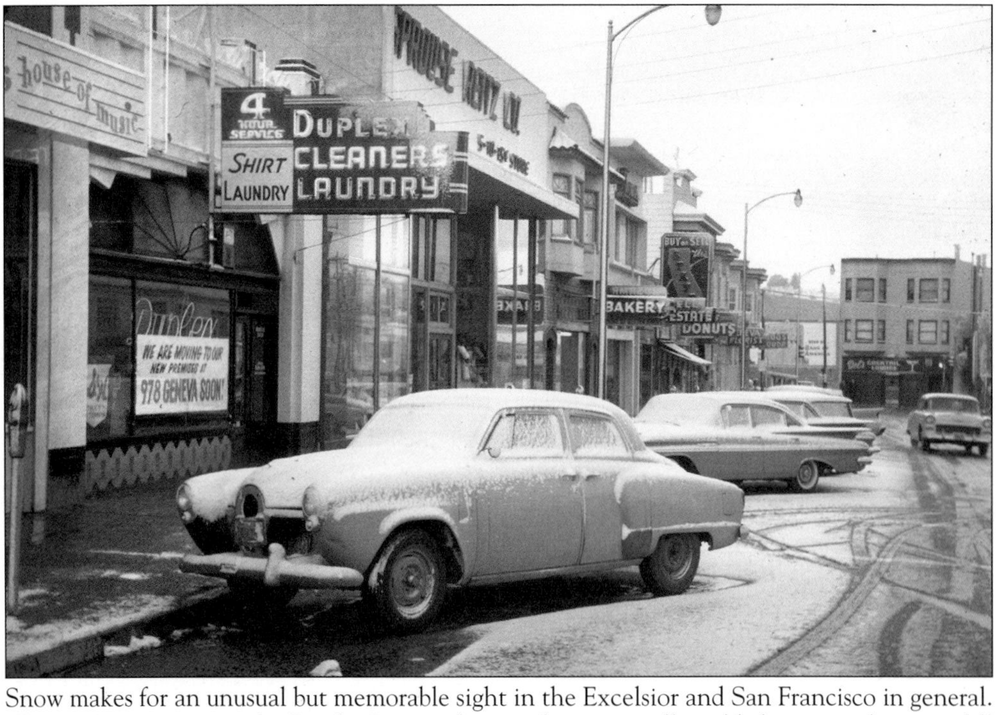

Snow makes for an unusual but memorable sight in the Excelsior and San Francisco in general. This city's proximity to the Pacific Ocean, along with its generally mild climate, makes snowfall an extremely rare occurrence.